PERESTROIKA-ERA POLITICS

Contemporary Soviet Politics

PERESTROIKA-ERA POLITICS
THE NEW SOVIET LEGISLATURE
AND GORBACHEV'S POLITICAL REFORMS
Robert T. Huber and Donald R. Kelley, eds.

CRACKS IN THE MONOLITH
PARTY POWER IN THE BREZHNEV ERA
James R. Millar, ed.

THE SOVIET CONSTITUTIONAL CRISIS
CONSTITUTIONAL REFORM AND
THE POLITICS OF LAW IN THE USSR
Robert Sharlet

EXECUTIVE POWER AND SOVIET POLITICS
Eugene Huskey, editor

PERESTROIKA-ERA POLITICS

POLITICS The New

Soviet Legislature and

Gorbachev's Political

Reforms

 **Robert T. Huber**

E D I T E D B Y

and **Donald R. Kelley**

M. E. Sharpe, Inc.
Armonk, New York London, England

Library of Congress Cataloging-in-Publication Data

Perestroika-era politics: the new Soviet legislature and Gorbachev's political reforms
Robert T. Huber, Donald R. Kelley, editors
p.   cm.
Includes bibliographical references
ISBN 0-87332-829-9 (cloth)   ISBN 0-87332-830-2 (paper)
1. Soviet Union, Verkhovnyi Sovet
2. Soviet Union—Constitutional history
3. Soviet Union—Politics and government—1985-
I. Huber, Robert T., 1955 II. Kelley, Donald R.
JN6556.P47   1991
328.47—dc20
91-18983
CIP

Printed in the United States of America

The paper used in this publication meets the minimum requirements
of American National Standard for Information Sciences—
Permanence of Paper for Printed Library Materials, ANSI Z39.48-1984.

MV 10 9 8 7 6 5 4 3 2 1

CONTENTS

The Functioning of the New Supreme Soviet

ACKNOWLEDGMENTS

The rapid pace of change in the Soviet Union makes a volume like this both a daunting challenge and an exciting enterprise. The need to synthesize longer-term systemic trends with dizzying changes in the arrays of political actors and institutions makes social scientific work on the Soviet Union particularly difficult. Nonetheless, researchers both in academia and in government have taken the challenge.

The objective of this volume is to provide a more reliable foundation of knowledge for advanced research on the Soviet political system. The volume will fill a generally recognized gap in teaching materials on the new Soviet political institutions and formations. It will also help take stock of the possible future direction of the current political system for possible application to policy making.

The excitement of undertaking such a project is that the course of perestroika-era politics has made it possible to continue the critical effort to place the Soviet Union in a comparative analytical framework for the study of political systems. This volume is one of the very few that have drawn on the experience of comparative study of political institutions, particularly legislatures, to develop research programs that might enable us to understand better the nature and significance of political events in the Soviet Union. Comparative analysis of the Soviet experience also enriches the existing literature by suggesting anomalies, confirming some established hypotheses, and modifying others.

The pursuit of this endeavor has required many hands. Appreciation must clearly go to my co-editor, Professor Donald Kelley, whose leadership in organizing a panel on emerging political institutions at the 1989 meeting of the American Association for the Advancement of Slavic Studies provided the inspiration for preparing this volume. Professor Kelley was also quite helpful in reviewing the conceptual framework and coordinating the research activities of individual authors.

I would also like to thank individual contributors to this volume. While preserving their independence in the pursuit of research, they were most cooperative in working out suitable divisions of labor for an immense and deeply interrelated subject matter. Their indulgence in tolerating the frequent reminders of the editors for meeting deadlines is also appreciated.

The scholarly content of the volume, of course, would have remained unfulfilled without the practical and highly effective contributions of Sarah Tarrow, Rose London, and Patricia Kolb in preparing the manuscript for publication and suggesting editorial changes along the way. All too often, self-important authors overlook such contributions. The consummate skill of these colleagues, as well as their commitment, good-naturedness, and toleration of idiosyncratic editors and authors was quite frankly indispensable for bringing this volume to publication. All of them are genuine professionals and reflect credit on those who have the opportunity to work with them.

Words of appreciation are also in order for the Social Science Research Council, particularly its president, David Featherman. Professor Featherman's leadership in implementing a new professional development program for Council staff afforded me both the time and the funding to pursue the preparation of this volume in a timely manner. The development of such a program is but one example of Professor Featherman's commitment to advanced research in the social sciences across its many disciplines, areas, and methods of inquiry, and to the training of scholars, both within the Council and outside it, to achieve that purpose in a focused and effective way.

Finally, the support of my wife Lois and my sons Jeremy and Joshua remains a critically sustaining energy for all my professional work. They bear the brunt of many, sometimes conflicting commitments with grace and encouragement. Only they know how much I depend on them.

Robert T. Huber

PERESTROIKA-ERA POLITICS

1

INTRODUCTION
The New Soviet Legislature:
How Ideas and Institutions Matter

Robert T. Huber

Social scientists have long disagreed about the role ideas play in politics, particularly in times of transition or crisis. This disagreement has been evident in many cases where the struggle of ideas has clearly produced policy changes, but the role that can be assigned to new ideas as opposed to more settled institutional interests in effecting the changes is difficult to assess.[1]

To date, there has been no integrated effort to explore the role ideas have played in the systemic transition now under way in the Soviet Union. Why is such an effort important? Because the beliefs, values, and principles that are a part of *glasnost'*, *perestroika*, *demokratizatsiia*, and "new thinking" in foreign policy, as well as transplanted conceptions of civil society and particularly the concept of separation of powers, have had an unmistakable impact on both individuals and institutions in the Soviet political system. Such an impact cannot be understood merely by regarding such ideas as the product of institutional interests or actors in place at the time of Mikhail Gorbachev's accession to power in 1985.

To argue that the ideas of the post-1985 period are simply "hooks" used by elites to advance their own interests is to lose much of the richness and context of today's Soviet politics and society. Such an approach was very popular in explaining Soviet politics of an earlier period. On the eve of Gorbachev's accession, no one would have suggested that the ideas we now accept as essential to understanding Soviet politics would develop in the years ahead.

Indeed, most scholars and policy makers were content to accept political outcomes in the Soviet Union as the product of entrenched individuals and institutions who preferred the status quo or only marginal change. Politics dominated by the Communist Party and tolerant of only a highly controlled pluralism of ideas was thought to explain adequately the political life of the country. Most observers had confidence in the party's ability to assimilate demands for modifications in policy within an existing political structure.

Studying only institutions and the policy-making process, as if the ideas and preferences of individuals were only the modeling clay of policy outcomes, produces a very distorted analysis. The stagnation of this approach produces either woeful unpreparedness for the dynamics of political change or after-the-fact explanations of policy changes that argue that institutions and individuals were really in favor of those changes all along.

To be sure, the debate about the role ideas play in politics and policy making has not been settled. The scholarly literature does, however, offer a number of hypotheses positing a role for ideas in the making of policy, hypotheses that will find both support and some counterevidence in the chapters that follow. Here are some of the hypotheses.

1. Ideas change the way actors define their worldviews and preferences by helping them to define meaning, to discern order and disorder, and to formulate beliefs, values, rules, and expectations.

2. Ideas are conditioned by and have impact on the way individuals, institutions, and their constituent interests are organized and deal with problems within their purview.

3. Ideas affect the structuring of policy-making agendas in both a limiting and a delimiting way, thereby suggesting tracks on which practical solutions will be channeled.

4. Ideas provide clues to a range of multiple equilibria in policy outcomes and the diversity of social, economic, and political forms present in those outcomes, as well as clues about their prevalence and enforcement or their failure to take root in the same or differing institutional settings.

5. During times of crisis or transition, ideas enable policy makers to reduce uncertainty and build consensus outcomes, or conversely, can restrain successful efforts to overcome uncertainty and instability.

6. Ideas frame the way policy makers signal commitments and structure strategies for reaching preferred outcomes.

7. Ideas enrich our understanding of outcomes, particularly since their implementation can be subject, for a variety of reasons, to lag times of long duration during which constraints to their acceptance are lowered.

8. Ideas are contested and their implementation can produce unexpected or unanticipated outcomes that in turn give purpose to differing ideas and policy-making preferences both within and across institutions.

The above hypotheses attest to the analytical richness the study of ideas can have for the conduct of research on political systems. But simply to posit a role for ideas is a rather modest scholarly objective. Many scholars can readily concede, whether they favor an ideational or a rational actor perspective, that in a general abstract sense both ideas and institutions matter. Far more useful is an effort to explore *how* they matter in concrete and disaggregated ways, what the ideas are and what led to their acceptance, how they are being practically implemented, the social context of implementation, and its effects on outcomes.

Moreover, it can be persuasively argued that ideas have played an important *causal* role in certain political outcomes, or at least helped make possible a range of outcomes. These ideas have also been a causal factor in the practical implementation of certain policies and in some instances the institutionalization of policy making generally.

The essays that follow seek to demonstrate not only the ways but the means by which the ideas of the Gorbachev period have had impact. The main focus of analysis is the major institutional changes under way since 1989 in the national legislature of the Soviet Union,[2] the Congress of People's Deputies, but particularly the Supreme Soviet.

The functions and processes that legislatures undertake help us understand why they are often important institutions in their own right, particularly during times of systemic transition. Legislatures are a recruiting ground for emerging political elites. Legislators may serve as representatives of the public in dealing with unelected elites in the executive bureaucracy. The legislature can serve as an institution through which societal groups form coalitions and political parties to promote or frustrate social action and change, channel or harness dissent, and challenge or reinforce regime legitimation.

Finally, legislatures can often become the arena in which judgments are made about *what* functions governments will or will not carry out for the society. The legislature is, as Robert Sharlet points out in his chapter in this volume, part of "the value-rich environment of entwined supporting sociolegal networks . . . underpinning a democratic system."

Thus, a legislature cannot be studied in a vacuum. Processes and institutions outside the legislature matter and deserve careful attention. In the Soviet context today, such issue areas as the direction of constitutional reform, the evolution of the electoral system, the legislative process, the emerging political parties and their interaction with the existing party-administrative structures, legislative-executive relations, the development of legislative power in specific issue areas, must be studied to understand credibly how the Soviet national legislature impacts and is impacted upon by *perestroika*-era politics.

The volume has chapters in all of the above issue areas. It is divided into a tripartite framework encompassing (1) the new legal framework that defines the legislature (the ongoing constitutional debate, electoral procedures and outcomes, and legislative organization and practice); (2) the formation of new parties and political groupings both within and outside the legislature (parties of the left, the right, and proto-partisan interest groups and national fronts); and (3) the functioning of the new Supreme Soviet (the state of legislative-executive relations, legislative oversight vis-à-vis the Soviet executive bureaucracy, and case studies of legislative action on both domestic and foreign policy issues).

A background theme in many of the chapters is the often competing rather than reinforcing development of politics and political institutions at other levels of the system. The volume also provides rich and heretofore unavailable taxonomic detail on the new political parties, and the rules of legislative debate, referral, amendment, and enactment.

As stated earlier, in addition to being a study of institutions, the volume seeks to explain the impact of ideas in the Gorbachev period and how those ideas have mattered for outcomes. The volume considers these ideas in the context of a series of hypotheses described earlier about the impact of ideas on policy making. For example, Sharlet's chapter on constitutional reform points out how the idea of movement toward a law-based state transforming society has changed the world views and preferences of policy makers, enabling and empowering new elites to declare autonomy for their regions and republics, and helping to create a new set of beliefs and values concerning sovereignty, regime legitimacy, private ownership, and the status of independent associational groups in policy making. The article also explores how changed conceptions of order and disorder as perceived by both the new elites and institutions and their established counterparts have affected the constitutional debate.

Viktor Danilenko's chapter on electoral reform demonstrates how ideas are conditioned by and have impact on the way problems are dealt with by policy makers and policy-making institutions. While as Danilenko points out, electoral legislation was designed to increase political participation, improve systemic responsiveness to public opinion, and change the composition and outlook of the previous national legislature, the impact of these ideas was diluted in various ways. Problems encountered in bringing about intended effects included a lack of political and legal experience in promoting institutional change, compromises in the law made necessary by the clash of reforming and reactive forces in the political system, and efforts to undermine the representativeness of nomination procedures.

Nonetheless, Danilenko argues firmly that the first contested national parliamentary elections since the early days of the Revolution did produce important results and impacted heavily on the approach of elites to political problems. In place of "the old talk about 'monolithic unity' . . . a real, vital society emerged, full of different and sometimes conflicting interests."

Stuart Goldman's chapter on the legislative process shows how ideas change the way policy-making agendas are structured in both a limiting and a delimiting way. The proposals enunciated by Gorbachev in 1988 for the revitalization of the Soviet national legislature, in Goldman's view, had multiple objectives: establishing a more consensual legal foundation for promoting economic reform, increasing popular accountability for elite decision making, providing an alternative institutional structure for isolating opponents of reform within the Communist Party, and enforcing and giving greater meaning to the concept of "socialist legality."

The evolution of the legislature to date has resulted in at least partial achievement of these ideas. For example, the legislature has insisted on making final override votes on vetoed legislation, a two-thirds voting requirement for the imposition of a state of emergency, and the ability to reject the agenda for legislation proposed by the presidium of the Supreme Soviet. Nonetheless, ideas of legislative power have also been delimited by Gorbachev in terms of agenda setting and the arbitrary control of legislative power that he has exercised through the presidium.

Donald Kelley's chapter on the factionalization of Soviet politics demonstrates how ideas frame the way policy makers signal commitments and structure strategies for reaching preferred outcomes. The reduction of power located in the Communist Party that was a consequence of *glasnost'* and *perestroika* had a major impact in the decision to agree to the abolition of the constitutionally mandated leading societal role for the party. This decision led to the demise of the Communist Party as the ultimate aggregator of interests and signaler of political commitments in the Soviet political system.

In the process, a whole range of strategies for attaining favorable political outcomes have arisen, along with a staggering array of structures (60,000 informal public organizations, a myriad of political parties, popular front coalitions, splits within the Communist Party, and the formation of decentralized communist parties at the republic level). As Kelley points out, the structuring of strategies and signaling of commitments brought about by the ideas of the Gorbachev period have at least for the present created a situation in which elites in various new institutional structures "seem better able to articulate demands, spawn new political entities that zealously set themselves apart from others in the political spectrum, and press for solutions to real and imagined grievances than to generate mechanisms that produce political consensus, working coalitions within the legislature, and viable national leadership."

Joel Moses's chapter on the new right-wing political parties demonstrates how the implementation of ideas can be subject to lag times of long duration. Like Kelley, Moses points to the idea of removing the monopolization of formal political power by the Communist Party as being a pivotal event in political party formation. This idea in turn also made possible a whole range of ideas heretofore considered unsuitable for appropriate political discussion or implementation. Moses describes in detail a furious political debate now under way to define a symbolic "turning point" in Russian history, to establish a new "conventional wisdom" about the country's past and thus to legitimate a future path. As Moses points out, a debate about ideas has been spawned in *perestroika*-era politics, centered around "the reasons for the crisis and the point at which things began to go wrong and a course of actions was taken that led to the present political crisis threatening the very survival of the nation."

Michael Urban's chapter on the new left-wing political parties shows that, particularly during times of crisis or transition, ideas enable policy makers either to build consensus outcomes or to restrain successful efforts in this direction. Urban argues persuasively that despite the presence among members of the Soviet democratic left of new ideas about the direction of economic activity and the political system that regulates it (constitutional democracy, social democracy, economic liberalism, regulated market economy, welfare-state capitalism, nonpartisan civil and military bureaucracy), these ideas to date have not contributed to an emerging societal consensus about political forms.

Rather, ideas about the future promulgated by new left-wing parties, in Urban's view, "are themselves expressions of the society in which they have emerged." Thus, the new parties are frustrated by the legacy of the past in representing interests and social forces, aggregating demands, and allocating resources. In many instances, even as they engage in tumultuous charges against each other concerning "collaboration" with the Communist Party, the tactics and strategies of the new opposition parties have often emulated the target of their scorn.

Emerging out of a political reality in which one party not only ruled society but sought to define its functions, new parties are torn between a need to extirpate one-party rule and the need to organize effectively against the remnants of that rule. The entrenched ideas characterized by stark pretensions of the old Communist Party to representation of all of society have frustrated the new political parties' ability to be candid about their desire to express and implement the policy preferences of social groups. This process has produced in turn a somewhat strange disassociation of parties from the social groups they purport to serve.

Eugene Huskey's chapter on legislative-executive relations demonstrates how ideas fare in institutional settings and how the diversity of differing social, economic, and political forms mitigates the effects of both ideas and outcomes. Inherent in the ideas of *perestroika*-era politics has been, as Huskey points out, "the struggle [by legislatures] over the centuries to influence and restrain the power of the executive."

The idea of restraining executive power through the approval of ministers and their accountability through public discussion found resonance in the revitalized Soviet parliament and gave meaning to its activities. Nonetheless, these ideas were not well received in the older and more adroit executive institutions, which found procedural means to resubmit ministerial appointments already rejected or remove those already approved.

Moreover, Huskey argues that efforts by the Supreme Soviet to use its law-making powers more extensively have been confronted by ministerial efforts to overwhelm statutes through the traditional practice of immersing Soviet society "in a sea of normative acts issued by the Council of Ministers and its constituent ministries." While this ocean of regulations, both written and unwritten, well known or little known, has been mitigated somewhat by legislative efforts at enhanced oversight and legal prohibitions on the recourse to regulation writing, Gorbachev's own method for dealing with ministerial interference has been to enhance the power of the office of the president through the issuance of decrees. Such a power clearly undermines legislative power, but not necessarily that of the executive bureaucracy.

Thomas Remington's and Robert Huber's chapters on the Supreme Soviet's legislative activities with respect to laws and oversight concerning the media and defense and foreign policy deal with the ways ideas become institutionalized, drawing on a comparative framework for evaluating institutionalization. Both chapters also show how ideas become implemented, are contested, produce unexpected outcomes, and generate differing policy-making preferences.

In Remington's chapter, the political environment encouraged by the promulgation of *glasnost'* emboldened legal scholars to advocate the widening of media access to information from official organizations. However, the policy-making process, which in the past had often frustrated initiative and boldness in the presentation of policy options, was transformed by the idea and new institutional reality of a revitalized parliament. In Remington's view, the Supreme Soviet and several of its committees played a critical role in articulating and framing legislative provisions dealing with the expansion of access rights, the rights of a citizen to establish a newspaper, and the nature of ownership rights.

This somewhat unanticipated outcome, given the ability of conservatives to restrict the rights of the media through the previously institutionalized, party-centered decision-making process, produced a reaction within the parliament's presidium and the Communist Party apparatus. After seeking to short-circuit a liberal media law through the presidium's well-known arbitrary means of controlling the legislative process, compromises were achieved that, in Remington's view, enabled advocates of expanded media rights to establish "a legal mechanism for media organizations to declare their independence of state and party owners." In this way, ideas helped create new institutions that changed policy formulation, contestation, implementation, and outcome.

The same can be said for the discussion in Huber's chapter on the Supreme Soviet's approach to defense and foreign policy issues. The ideas contained in the "new thinking" in Soviet foreign policy, including the principle of greater public accountability in defense and foreign policy decision making, led to greater activism by the new Supreme Soviet in conducting oversight on such issues. Through the parliamentary "question hour," and the right of the parliament to approve executive nominations, make laws, approve treaties, and authorize the use of force, the executive has been rendered more publicly accountable than was the case before the revitalization of the Supreme Soviet.

The implementation of the ideas of the Gorbachev period has clearly produced unintended outcomes in terms of legislative actions in defense and foreign policy. The power to question and perhaps even limit executive policy making on such critical issues as German reunification and the Persian Gulf has not been exercised by liberal deputies but rather by the conservative Soiuz faction. Liberal deputies have also been checkmated in their more aggressive efforts to reorganize and restructure the Ministry of Defense. The promulgation of new ideas has produced contestation, which while not yet impacting significantly on outcomes, has clearly made possible the articulation of differing ideas and policy-making preferences in the executive ministries and parliament.

To be sure, this introduction provides only a thumbnail sketch of the chapters that follow and how each of them demonstrates the impact of ideas on policy making. The reader is invited to reflect carefully on each chapter, for all of them contain evidence of not only one but many of the hypotheses discussed earlier and how they are brought to bear in the current transformation of the Soviet political system.

Moreover, the chapters also shed light on how ideas have mattered and how future practical implementation will have causal effects on outcomes. For Sharlet, in the area of constitutional reform the ideas most likely to promote a stable equilibrium are those that would promote what he calls a " 'fusion constitution,' bonding Russian values and Western ideas into at least semi-democratic institutions, rather than trying to transplant American institutions prematurely into still infertile Soviet soil." In order to deal with the "war of the laws" problem, characterized by a myriad of geopolitical entities claiming the right to make and enforce laws, Sharlet points to ideas promoting "plural conceptions of ownership and civil society, and its vision of a more decentralized, federal system," as best able to deal with the dilemmas and contradictions of *perestroika*-era politics.

Danilenko's chapter points to ideas that stress political competition as essential to building responsive representative institutions. The threat of removal from office under public or legislative pressure seems a critical, galvanizing idea in the current Soviet political setting, as is the corresponding idea of multiple political parties that compete regularly for political power rather than claiming ownership of such power. Such parties must be conditioned by the idea that they are, in Danilenko's words, "just one of many competing political forces rather than a mighty dictator."

Goldman's chapter similarly points to the idea of a separation of powers, and its still underdeveloped institutionalization, as critical to future political outcomes. He argues that for all the flaws in the performance of the new Soviet parliament to date, the current situation "is far removed from the highly centralized circular flow of power exercised by the ruling party elite only a few years ago." In Goldman's view, how the idea of a separation of powers fares, and its institutionalization in legislatures at the national, republic, and local levels, is critical to understanding future political outcomes.

In his chapter, Kelley describes four scenarios for the coordination of policy (a reformed democratized party, multiparty noncommunist coalitional government, parliamentary government, and strengthened presidential control). He argues that the ideas that facilitate interest aggregation in various policy areas will emerge successful. At the time of this writing, the idea of a strong executive, certainly an old idea indeed in the Soviet/Russian political environment, seems to be prevailing. In this sense, Kelley's article is extremely helpful in reminding all of us of the constraints new ideas have in changing policy outcomes, and the strong possibility that in many issue areas, older ideas will have considerable staying power.

Moses, too, emphasizes the role of entrenched and already institutionalized ideas. Deteriorating economic conditions, the failure of official reforms and of liberal political actors outside the Gorbachev circle to address those conditions effectively, and the organizational weaknesses of the Soviet left suggest that "any conclusion that democracy has triumphed irreversibly over the antidemocratic right would be extremely premature." In pluralist systems, Moses argues, stability is conditioned on certain factors (narrow differences in values, long-term economic growth, and a relative absence of ethnic-religious pluralism and communal conflict) not characteristic in the present-day Soviet Union. Ideas promoting multiparty political structures at this stage are therefore not likely to become institutionalized.

Urban's chapter also focuses on how old ideas shaping institutions and policy outcomes have retarded the creation of Western-style political parties. So far, the idea of parties as concrete channels and representatives of major social groups and aggregating, cross-cutting agents of interest have not been falling on fertile political ground. Without the institutionalization of such ideas, long-entrenched ideas about the divisiveness of factions, one-party notions of representing and leading all of society, and the resort to conspiratorial recriminations against political opponents, will continue to have broad resonance. Moreover, such ideas may over the long term crowd out multiple party formation in favor of another all-encompassing ruling structure.

In the area of legislative-executive relations, Huskey stresses the idea of executive accountability to the public through the legislature's oversight and law-making responsibility as central to the relevance of the legislature in the future. The struggle to restrain executive power will be played out over such ideas as the separation of powers, investigatory legislative powers, and the right of the legislature to demand policy-making information from the president and his ministries. The debate over these ideas and its outcome will provide key barometers of the state and direction of systemic crisis. Their resolution will also tell us much about the future political structure of the Soviet Union.

Finally, in both the Remington and Huber chapters, ideas about the scope, content, and process of legislative activity are seen as important in determining outcomes in issue areas. In both cases, the conviction among some parliamentarians that law-making, treaty-making, and policy-review mechanisms should be used vigorously to shape the content of laws and policy implementation did make a difference in critical issue areas.

Whether such ideas become institutionalized through agenda-setting, the defense of prerogatives, increased resources for staffing and oversight activities, the development of full-time legislators and complex functional infrastructure, systematized rules and norms of behavior, regularized recruitment, images of effectiveness, and other factors will shape the way issues are discussed and policy options are chosen. Furthermore, as Huber points out, such ideas are also central to the positioning of the new Soviet legislature along a continuum of possible institutional outcomes (active, vulnerable, reactive, marginal, and minimal legislatures) seen in the rise and fall of parliaments throughout the world.[3]

As this volume goes to press, the complex processes of *perestroika*-era politics, including the place of the new Soviet legislature in those processes, are still unfolding. Social scientists studying the contemporary Soviet Union have encountered the considerable occupational hazard of trying to come to grips intellectually with a moving target.

Clearly, this volume does not escape this problem. In August, 1991 a group of political conservatives led ostensibly by Vice-President Gennadi Ianaev replaced President Gorbachev and attempted to impose by force a new government which sought to reverse many of the political changes and institutional reforms described in this volume. Clearly, the ideas of the *perestroika* era are being contested, with some rejecting and resisting by force new ideas and fundamental change.

New ideas of a law-based state, the legislature as a key institutional foundation for that state, toleration and encouragement of multiple political institutions, accountability of the state to its citizens through electoral and regulatory means, and a competitive political and policy making process are under challenge by individuals and institutions that seek to reverse the spread and effective implementation of those ideas. Instead, more traditional ideas of centralized political power, a single-party ruling structure, delegated administrative control of the economy, and a minimal legitimating legislature are once again being offered by some policy makers as the only practical means to rule the Soviet Union.

No one can predict the outcome of this power struggle at this juncture. However, one must doubt that the ideas, individuals and institutions that have developed in the *perestroika* era can be suppressed successfully in the long term.

Whatever the immediate short-term outcome of the coup d'etat of August, 1991, this volume offers both scholars and students a unique compilation of updated information on a variety of political processes now under way in the Soviet Union, particularly concerning the fledgling legislature. Additionally, the volume provides a framework for considering how the ideas of the *perestroika*-era have shaped and been shaped by institutions, how those ideas have sometimes mattered, and sometimes have not, and how they have been accepted, resisted, or incorporated in new forms.

Significantly, the articles in this volume also provide clues as to what ideas could lead to practical implementation and have a causal effect on a variety of possible outcomes. With these tools in hand, the reader is hopefully far better prepared to anticipate upcoming struggles of ideas and institutions, and their impact on the future direction of the new Soviet national legislature and the Soviet political system as a whole.

Notes

1. The author is heavily indebted to Judith Goldstein, professor of political science at Stanford University, and Robert Keohane, professor of government at Harvard University, whose outstanding work on the impact of ideas on policy making helped frame many of the hypotheses outlined in this article. For more on this general subject area, see Judith Goldstein and Robert O. Keohane, "Ideas and Foreign Policy" (draft introduction to conferences on the role of ideas in foreign policy sponsored by the Social Science Research Council, January 18-20, 1990, and April 19-20, 1991).

2. It is recognized that the term "legislature" is fraught with difficulty because other terms for the institution, particularly "parliament," are often used with identical meaning. One standard definition of a legislature, "a predominantly elected body of people that acts collegially and that has at least the formal but not necessarily the exclusive power to enact laws binding on all members of a specific geopolitical entity," helps to clarify the problem somewhat.

Nonetheless, an examination of legislatures globally reveals a rather diverse set of institutions called legislatures, parliaments, assemblies, and other terms. Their functions vary with degrees of law making, policy making, representation, and interest aggregation and legitimation activities. By focusing on what legislatures or parliaments do instead of what they are called, the reader is better able to study the processes under way in the Soviet national legislature without stumbling over what is an admittedly loosely defined term. For more on these points, see Michael L. Mezey, *Comparative Legislatures* (Durham, NC: Duke University Press, 1979), pp. 6-24.

3. For more on this typology of legislatures and definitions of each type of legislature and policy-making activities within, see Mezey, pp. 6-143.

THE NEW LEGAL FRAMEWORK

2

THE PATH OF CONSTITUTIONAL REFORM IN THE USSR

Robert Sharlet

The era of *perestroika* or "restructuring" began in the mid-late 1980s with high hopes that law would become the defining characteristic of the period, institutionalizing the great changes Mikhail Gorbachev promised for the Soviet system. As a lawyer himself, Gorbachev frequently referenced the law as the preferred medium for transforming state and society. Moreover, law was to be counted on to give the reforms durability and longevity or, in the word favored at the time, "irreversibility."

As the Soviet Union proceeds into the 1990s, law has lost some of its luster, becoming part of the problem of reform instead of part of the solution. Indeed, the "war of laws" has become a codeword for the contemporary dilemma of Soviet politics: the country has been wracked by collisions between federal or all-union law and diverse, contrary republic laws. The result is that the Soviet legal system--heretofore a top-down, centralized, well-oiled mechanism--has been paralyzed in many aspects by implementation failure, with neither central nor local laws working effectively. How did this situation come about?

Gorbachev's domestic restructuring program was initially fashioned out of three policies. While it has been generally agreed at home and abroad that Soviet economic reform has failed to date, there has also been a consensus that the other two component policies, *glasnost'* and democratization, have been successful beyond the elite's expectations in changing the political landscape of the USSR. In fact, from the point of view of the formerly unchallenged incumbents of power, these policies have been too successful.

Soviet conservatives have begun to equate *glasnost'* and democratization with the dreaded term "destabilization." The Russian republic's Communist Party chief has spoken of *glasnost'* unleashing "informational terrorism,"[1] while for the outgoing prosecutor-general, democratization had led to "intoxication with pluralism."[2] In the early 1990s even Gorbachev had begun to back away from his own policies, castigating his radical opponents for carrying these ideas to "absurd lengths" which, he argued, were "deforming the democratic process."[3]

The reasons for conservative dismay were evident. Initially, spontaneous political groups and eventually entire union republics had seized upon Gorbachev's liberalizing policies to pursue their respective ethnic nationalist and, in several cases, secessionist agendas. Beginning in the late 1980s, the newly reformed republic legislatures had begun to challenge the legislative hegemony of the restructured all-union parliament in Moscow. First the union republics passed language laws ensuring that the language of the titular nationality,[4] and not Russian, would be the official tongue of the republic. The next step was to declare the preemptive right of the republic parliament to ratify federal legislation before it could take effect on the republic's territory. Inevitably, some of these more independent republic legislatures gradually began to enact ethnically exclusive laws on citizenship and immigration in order to delimit Russian influence in their midst.[5]

By the end of 1990, all fifteen union republics, and most of the USSR's autonomous republics as well, had declared their sovereignty within the Union, and a few union republics, following Lithuania's example, indicated their intention to set a course for full independence. Thus, openly contending parliaments, a parade of sovereignties, secessionist fever in some regions, and what the former Soviet foreign minister Eduard Shevardnadze called the "war of presidents" between Gorbachev of the Union and Boris Yeltsin of the Russian Republic[6] intensified the war of laws, diminishing the authority of the law throughout the crisis-riven USSR.

As the legal system became more complex--for example, with so-called "parallel" structures such as competing union and republic procurators or chief prosecutors in the more independent-minded republics--Gorbachev and the reformers placed their confidence in constitutional reform to disentangle and reallocate authority between the center and the provinces. A reformed all-union constitution incorporating the vast changes brought about by *perestroika* was seen as the way to resolve the crisis in the law itself. The revised constitution would become the wellspring of a "law-governed state," which in turn would midwife a market economy, at last bringing to life desperately needed economic reform. Thus, the new Soviet Union would ride a crest of constitutionalism to a bright, shining future within a multiethnic state. The chaos at the door would be banished, so Gorbachev hoped, but has he underestimated the task of constitutional reform in the USSR?

Is There a Constitution in the USSR Today?

It may seem strange to ask whether an operative constitution exists in the Soviet Union at this time. An obvious answer would be to refer to the USSR Constitution of 1977.[7] The fourth Soviet constitution, the 1977 document presided over by Leonid Brezhnev, subsumed basic features of Lenin's constitutions of 1918 and 1924 and Stalin's constitution of 1936. For law reformers of the post-Stalin period, the new Constitution of 1977 appeared as the logical culmination of a long train of legal reforms begun by Nikita Khrushchev in the mid-1950s after Stalin's death and carried on by Brezhnev after Khrushchev's ouster in 1964.[8] Although the document was the product of a one-party dictatorship and fell well short of Western democratic constitutional standards, it was a significant improvement over its Stalinist predecessor, which, heavily amended, had remained in force nearly a quarter of a century after Stalin's death in 1953. As such, the 1977 Constitution exemplified the continuing trend toward the juridicization of the Soviet system as the post-Stalin Communist Party, having eliminated political terror as a means of governance, increasingly began to rely on law as a method for regulating its subjects and controlling Soviet society.[9]

Extensively and repeatedly amended since late 1988, the 1977 Constitution by the early 1990s looked like a patchwork quilt of ideas from East and West. Leninist and Stalinist substructures underlying Brezhnevist superstructures commingled with Gorbachevian reformist themes and even Western constitutional concepts. Depending on which part of the Constitution one looks at, a case can be made that it remains an operative document or, conversely, that it has become a hopeless anachronism.

For instance, present policy if not yet practice has relegated the Preamble to the proverbial museum of history. True, one might ask who pays attention to constitutional preambles, but in the USSR, ideas have long been used as weapons and, at the very least, as ideological touchstones. The Preamble begins with the Bolshevik Revolution of 1917, proclaims the creation of a new type of state for the building of socialism and communism, and asserts that mankind's "world-historic turn from capitalism to socialism" had begun.[10] The Preamble goes on to extol a Soviet society of "mighty productive forces," "advanced science," "mature socialist social relations," the "fraternal cooperation" of all nationalities, and "a high degree of . . . ideological conviction." The Preamble closes with the Communist Party-led Soviet state having as its supreme goal "a classless communist society."

On the other hand, a perusal of the Constitution's initial chapter on "The Political System" gives one simultaneously a view of the recent past, a sense of the present, and a glimpse of the Soviet future. The "Legitimacy" clause (Article 1) still speaks of a socialist state and locates its source in the workers, peasants, and intelligentsia, not to mention all of the Union's constituent nations, surely now the Achilles heel of Soviet legitimacy. In addition, a place must now be found in the scheme of Soviet popular sovereignty for the newly arisen multi-million force of legal private entrepreneurs. The "Power through the Soviets" clause (Article 2), heretofore a facade for Communist Party rule, looks more promising since the relatively free elections of 1989-90, but the local soviets have proven too large and cumbersome for effective municipal administration and will need to be substantially redesigned. The "Democratic Centralism" clause (Article 3), previously a feature of centralized Soviet government, has become a "dead letter" in view of the raging "war of parliaments."

Progress has been made toward the fuller realization of the "Socialist Legality" clause (Article 4), but the old administrative-command system still lives on in the bureaucracy and the ongoing "war of laws" compounds the problem further. The "Discussion and Referendum" clause (Article 5), earlier confined to a half-life, has now been fully activated with the passage of the referendum law and the holding of the first national referendum in 1991. Article 6, on the Communist Party hegemony, has been one of only two clauses in Chapter One to be amended. In probably the most significant amendment of the Constitution to date, the party was deprived of its domination of the system in 1990 and a constitutional door was opened to the emergence of a multiparty system in the USSR.[11] Gorbachev's democratization policy has substantially transformed and augmented the "Mass Public Organizations" clause (Article 7) which in the past essentially meant Communist Party-controlled organizations. The explosive growth of new independent associational groups in the USSR, some 60,000 by the 1990s, has given this revised clause important new meaning. One of the innovations of the 1977 Constitution was the "Labor Collective" clause (Article 8), which effectively created a new Communist Party-controlled adjunct to management under the guise of workers' participation. The necessary enabling legislation was passed later, during Iurii Andropov's short rule (1982-84), but the rash of strikes by coalminers since the summer of 1989 has given this humble clause dynamic new content.[12]

The final provision of the Constitution's first chapter, the "Socialist Democracy and Political Culture" clause (Article 9), has provided the biggest surprise, surely beyond anything Brezhnev and his constitutional draftsmen could ever have imagined. Essentially, this clause was intended to afford a glimpse of a more open Soviet society in the distant future. Article 9 anticipated, among other things, more civic participation, respect for public opinion, a more activist society, greater *glasnost'*, and increased democracy. While recognizing that the Soviet Union still has a considerable distance to go to perfect these features of a civil society, it should be acknowledged that the ideational seedlings of this long-dormant clause have begun to take root.

As this brief analysis of just the opening parts of the extant Soviet constitution suggests, the answer to the question posed at the beginning of this section is neither easy nor obvious. A simple solution would be to say "No," there is no operative constitution in the USSR today. Change has been moving too fast, everything has been in flux, and the confusion, political and constitutional, has become too great; hence, the Soviet Union has become a state without a legal rudder, a normative charter.

However, a persuasive case can also be made for arriving at "Yes," through at least five partial answers or affirmative perspectives on the question of constitutional order in the contemporary USSR. One could begin by saying that the Constitution of 1977, although a "Rube Goldberg" contraption in the context of world practice, has remained a functioning constitutional document. Or, one might construe the present Soviet constitution as a combination of the amended 1977 instrument and the aggregate of Gorbachev-inspired federal legislation, some of which has mainly operationalized constitutional "dead letters," while other statutes have effectively eclipsed some of the core ideas of the 1977 Constitution.

Yet another affirmative perspective would be to argue that a kind of phantom "transitional constitution" has somehow been at work out there in public space, or at least in Gorbachev's mind. He has indeed spoken of the Soviet Union being between constitutions, so to speak, in transition from the "old" to a "new" constitution.[13] Complementing this perspective, one might suggest that the Soviet Union may be operating under an unwritten constitution, comprised of the flotsam and jetsam of Gorbachev's many policy speeches with their soaring and searing rhetoric, conveying his metaphors, critiques, construals, zig-zags, advances and retreats. Thus, to the question "What is the Soviet constitution," Gorbachev might figuratively reply "C'est moi."

One further perspective would be that the Constitution of the USSR today could be construed as the composite of the patched-up federal document and all of the revised and amended union republic constitutions, some of which, like the draft RSFSR Constitution of 1990,[14] differ markedly in letter and spirit from the union constitution. Of course, if this position is adopted, one may have to concede a tangle of constitutional conflicts between Moscow and the republic capitals, and, quite possibly, the fundamental ungovernability of the USSR by normal, noncoercive means.

This leads to the final hypothetical situation of a biconstitutional order in the contemporary USSR. How might one arrive at this conclusion? If one defines the center's constitutional claims as "thesis" and the various republics' constitutional responses as "antithesis," then Gorbachev's draft Union Treaty of 1990, and the 1991 referendum victory of its revised version, might be considered as his attempt at dialectical "synthesis."

The difficulty with such a neat intellectual outcome, however, is that a number of union republics formally declined to participate in the first all-union referendum, meaning that they may still be subject (at least in

Gorbachev's mind) to the original Union Treaty of 1922 as embedded in sections III, V, and VI of the 1977 Constitution. Thus, a bi- or dual constitutional system might conceivably arise in the Soviet Union, a bizarre outcome that sooner or later would either require radical grafting by force or a deft surgical separation of the two incompatible systems.

Is Constitutionalism Emerging in the USSR?

In recent years it has become politically fashionable in the Soviet Union to borrow from the American experience, be it fast food or constitutional government. Even the KGB chief has cited US national security legislation to justify similar authority for the Soviet secret police.[15] All of this has constituted a sharp turnabout in the Soviet mindset, since, until the mid-1980s, American institutions, the epitome of "bourgeois democracy," were consistently subjected to scholarly criticism in the USSR. The American Constitution with its "grandiloquent, . . . vague language," constantly in need of judicial interpretation, was always seen at odds with Soviet jurisprudential canon on constitutions and the courts.[16]

The reception of Western ideas will likely prove to be more difficult than the Soviet leadership has imagined. Hoary concepts such as democracy and markets, which have evolved gradually in the West, have been grasped in the USSR mechanistically at best, in a manner reminiscent of Soviet technology-borrowing during the interwar period. Gorbachev and others have facilely spoken of these ideas with little apparent awareness of the encrustations of time and tradition, policy and practice, which have shaped their contemporary meaning in the United States and the Western democracies. Particularly absent in the current Soviet rush to embrace modernity has been the realization that a market economy, for instance, has never been freestanding, but has always operated within a value-rich environment of entwined supporting sociolegal networks encompassing concepts of property, risk, liability, service, quality control, and even bankruptcy. Some of these values, like the substratum of values underpinning a democratic system, cannot be easily transplanted and may well have to be "grown" organically over time within the indigenous culture.

In the past few years, Gorbachev has begun complaining that certain Western-style practices, such as the rapid accumulation of wealth by the new Soviet entrepreneurs or insistent calls for his resignation by the "opposition," have been carried to excess in the Soviet Union and required curbing. His complaints have probably echoed a broad spectrum of public opinion, reflecting the subtle collisions between deeply entrenched Russian and Soviet values and popular Western ideas of government and economy, as the latter have undergone cultural reinterpretation by the invisible filters of the receiving society. These caveats may be early indicators that the Russian body politic has begun to reject as alien some of the Western ideas so hastily grafted onto it in the early enthusiastic years of *perestroika*.

Few other tasks on the Soviet reform agenda will probably be as complex or take as long as the importation of Western constitutionalism into a country with such a long history of legal nihilism and unchecked power.[17] Compounding the task is the absence of a definitional consensus among Western theorists on the historical origins, evolution, and content of constitutionalism, which has become more a constellation of ideas than a single concept.[18] The dilemma, as expressed by one American scholar, is that "Constitutionalism is one of those concepts, evocative and persuasive in its connotations yet cloudy in its analytic and descriptive content, which at once enrich and confuse political discourse."[19]

Nevertheless, as Soviet jurists have figuratively surveyed the terrain of Western constitutionalism, certain salient features surely have become apparent to them. Fundamentally, they will have recognized the contractual nature of a democratic constitution as an instrument through which the people convey legitimacy and empowerment to government, which in return performs vital social functions on behalf of the entire society. Implied in such a social contract have been limits and restraints on the powers delegated to government, in order to ensure the freedom and viability of the civil society embodied within the constitutional system. Spatially, the constitutionalized civil society has rested on a dichotomy between social and political domains, or the private and public spheres of life, within both of which the rights-bearing individual has been the cynosure or center of the constitutional universe. A final minimum condition for the reception of constitutionalism would be the necessity of understanding that a democratic constitution has never existed in a vacuum. Just as a market economy functions within a broader market society, constitutionalism has required a supportive political culture, a set of attitudes, beliefs, and sentiments that join the theme of limited government with the values of individual self-restraint and civic compromise.

Needless to say, if Gorbachev and those around him have fully understood the implications of their quest for constitutionalism as the housing for a law-governed state and civil society, they will have recognized that the journey ahead will be arduous and long. Possibly, the constitutionalist theses of two prominent Western political philosophers, the eighteenth-century Irish-born British statesman Edmund Burke and the twentieth-century German-born American scholar Carl J. Friedrich, could be of assistance in the Soviet Union's great undertaking. Burke offered the perspective of a unique path to constitutionalism, while Friedrich advocated the concept of constitutional development as a dynamic process. Thus, for Burke "each human society is founded upon [a] historically unique set of organically integrated and evolving values and institutions," and "these deeply rooted customary and traditional norms are incorporated into the constitution of the community."[20] Friedrich, over a century and half later, spoke of the " 'experimental' character of constitutionalism," the idea "that every constitution is continually changing and that the making of a constitution is a continuous process."[21]

How then could Burke and Friedrich be of intellectual assistance to Gorbachev, the aspiring constitutionalist? Under Gorbachev, the language of Soviet politics has undergone radical change in the past several years. Whereas from Lenin through the last of the old guard leaders, Konstantin Chernenko (1984-85), the principal terms of reference were Marx and *partiinost'*, or party-mindedness, Gorbachev has primarily described the present and projected the future in terms of *zakonnost'*, or legality, and constitutional reform. Gorbachev's speeches have been replete with proposed legal solutions to chronic Soviet problems that in the past, if even acknowledged, were handled *in camera*, in Communist Party offices. Gorbachev's exceptional sense of legal efficacy has been readily apparent in his many texts, in nearly all of which he has referred to a pending new law, a law just passed, or a law to be drafted. In his policy mind, law to a great extent became a panacea for *perestroika*'s tasks.

Beyond this, especially since the first major wave of constitutional amendments of 1988, which restructured the legislative process and the electoral system, Gorbachev has regularly invoked the "constitution" both in the corridors of power and in his new relationship between president and nation. The main question for us then becomes, what has he really been saying in these instances, what does he mean by his repeated invocations of the Soviet constitution?

Gorbachev has had a tendency to reference the constitution in polar ways. At one extreme, the constitution has been invoked as a political symbol conferring legitimacy on the speaker (much the way the conch was used in William Golding's *Lord of the Flies*), or as a tribal totem the mere brandishing of which might resolve conflicts and solve problems. In this style, Gorbachev's tone has become incantatory as if in performance of a public ritual, perhaps in worship of a new Soviet cult, the cult of constitutionalism. Gorbachev has tended to envision the constitution in this usage as so many words and phrases gathered on parchment, so to speak, a dry, static image of the constitution as scepter or a mere ornament of power. Yet, as with his belief in the law generally, he has displayed an unwavering faith in the symbolic resonance of the constitution on which his claim to power rests, almost as if the constitution were a "magic carpet" that could whisk him and his troubled country to the elusive future.

At the other extreme, more common in the past few years, Gorbachev has used the constitution instrumentally to win a dispute, stem a challenge, or neutralize a foe; in a word, to wield power. In this usage, the constitution has been conceptualized pragmatically as an open, mutable document or a living institution. As such, Gorbachev has tried to maneuver within its precincts all but the most intractable conflicts (those that have required the application of short-term force, such as the riots in Uzbekistan in 1989 or the widespread communal violence between Georgians and South Ossetians in 1991). Thus, the constitution has been transformed into a political arena or a place for negotiation with its own special due-process rules. Implied has been the idea of the constitution as a macropolitical process designed to blunt sharp confrontations and mute unbridled discourse in the interest of peaceful conflict resolution.

In Gorbachev's skilled hands, the constitutional process has become a civilized political game in which all the principal players but one must accept limitations on their power. In constitutional theory, the republics must yield to the Union, the party (since the revision of Article 6) to the state, and the state to the presidency (since the introduction of the office in 1990). Theoretically, this limitationist aspect of constitutionalism has been intended to apply to all governmental actors in the USSR, even to the president. The "catch" has been that President Gorbachev has interpreted the rules, rolled the dice, and generally manipulated the constitutional game to his preferred ends, which increasingly in the early 1990s have seemed to focus on the maintenance of his own personal power.

In the few instances where the rules have not worked for him, Gorbachev has cavalierly made *ad hoc* exceptions to achieve his desired outcomes, for example demanding a second parliamentary vote in late 1990 after his candidate for the new vice presidency failed to gain the necessary majority in the first round, or earlier in the year, by ramming through the legislative process a "midnight" law on secession that imposed a five-year waiting period in the wake of Lithuania's proclamation of independence.[22] Wielding the nascent Soviet constitutionalist doctrine more as a political weapon than as a jeweled scepter, Gorbachev has progressively divided the Soviet political universe into the friends and foes of the president, placing those who act constitutionally in one camp and those guilty of "anticonstitutional" behavior, the successor term to "anti-Soviet behavior" of the recent past, in the opposing enemy camp. In effect, Soviet politics may once again turn into a zero-sum game.

As the first President of the USSR, Gorbachev has come to think of himself as the indispensable Soviet leader, and has been partially remiss in his duty to nurture the seedlings of constitutionalism in the Soviet Union by his evasive unwillingness to accept limitations on his personal power from any quarter. Otherwise, he has significantly helped lay out the framework for a constitutionalist future by approaching the constitution as an open document and a transitional vehicle within which to conduct political negotiations with challengers to the center and the Union. If he or his eventual successor will take the next steps along the path demarcated by Burke and Friedrich, there could ultimately be hope for the future flowering of Soviet constitutionalism.

To get beyond the troubled present, however, the constitutional process will need to be reconceptualized as a long-term dialogue between the past and the future, between Russian tradition and the Western theory of limited government. In the mid-run, the optimal possibility might be what I would call a "fusion constitution," bonding Russian values and Western ideas into at least semidemocratic institutions, rather than trying to transplant American institutions prematurely into still infertile Soviet soil. In the long run, an ideal scenario would be to establish the Soviet constitution-making process as an open, continuous system for renegotiating the fluid and shifting power relationships between citizen and state, executive and legislative institutions, and the center and peripheries of the Union within the rapidly changing USSR.

Making a New Soviet Constitution

When Gorbachev first began to introduce legal reforms to accommodate his planned economic and social reforms, there was an *ad hoc* quality to the endeavor.[23] New laws were patched into the system almost randomly and often on the basis of political expedience.

True, Gorbachev and his team produced an extensive legislative agenda for law reform in the summer of 1986.[24] However, although the agenda included several dozen projects spaced out over the forthcoming five-year period, it soon proved inadequate to chart the changes both wrought and sought by Gorbachev under his programmatic theme of restructuring. Thus, nearly every major Gorbachev speech has emended the agenda with new legislative projects, or altered priorities in the long-term timetable for enactment. By 1988, the further impetus given to law reform by the nineteenth party conference, particularly the proposal to create a law-governed state, set in motion the process of replacing the 1977 Constitution itself.[25] A year later, a Constitutional Commission was created for this purpose by the first session of the newly elected USSR Congress of People's Deputies.[26]

The idea of writing a new union constitution had seemed clear enough, but the task so far has turned out to be politically and juridically more formidable than expected. In the spirit of *glasnost'*, a lively discussion has emerged in the press and the law journals over the nature and direction of constitutional reform. Fundamental questions have been raised to which there have been diverse answers, but, unfortunately, no consensus as to how to proceed. Should a new constitution be a document of change and break with the vestiges of the Stalinist system, or should it represent a degree of continuity, carrying forward constitutional baggage from the past as each of its predecessor documents had done? More likely, there will be both constitutional change *and* continuity, but which elements of the antecedent system should be carried forward?

This is an especially knotty question, since radical and liberal reformers have been constantly advocating the acceleration and deepening of the reform process, while Gorbachev, the centrist, with the conservatives pressing from the right to slow the process down, has been acting as a presidential "brakeman," doing the minimum necessary and the maximum feasible politically.[27] As a shrewd politician, Gorbachev has never been inflexible, moving as needed with the political tides. Thus, for example, while he initially dug in his heels against the radicals' push for a multiparty system to replace the Communist Party's monopoly on political activity, by 1990 he had yielded, endorsing the revision of constitutional Article 6, the "Party hegemony" clause.[28] Similarly, as he has felt the undertow of the new, more turbulent politics of the USSR, Gorbachev has temporized and switched positions several times on the issue of privatization of property, especially of land. Needless to say, this heady political volatility could only make the constitution-drafting process infinitely more difficult.

Other basic questions swirled through the political environment with no individual or group, least of all the declining Communist Party or the fledgling Soviet parliaments, able to give the constitutional commission a clear sense of direction. For instance, presumably there was to be a new constitution, but a constitution of what? Socialism, democratic socialism, modified capitalism and semidemocracy, or some vague "third way"? Clearly, the Soviet Union has generally rejected the sociopolitical features of state socialism; on this there has been a broad consensus within the political class (with the exception of the extreme reactionaries). But as to what alternative belief system the country should adopt or at least move toward, dissensus has prevailed. The "left," with its embrace of complete capitalism and unrestricted democracy, has been offset by the "right," with its reluctance to give up on the economic aspects of socialism in one form or another. Trying to maintain his political balance in the middle has been Gorbachev, who has tried to combine the best of the two worldviews of East and West. Since the writing of a constitution involves much more than the parsing of juridical phrases, this absence of a consensual political and social belief system has injected further confusion into the process.

A similar first-order issue that has yet to be resolved has been the functional question: a new constitution for what? Should it be a reflective document? The constitutions of 1918, 1924 and 1936 were purely reflective instruments while the 1977 document was mostly so (with the exception of Chapter 3, on the social system, which was largely inspired by the utopian perspective of Khrushchev's 1961 Party Program).[29] Should a new Soviet constitution reflect the configuration of power in the country, if anyone could actually define it with a measure of accuracy and a degree of longevity?

Or, should a new constitution be essentially normative in character, following the now admired model of the American Constitution? If, indeed, a normative, open-ended document could be drafted, what should be normativized, or for what purpose should the constitutional norms be created: to provide political and social space for emergent processes, to promote socioeconomic growth (or consolidation?), or as an interim framework for a lengthy transition . . . to what (socialism, capitalism, a "third way")? These are not incidental problems in the drafting of a constitution since their resolution will affect the length, scope, degree of detail, and, of course, the content of the resulting document--not to mention the question of whether it would be intended as a permanent constitution American-style, or another in a line of constitutions, Soviet-style.

Finally, another politically sensitive and as yet unresolved issue concerning the making of a new Soviet constitution has emerged since the empaneling of the constitution commission. Who should be the authors of the draft constitution--the formal, appointed draftspersons, or should other formal and informal political actors participate directly as well? Should the USSR Supreme Soviet issue fresh directives to the commission, updating its generic mandate, or should new instructions emanate from the president and the Federation Council, with its representation from the union republics? Should opinion polls be consulted, or perhaps a formal discussion opened in the national press as to what the public would propose for the thematic content of a new constitution?

The intelligentsia and the academic establishment have of course been represented on the constitutional commission; in addition, some of the dozens of proposed drafts for the union constitution (as well as for the new Russian Federation constitution, also being formulated)[30] have arrived in the commission's mailbox from various "think tanks" around the country such as the Saratov Juridical Institute as well as from prominent individuals such as the late Academician Sakharov[31] and the deputy chairman of the Russian Republic Supreme Soviet.[32] In the crosscurrents of contemporary Soviet politics, however, should the public also be more directly involved in the drafting process, through such groups as the popular front Rukh in the Ukraine, or the extreme left and right fringe groups such as Democratic Union and Pamiat'? And what about the voice of the inchoate "masses" such as the strike committees of the mining regions, which first emerged in the summer of 1989 with a mix of economic and political demands, including the demand that Article 6 constitutionalizing Communist Party dominance be repealed.[33]

Obviously, a kind of cacophonous constitutional convention writ large has been under way in the Soviet Union for some time now, with a Babel of voices and few clear answers to a number of fundamental questions. If a new constitution is eventually to be written and ratified, however, and if Gorbachev or a possible future successor is to have any hope of politically navigating the draft document through the reefs and shoals of the uncharted new Soviet political system, then some solutions to the several systemic queries raised here will need to found.

The Union Treaty as a Proto-Constitution?

With all the attendant problems with which the constitution-making process has been fraught, work on the document has understandably slowed as Gorbachev has had to turn his attention to and struggle with the worsening economic crisis and the secessionist forces roiling Soviet life and tearing the USSR apart in the early 1990s. His position has been that the critical state of the economy has been intensified by the progressive breakdown of public authority as a result of the fractious disintegration of the multiethnic Soviet state.

Gorbachev's solution was to rush through a draft of a new Treaty of Union in late 1990 and to call for the first-ever national referendum on whether to restructure the Union along more genuinely federal lines.[34] The proposed treaty, intended to replace the original Leninist version of 1922, represented an improvement, but basically offered only *de jure* acknowledgment of the new *de facto* relationships already forged between periphery and the center by many of the union republics against Moscow's will. Little new ground was broken by the proposed document and for the more rebellious republics, Gorbachev's treaty had been too little, too late. Six of the fifteen refused to conduct the referendum on their territories.[35] Nonetheless, Gorbachev campaigned vigorously for "renewing" the Union and keeping the USSR together. A more liberal, revised version of the draft treaty was released on the eve of the referendum, which, with its loaded, motherhood-type question, predictably passed by a sizable majority in March 1991.[36]

Gorbachev's problems would not end there, however. A number of the participating republics and even several sub-republic units had added their own questions to the referendum, very much clouding the meaning of his victory in terms of the future of the USSR. Of the nonparticipating republics, Lithuania and Georgia reaffirmed their intention of seeking full independence, while Armenia served notice that it would conduct its own referendum under the new union law on secession, thus setting in motion its eventual separation from the Soviet state.[37]

Meanwhile, the revised treaty of 1991 has limned the contours of a new union constitution, and Gorbachev has appeared ready to seize the mandate from the referendum, such as it was, to try to move ahead again with the creation of a new fundamental law for the Soviet state. His hopes for the future will no doubt rest on a constitution that could ideally hold the union together or, at least, provide him with greater legitimacy to use his extraordinary police powers to block the exits if necessary. In this spirit, the revised Treaty of Union, with its celebration of the individual and human rights, its promise of a plural concept of ownership and a civil society, and its vision of a more decentralized federal system, may, as implied in Article 9 of the treaty, provide the urgently needed sense of direction and renewed political momentum for creating a constitution compatible with the evolving shape of the Soviet Union. It reads:

> The Union Treaty is the basis of the USSR Constitution. The USSR Constitution shall be adopted by a Congress of representatives party to the treaty. The USSR Constitution may not contravene the Union Treaty.[38]

Finally, in the pursuit of constitutionalism, the treaty, as a proto-constitution, has also provided for a Constitutional Court (Article 17). What the new court's enforcement powers would be, especially against presidential decrees deemed unconstitutional, will have to await further negotiations.

Crucial questions still remain. What will become of the republics that chose not to be parties to the treaty, but may not in the foreseeable future succeed in gaining their independence? Will Moscow really try to stand astride a biconstitutional system and govern the holdouts according to the old constitutional rules? And an even more elementary question: Is it possibly too late for the union state as the world has known it? Has the internal crisis gone beyond the point of no return? Or, to put it more directly, can the chaos of contemporary Soviet reality be constitutionalized?[39]

Notes

1. I.K. Polozkov's speech to a Communist Party group, *Sovetskaia Rossiia*, 6 February 1991, p. 1.

2. Interview with A.Ia. Sukharev in *Rabochaia tribuna*, 27 October 1990, in *JPRS Report--Soviet Union: Political Affairs*, 18 December 1990, p. 54.

3. Gorbachev's speech in Mogilev, BSSR, *Moskovskaia pravda*, 2 March 1991, p. 2.

4. E.g. in the Moldavian union republic (renamed Moldova), Russians and other nationalities live as ethnic minorities. Moldovans constitute the titular nationality; their language is Romanian.

5. See, e.g., the Moldovian bill on citizenship, which restricts citizenship to those individuals who lived on the territory before annexation by the USSR on June 28, 1940, and their descendants. See *FBIS, Daily Report: Soviet Union*, 27 November 1990, p. 81.

6. E.A. Shevardnadze quoted by *Los Angeles Times* in *The Daily Gazette* (Schenectady, NY), 21 February 1991, p. A1.

7. See Robert Sharlet, *The New Soviet Constitution of 1977: Analysis and Text* (Brunswick, OH: King's Court, 1978).

8. See Robert Sharlet, "Soviet Legal Reform in Historical Context," *Columbia Journal of Transnational Law*, 28, no. 1 (1990), esp. pp. 5-6.

9. See Robert Sharlet, "Constitutional Implementation and the Juridicization of the Soviet System," in Donald R. Kelley, ed., *Soviet Politics in the Brezhnev Era* (New York: Praeger, 1980), ch. 8.

10. See Sharlet, *The New Soviet Constitution of 1977*, pp. 73-79.

11. For the amended version of Article 6, see *Current Digest of the Soviet Press*, 42,

no. 14 (1990), p. 20.

12. See ibid. for the revised Article 7. On the first waves of coalminers' strikes, see Peter Rutland, "Labor Unrest and Movements in 1989 and 1990," *Soviet Economy*, 6, no. 4 (1990), 345-84.

13. See "Excerpts from a Speech by Gorbachev Before the Lithuanian Communists," *New York Times*, 15 January 1990, p. A9.

14. See the draft Constitution of the Russian Federation, *Sovetskaia Rossiia* 24 November 1990, pp. 1ff.

15. For Vladimir Kriuchkov's general reference to U.S. security legislation, see "Nachalos' obsuzhdenie zakona o KGB," *Izvestiia*, 5 March 1991, p. 1. For his specific reference to U.S. wiretap law, see his speech to the Supreme Soviet as carried by TASS, in *FBIS, Daily Report: Soviet Union*, 6 March 1991, p. 25.

16. Richard M. Mills, *As Moscow Sees Us: American Politics and Society in Soviet Mindset* (New York/Oxford: Oxford University Press, 1990), pp. 206-07. For an example in the recent transition in Soviet scholarship on the U.S. Constitution, see the chapter by A.A. Mishin, the leading Soviet specialist, in A.A. Mishin and E.F. Iaz'kov, eds., *Konstitutsiia USA: Istoriia i sovremennost'* (Moscow: Iuridicheskaia literatura, 1988), ch. II, part 2.

17. See Andrzej Walicki, *Legal Philosophies of Russian Liberalism* (Oxford: Oxford University Press, 1987), ch. 1.

18. See the diversity of interpretations in J. Roland Pennock and John W. Chapman, eds., *Constitutionalism* (NOMOS XX) (New York: New York University Press, 1979).

19. Thomas C. Grey, "Constitutionalism: An Analytic Framework," in ibid., p. 189.

20. Ibid., p. 204.

21. Paul Sigmund, "Carl Friedrich's Contribution to the Theory of Constitutionalism-Comparative Government," ibid., p. 35.

22. G. Ianaev was elected vice president in December 1990. Lithuania declared its independence on March 11, 1990, on the eve of the opening of the Third Extraordinary Congress of People's Deputies, which began the next day in Moscow. The principal agenda item was the question of creating a strong executive presidency equipped with emergency powers. Within a few days, the law on the presidency had been rushed through, with at least one deputy objecting to the unseemingly speed of the process; at the same time, the question of a law on secession was added to the agenda and a secession law (or a nonsecession law, as another deputy termed it, given its many impediments to separation) passed within a few weeks. This has become typical of expedient law-making or "just-in-time legislation" under Gorbachev. For excerpts of the debates at the Congress, see *Current Digest of the Soviet Press*, 42, nos. 11-15 (1990).

23. See Robert Sharlet, *The Soviet Constitutional Crisis: Constitutional Reform and the Politics of Law in the USSR* (Armonk, NY: M.E. Sharpe, forthcoming), ch. 4.

24. See "O plane podgotovki zakonodatel'nykh aktov SSSR, postanovlenii Pravitel'stva SSSR i predlozhenii po sovershenstvovaniiu zakonodatel'stva SSSR na

1986-1990 godu," *Vedomosti verkhovnogo soveta Soiuza Sovetskikh Sotsialisticheskikh Respublik*, no. 37 (10 September 1988), art. 783, pp. 729-36.

25. See "Resolution of the 19th All-Union CPSU Conference: On Certain Urgent Measures for the Practical Implementation of the Reform of the Country's Political System," *Current Soviet Policies X: The Documentary Record of the 19th Conference of the Communist Party of the Soviet Union* (Columbus, OH: CDSP, 1988), 5, pt. 2. The resulting constitutional reforms in late 1988 revised one-third of the 1977 Constitution, including the creation of the Congress of People's Deputies.

26. See debates in *Current Digest of the Soviet Press* 41, no. 33, pp. 25-26.

27. See the insightful analysis of American presidential behavior during the Vietnam war in Leslie H. Gelb and Richard K. Betts, *The Irony of Vietnam: The System Worked* (Washington, DC: Brookings, 1979), Part Three, chs. 9 and 10.

28. See *Current Digest of the Soviet Press*, 42, no. 14 (1990), p. 20.

29. See Sharlet, *The New Soviet Constitution of 1977*, p. 14.

30. See *Sovetskaia Rossiia*, 24 November 1990, pp. 1ff.

31. See "Sakharov Draft Constitution," *JPRS Report--Soviet Union: Political Affairs* (19 January 1990), pp. 1-5. The late Academician Sakharov had been elected a member of the all-union Congress's constitutional commission. His draft had been one of the documents considered by the Russian Federation constitutional commission.

32. R. Khasbulatov's draft constitution was referred to in an interview with President Z. Gamsakhurdia of Georgia in *Vestnik Gruzii*, 21 February 1991, in *FBIS, Daily Report: Soviet Union*, 22 March 1991, p. 71.

33. See Rutland, "Labor Unrest," p. 364.

34. The all-union referendum on the draft Union Treaty of 1990 was scheduled for March 17, 1991. In the spirit of expedient law-making, the necessary new law on conducting a referendum was passed just in time. See the text in *Izvestiia*, 7 March 1991, pp. 2-3.

35. The six republics which did not participate in the referendum included Armenia, Estonia, Georgia, Latvia, Lithuania, and Moldova.

36. The referendum on union received approximately 80 percent approval, but the meaning of the mandate was clouded by various alternate and supplementary questions added on in certain cities, regions and union republics.

37. Armenia has signaled that it will be the first union republic to attempt to proceed to independence through the machinery of the 1990 law on secession. A required republic-wide referendum on the question has been scheduled for fall 1991.

38. For the text of the 1991 revised draft Union Treaty, see *Izvestiia*, 9 March 1991, p. 2.

39. By spring 1991, the chaos had driven Gorbachev to parley with the leaders of nine of the republics, including Yeltsin. Agreement was reached on further revisions of the draft Union Treaty. Once this would be accomplished, work on the new all-union constitution would resume. See "Gorbachev Yields on Sharing Power and Cuts in Prices," *New York Times*, 25 April 1991, p. A1. Was Gorbachev engaging in expedient politicking since Party conservatives were also calling for his resignation from the Party leadership, or will the fragile anti-crisis coalition hold?

3

ELECTORAL REFORM

Viktor Danilenko

The Process of Electoral Reform

A dramatic overhaul of electoral legislation was the first step toward a sweeping political reform in the USSR. It had three basic purposes. First, instead of remaining obedient dummies, voters were to play an active political role; their votes were to be decisive, actually determining the outcome of an election campaign. Second, the political nature of elections as such was to be changed so that elections would become a means of expressing the genuine will of the entire population and the political sentiments and expectations of society rather than an instrument for manipulating popular aspirations and forcing representative bodies to fit into the required sociopolitical patterns. Third, it was necessary to change the composition of the legislature and other representative bodies to replace the old preselected or "favored" members with strong, independently minded, and authoritative people. This was to be a major guarantee of a renewed and important role for the legislature in the constitutional structure of power.

The general political idea behind the electoral reform was to make the public at large a political driving force, to create a powerful momentum to move ahead and break conservative resistance. Once released, popular political activity was to be used as a lever for further progressive transformation of the Soviet Union. Without this, the intentions of the authors of *perestroika* could not be realized. Voters, incidentally, took a while to grasp this. The 1989 election campaign started off as dull and passive as usual, and some time elapsed before the campaign gathered momentum.

In fact, the changes in the electoral system were neither as profound nor as consistent as might be hoped, due to some particular circumstances.

First, the new legislation was obviously drafted in haste, although the scope of the reform was very extensive, covering the entire constitutional structure of power in addition to the electoral system. After a late start, and having spent over two years getting their bearings in the new situation, the national political leadership was in a hurry to catch up. This could not but affect the quality of research and the proposals that were prepared.

Next, there was a lack of appropriate political and legal experience. Democratic institutions had never existed before in the USSR, so there had never been any need to look into the legal mechanisms of their functioning. No wonder, then, that factors were not properly analyzed, coordinated, or optimized.

We need to keep in mind how the reform was drafted. Essentially it was prepared within the machinery inherited from "pre-*perestroika*" times i.e., in the traditional "apparatus" way. The drafters of the legislation remained anonymous, and the final decisions were taken in tranquil offices inaccessible to ordinary people, behind closed doors. The draft bills were pushed through a process of "nationwide discussion" that had been perfected during the "years of stagnation." Although groups of workers might submit hundreds of thousands of suggestions and amendments to the proposed legislation, these were almost without exception ignored, while it was always possible to incorporate any changes desired by those in the corridors of power. The draft legislation for the electoral reform was considered and adopted by the old Supreme Soviet--obedient, controllable, and never daring to criticize let alone reflect whatever came down from on high. Of course, this time everything looked a little different and the deputies did make amendments, but these were mainly concerned with technical details of the legislation and made no qualitative change in the text submitted.

Finally, and most important, the 1989 constitutional reform was a reflection of the actual balance of domestic political forces--the progressives favoring *perestroika*, and the conservatives opposing it. Much of what is routine today was initially approached with caution and apprehension not only at the top but also at the grass-roots. The new legislation put in sharp relief the transitional situation: progressive ideas calling for a dramatic change started to materialize in specific legislation, but had not gained enough strength and public support to have a decisive influence on the political content of these legal instruments. That is why the new legislation, in general terms, contained both a strong positive side working for *perestroika*, and a weak negative side rooted in the interests of its opponents. There were also a lot of compromise provisions and formulas lending themselves to different interpretations ranging from a bureaucratic to a consistent democratic one. In practical terms, this meant that the law could function differently (depending on the balance of forces and interests) in various areas and regions of the country, which was quite evident in the 1989 campaign.

The implication of this was that the law could be changed if there was a shift in the national balance of forces. This expectation was realized. The electoral legislation has already been amended on numerous occasions, each time becoming more consistent and democratic. Moreover, as political and legal experience accumulated, it became possible to raise the issue of fully redrafting the legislation before the next elections--an issue falling within the competence of the Constitutional Commission of the Congress of People's Deputies. There is no doubt that in its present form, the legislation seems wanting and imperfect, though against the backdrop of pre-*perestroika* times it represents a gigantic step ahead, radically changing both the institutional system of power and the overall domestic political climate.

The New Electoral Procedures

What is the current electoral system all about, and what are its salient features?

First of all, it introduced the mechanism of electoral alternatives, i.e., elections are held on a competitive basis and ballots feature several candidates running for one seat, or mandate. Thus, a voter may actually choose among contenders rather than just cast a vote. The Soviet Union has never had anything of this kind before. However, a reservation is in order. Having resolutely opened a door for a new political practice, the law unfortunately has not barred the previous one. According to Article 100 of the Constitution, a ballot may contain "any number of candidates," which means that a single-candidate ballot is permissible. The latter option runs counter to the logic of the reform, but this was an unavoidable concession to conservatives. During the 1989 election campaign it became clear just who needed this loophole. As of the official registration date one-fourth (!) of the 384 constituencies had a single candidate, and in the majority of cases those unchallenged contenders were high-ranking local party and government officials. The Congress of People's Deputies later tried to remove the ambiguity by requiring that ballots include no less than two candidates, but the effort has so far failed and will have to be taken up in the future.

The new electoral procedure required that the election campaign be extended from two to four months (even a six month schedule was suggested), and all stages of the campaign were strictly defined: the first month--setting up bodies in charge of elections (electoral commissions); the second--nominating candidates; the third--officially registering the candidates; and the fourth--election campaigning by the officially registered contenders for deputy mandates. The disadvantage of this scheme is the limited nominations period. This is a crucial stage of the whole electoral procedure and it would be advisable to extend it. At least, such is the opinion of many experts and voters alike (46 percent of those polled during the national debate over the draft electoral legislation supported the idea).

Nominations

The right to make nominations belongs to workers' collectives (they now come first in the constitutional listing); nongovernmental organizations; collectives of technical high schools and higher education institutions (not previously included); local meetings of voters (not previously included); and servicemen in military units. In other words there are now many more bodies entitled to nominate candidates. Consequently, a considerably larger part of the population can now take a more active part in the election process, which should guarantee a much wider social range of candidates.

The nomination of candidates by workers' collectives is a form of representative authority typical of the Soviet Union alone. The 1936 Constitution made no such provision, reserving this right for public organizations. When this constitutional right was granted to workers' collectives in 1977, it served to reinstate the social nature of the Soviet state as one belonging to the working people and to enhance the political role of workers' collectives. (Additionally, it served to introduce at least a surrogate for pluralism under a rigid one-party system.) Such views further evolved even into an idea of holding elections on the basis of special industrial constituencies (which was enthusiastically supported by many workers). Several such experimental constituencies were created in the republican and local elections in spring 1990. In practical terms such an approach leads to enhanced producer power not only in the economy, which is typical of the system of administrative command, but in politics as well, and for this reason the majority of professional lawyers are bitterly critical of this provision. As civil society develops and a real multiparty system gains ground, the priority right of selecting and nominating candidates will probably shift toward public organizations, political movements, and voters' unions. Today it undoubtedly belongs to workers' collectives.

By contrast, one cannot but welcome the reintroduced right to nominate candidates in local communities. This right is implemented at voters' meetings at the community level which are convened by the local soviets of people's deputies together with district electoral commissions. A meeting is competent to nominate in the presence of at least 500 voters domiciled in the constituency. This figure has been attacked as being too high and curbing local initiative, and it would be advisable to lower it.

The new legal provisions helped to eliminate discrimination against the nonworking part of the population and permitted local communities to have their "own" deputy. Thus it gave an impetus to self-organization on a territorial basis. In a number of cases voters' meetings started functioning on a standing basis, voters' conferences and councils were established, and local elected leaders emerged, which could not but promote local self-government as well as a fundamentally new relationship between voters and deputies.

This new system of nominations is operating on only a limited scale, although it is tending to spread. During the 1989 elections the proportion of locally nominated candidates was very small (Boris Yeltsin was one such candidate); at the elections to the representative bodies in the autonomous republics in spring 1990 they already accounted for 7.3 percent, and in the elections to local soviets, for 18.2 percent.

Setting procedures for holding electoral meetings, the legislation provides for a possibility to nominate any number of candidates. A person is nominated when supported by the majority (over 50 percent) of those present at the meeting. It also introduces a fundamentally new provision--the right to set forth one's own candidacy. This was not envisaged before as it was not considered to be modest. Experience shows that mostly young and radical candidates availed themselves of the opportunity.

For electoral purposes the country was divided into two types of constituencies: the population at large was represented on the basis of territorial constituencies; and the union and autonomous republics, autonomous regions, and autonomous districts were specially represented on the basis of national and territorial constituencies.

A more democratic electoral process is promoted by a legal provision that to be nominated an individual must be domiciled or work locally when running in a territory-based constituency; or in the territory of the corresponding Union or autonomous republic, autonomous region, or autonomous district when running in a national territorial constituency (Article 37 of the Law on the Election of People's Deputies of the USSR). This provision aims at abolishing the formerly widespread practice of high-ranking members of the *nomenklatura* who would secure a deputy mandate by organizing their own "election" in some remote locality. This provision also ensures much better contact between deputies and the electorate. However, the legislation contains an "as a rule" reservation which leaves a loophole for apparatchiks who may still try to use a remote constituency as a springboard.

The institution of district electoral meetings was briefly included in the Constitution of the USSR. The meetings were to discuss nominations and to decide on presenting candidatures for official registration at the local electoral commission. The intent was to ensure a preliminary endorsement and selection of candidatures--of course, with the noble goal of choosing only the best.

The idea of endorsing candidates in a preliminary way is hardly objectionable. It affords voters a chance to become acquainted with the contenders, to take a closer look at their platforms, and to sort out haphazard candidacies enjoying no real support at the grass-roots level and representing narrow parochial interests. Thus, it also serves to raise the importance of elections as such, since only the most serious and competent candidates are left to participate. That is supposed to be the purpose of similar institutions in many Western nations; in particular, in the United States primaries have similar functions.

Yet, the specific legal solution to this problem turned out to be glaringly imperfect in the Soviet Union. Neither the ways to set up district electoral meetings nor their rules of procedure met democratic standards. In many cases such meetings became a barrier between candidates and voters, and the future of candidates was left to the discretion of a narrow, nonrepresentative, and sometimes specially selected group of electors. The administrative machinery stopped just short of overtly using district electoral meetings as an instrument to keep developments under control and hold off undesirable contenders. This, of course, could not but provoke an extremely unfavorable public attitude toward this institution and, in the final analysis, doomed it to failure.

The first step was taken by Estonia, where it was decided at the very outset of the election campaign not to hold district electoral meetings and not to curb free initiative of voters.[1] During the May 1990 runoff elections such meetings were abandoned practically everywhere. In December 1989 a constitutional amendment abolished the institution of district electoral meetings altogether, which may be undoubtedly regarded as another victory of the left forces.

Representation of Public Organizations

Another important innovation of the 1989 constitutional reform is the institution of special representation in the parliament for public (nongovernmental) organizations. This provision immediately gave rise to controversy. On the one hand, it may have some positive features. Public organizations have the right not only to propose legislation but may also, through their representatives, take part in the legislative process. This raises their social and political role and affords them the opportunity to defend the interest of their membership, often very large (e.g., trade unions, youth, women's organizations, etc). This may well have been a basic intention of the authors of the reform, along with a desire to weaken the hold of the prevailing one-party system.

On the other hand, however, this provision was not well thought out and its serious shortcomings immediately clashed with the overall nature of the reform and were subjected to violent attacks. The allocation of parliamentary seats to public organizations cannot but undermine the principle of equal suffrage. Group members receive an extra vote, and those who belong to several different organizations get several additional votes. Representation is also glaringly disproportional: a deputy for, e.g., a small artistic union represents a tiny fraction of the voters represented by a deputy for a territorial constituency.

The majority of voters are totally deprived of any opportunity to express their attitude toward candidates from nongovernmental organizations. What is more, the rank-and-file members are, with rare exceptions, left out of the process, and the leaders of the organizations monopolize both nominations and the endorsement of candidates. The situation in the Soviet Academy of Sciences in spring 1989 is a case in point. The seats were allocated in clear violation of elementary democratic standards, and the opinions of the rank-and-file researchers were ignored to such an extent that protests ensued. The candidates in the list did not reflect the tendencies existing in the scientific community and even failed to fill in the quota reserved for the Academy. A major scandal exploded and the lists had to be completely revised. Only then was the name of Academician Andrei Sakharov, among others, included.

As a rule, the candidates nominated by the public organizations find themselves in a very ambiguous situation. They do not have anyone to work with in their capacity as candidates, they have no one to explain their electoral platforms to, and they have no place to campaign, as the members of the organizations do not take a direct part in the voting or influence its outcome. More often than not, the leaderships of public organizations (including the Communist Party) nominated only as many candidates as seats, allowing for no competition.

In light of the above, it is no wonder that the public organizations in 1989 elected mostly apparatchiks, many of whom could hardly have succeeded if they had had to face the voters in an open, competitive election campaign. Thus, it was not unreasonable to conclude that this aspect of the electoral mechanism had been structured to legitimate a sort of privileged "apparatchik chamber." But it may be doubted that these deputies will be capable of playing an effective role in the work of the legislature.

Thus political experience throws doubt on the value of retaining special elections for the representation of public organizations. There are proposals to improve that institution by introducing, for example, direct elections of deputies from nongovernmental organizations by all the rank-and-file members of those organizations (thus leaving their executive bodies aside), or to grant them the right only to nominate candidates who will then have to stand in in open, nationwide voting. A more radical proposal would abolish these special elections altogether. In the USSR Supreme Soviet on October 24, 1989, 254 deputies backed this proposal in a roll-call vote (with 85 votes against and 36 abstentions). However, since this is a constitutional change, it was up to the Congress of People's Deputies to decide. The Second Congress was cautious. On December 20, 1989, it made special elections from nongovernmental organizations optional (that is, nonobligatory) for Union and autonomous republics; otherwise the situation was to remain unchanged until the next parliamentary elections. Thus, the left forces did not manage to win, but it may be a delay rather than a loss.

Territorial Representation

Territorial constituencies in parliament are now based on the number of voters instead of the total population. In the USSR the share of underage population differs considerable from territory to territory: in the Russian Federation they number less than thirty percent whereas in Uzbekistan and Tajikistan they account for over one half of the population (51.6 and 52.3 percent, respectively). Therefore, the new criterion enhances the principle of equal voting rights. In 1989 territorial constituencies averaged 257,300 voters.

The legislation removed the strict requirement to hold elections only in single-mandate constituencies (single-member districts). It has become more liberal, permitting (Article 95 of the Constitution) either single-mandate or multi-mandate constituencies at the discretion of the local authorities. In 1989 such multi-mandate constituencies were formed in a number of places and provided greater opportunities for local initiative. However, experience in elections has shown that the public greatly prefers alternative elections in single-mandate constituencies.

To make the election process more orderly and to limit possible abuses, the legislation (Article 40 of the Law on the Election of People's Deputies of the USSR) allows each candidate to run only in one constituency at a time. It is possible to run for seats in soviets at different levels, but no more than two mandates at a time.

The Central Electoral Commission, made up of 35 persons, now functions as a standing body. It is created by the USSR Supreme Soviet (taking into account proposals by the supreme governing bodies of the union republics) no later than four months before the elections and functions for the full five-year term. This ensures control over compliance with democratic procedures in case additional elections are necessary to fill mid-term vacancies.

The new legislation draws a clear line between an active suffrage and the right to take part in the voting. The latter, according to Article 96 of the Constitution, is not granted to mental patients who have been found incapable by the court, or persons held in detention facilities in accordance with a court sentence or the prosecutor's sanction as well as those sent by the court to compulsory medical treatment facilities. Such a distinction has never been made in legal terms before, which has, of course, distorted the overall picture of the elections (especially, in view of the official reports on 100 percent participation).

For the first time Soviet citizens working abroad got the right to meaningfully participate in elections. To this end, 281 constituencies were organized in 42 Soviet missions abroad, associated to 24 constituencies in the Russian Federation, Ukraine, and Belorussia. On the whole, about 134 thousand employees of Soviet missions abroad took part in the voting in spring 1989.

Campaigns

The new legislation has also changed the conduct of election campaigns. All citizens, workers' collectives, and public organizations have for the first time been granted the constitutional right to engage in advertising and promotion in favor of their "own" preferred candidate or against one they oppose. The 1936 Soviet Constitution did not mention the right to campaigning at all, while the 1927 Constitution only permitted campaigning in favor of a candidate.

Election campaigning is not limited to any specific time-frame except that campaigning is prohibited on the actual day of voting. The legal forms of promotion include meetings with voters, demonstrations, use of the media, distribution of posters, leaflets, etc. The local electoral commission and the local authorities are supposed to assist candidates in this respect. In fact, the legislation (Article 44 of the Law on the Election of People's Deputies of the USSR) requires all public nongovernmental organizations, heads of enterprises and institutions, and community groups to help candidates in organizing meetings with the electorate as well as in obtaining the necessary background or information materials.

Officially registered candidates are allowed to have up to ten representatives to assist them with the election campaign, to organize advertisements, promotion, and contacts with the media, and to represent the candidate's interests in various public organizations, etc. These campaign committees are a fundamentally new phenomenon in the Soviet political experience, and were an innovation of the elections of 1989.

In addition, candidates now have a legally protected right to put forward a program of future action. Such programs reflect not only the personal political views of the candidates but also take account of the wishes and instructions of the voters. Nearly all the candidates have taken advantage of the right to present their programs. This makes the pre-election struggle more dynamic and poignant, helps the voters to make more knowledgeable choices at the polls, and makes the deputies' behavior after the election more predictable.

All candidates enjoy the right of immunity. They cannot be prosecuted, arrested, or subjected to administrative measures on the basis of a court ruling without the consent of the Central Electoral Commission.

After their official registration candidates may be fully relieved of their working duties and functions so that they can dedicate their time entirely to meetings with voters. This makes their electoral campaign more vigorous and meaningful. Furthermore, from now on all relevant costs (including the payments of average wages or salaries to candidates) are to be borne by the state, paid out of the funds allotted for elections, rather than by enterprises, as was the case before.

There are some new features in the overall financing of electoral campaigns. The main principle has not been changed: all the expenses related to preparing and holding elections are paid by the state. The law unambiguously states that candidates shall not incur any personal expenses (Article 12, the Law on the Election of People's Deputies of the USSR). The state is to provide premises for holding pre-election activities, guarantee the candidates an opportunity to use the mass media, cover their transportation expenses (the candidates have the right to use all kinds of public transportation except taxis free of charge within their constituencies), etc. As virtually everything that is required to hold elections is the property of the state, these costs are rather small if measured by Western standards. For instance, the general elections held in the spring of 1989 cost the state 156.6 million rubles (including 600,000 rubles spent to organize the polling stations and 2 million rubles used to fund the candidates' campaigns). The runoff elections entailed additional costs totaling 22 million rubles. Thus, on the whole the state spent 92 kopecks per voter, which is a very modest figure.

Then, in December 1989, it became legal to finance campaign costs from private sources--voluntary contributions made by enterprises, public organizations, and individual citizens (Article 100 of the Constitution). In this case the legislation was catching up with political practice. However, direct financial support to specific candidates is prohibited. Funds may be donated only to an electoral commission, which shares them equally among all candidates running in a given constituency: "Candidates shall participate in the electoral campaign on an equal basis," the above-mentioned article of the USSR Constitution clearly states. Of course, official private contributions still remain extremely small; the important fact is that they are legally recognized.

The Mechanism of Elections

Finally, we come to the very mechanism of elections, to the electoral system in the narrow, institutional sense of the term: the procedure for voting and determining the results of the voting. A lot has been changed in this respect, too. The law introduces a complex multi-stage system of voting.

A new voting schedule has been introduced--from 7 a.m. to 8 p.m. (previously 6 a.m. to 10 p.m.). The layout of the polling stations has been changed: now the ballot boxes are placed in such a way that every voter has to pass through a booth to reach the box (previously such booths were placed along the sidewall and one could easily be seen going there, which inevitably influenced the principle of the secret ballot). According to the new legislation, votes are counted on the basis of the number of people who actually participated in the voting rather than on the basis of the total number in the voters list, as in the past.

To win, a candidate has to collect an absolute majority of votes of those actually voting, provided that more than 50 percent of voters in a constituency take part in the election. If there are three or more candidates in a race and none of them gets the required majority, a runoff election should be held within the next two weeks. In this case, only the two candidates who received the most votes during the first round remain on the ballot and a simple majority is required to win.

If no more than two candidates run in a constituency and no one wins a majority, or if an election is deemed ineffective (because less than half of the electorate takes part) or null and void (in case of a gross violation of the electoral laws), a new election is held. This implies that the entire procedure of nominations and official registration of candidates should be repeated within a two-month deadline. In this case, candidates who were not included on the ballot before have the right to seek nomination again. Voting is held at the same polling stations and on the basis of the same lists of electors, but the district and local electoral commissions may be formed anew.

In other words, this is the well-known majority electoral system with two rounds of elections. A similar system is used in many other countries-- France, for example--but the Soviet Union adopted a somewhat more complicated version. In 1989 three rounds of elections were required in many constituencies (theoretically, four rounds are a possibility, for instance if a runoff election is ineffective or null and void). The process takes too much effort and is hardly justifiable. In the future, it would be advisable to simplify it and reduce the process to the commonly accepted two-round majority system of elections. This will require an improved system of nominating and selecting candidates. This would be facilitated by a transition to a real rather than proclaimed multiparty system.

The Results of the Reform

The new electoral legislation has dramatically changed the nature of Soviet elections. This became quite clear during the 1989 parliamentary elections, which were a genuine breakthrough. There was an unprecedented surge of political activity at the grass-roots level. All segments of the population, including social and age groups that had never been socially active before, became involved. To a certain extent, this was due to the fact that candidates were locally nominated or came from public organizations. Many more enterprises and organizations proposed candidates and vigorously helped them in their campaigns. The opportunity to participate in elections was no longer perceived as an "honorary duty" but as a major political right to be defended to the bitter end.

The elections shed an entirely new light on Soviet society. The old talk about "monolithic unity" has vanished in the thin air. A real, vital society emerged, full of different and sometimes conflicting interests. For the first time, those interests were highlighted, introducing pluralism into political life. For the first time elections represented open political struggle, giving a hitherto inconceivable impetus to the whole political process.

The elections gave a powerful boost to the formation of a civil society in the Soviet Union. They accelerated differentiation of political forces, their self-awareness and self-evaluation. The struggle for the minds of voters (not for power at this juncture) helped to crystallize political trends that will most probably become independent political parties in the future.

The elections afforded an opportunity to take a fresh look at the role the Communist Party plays in the political process. These were elections prepared by the CPSU, held by the CPSU, and won by the CPSU, as it had no real opponents in the struggle for power. The overwhelming majority of the newly elected deputies--87.6 percent, i.e., even more than in the past--are members of the CPSU. Nonetheless, the situation has qualitatively changed. The elections showed that the political monopoly of the party in society and in the state had come to an end. New political forces are emerging that eventually will become equal partners in the political process. The electoral campaign signaled a departure from a rigid single-party system; in many cases electoral rivalry was in essence a struggle among parties. The elections politically and psychologically paved the way for the March 1990 rejection of the constitutionally fixed "leading role" of the CPSU in Soviet society and a juridical recognition of a multiparty system.

Finally, these were the first elections in many decades in which the voters had a real choice among contenders and could feel that their votes represented an act of serious political consequence.

But from these gains, the 1989 elections also had quite a few negative aspects. A large proportion of voters were deprived of an alternative; they participated in elections with a single candidate on the ballot. Thus, the political rights of those millions of voters were *de facto* limited.

The party and government machinery exerted strong pressure on the electoral campaign, unscrupulously using anything to defend their interests. According to the press, in many cases party and government bodies followed the old principle requiring that candidates be nominated by workers' collectives only after their preliminary endorsement. Executive committees of local soviets often sought to usurp the functions of electoral commissions (which for some curious reason were located mainly on the premises of the executive committees). In many cases officials violated the legislation concerning local community meetings of voters (sometimes disrupting such meetings altogether). In quite a few cases district electoral meetings were used as an instrument for electoral scheming, as their audiences and procedures were manipulated by the government and party apparatus. Candidates were put under pressure or even blackmailed to withdraw from their races, leaving a local party or government leader the only candidate on the ballot. A more subtle approach was to allow a weak candidate on the ballot as a challenger.

The scope of the illegal practices may be illustrated by the fact that the

Central Electoral Commission alone received over 14,500 letters and telegrams with complaints about violations of voters' rights. Yet no one has ever been prosecuted for these violations, as those responsible were basically the people in charge of organizing the elections.

In many cases the contenders' behavior was questionable. Electoral debates were often at a level leaving much to be desired. There was widespread use of so-called "black propaganda," i.e., slander against other contenders, political labeling, dissemination of deliberately falsified information, etc. Sometimes a real "poster war" broke out. Overnight, fences and walls would be covered with posters promoting one candidate while the posters of an opponent were destroyed. "Experts" in tough electoral tactics emerged. Sometimes it was even necessary to maintain law and order during electoral activities.

The weakness of the electoral campaign consisted in the clearly unequal footing of candidates. For example, a candidate from a large enterprise could use official transportation and make speeches in more comfortable and better equipped meeting rooms; his programs were printed on nice paper and got larger circulation, etc. The electoral campaign of local party and government leaders was in fact served by the entire local propaganda machinery. A locally nominated candidate could not even dream of all this: it was much harder for him to defend his views and remain competitive. It was precisely for this reason that after the elections in December 1989, the Constitution was amended to require "an equal footing" for all candidates in an electoral campaign.

The list of the negative aspects in the 1989 electoral campaign could be continued. They stem from the lack of a democratic tradition, an insufficient overall level of political education, and deficiencies in the electoral legislation. This legislation can obviously help to rectify many of the flaws if developed and improved. What is of primary importance, however, is that the electoral reform raised the political process in the Soviet Union to a qualitatively new level, and Soviet citizens are now capable of forming the main governing bodies in a democratic way, i.e., by a free expression of popular will after an open competition of various social and political forces.

Voting Results

The following statistics on the results of the first parliamentary elections give clear evidence of how profound the change really was.

In all, 172.8 million people took part in the voting, i.e., 89.8 percent of eligible voters (the 1989 electoral lists contained 192.6 million people).

On election day, 2,895 candidates were registered in 1,500 territorial and national constituencies, which makes for an average of two contenders for every mandate. More specifically, 384 constituencies (i.e., over 25 percent) had one candidate, 953 constituencies had two candidates, 109 constituencies had three candidates, and 51 constituencies had from four to eight candidates. A high of twelve contenders for one mandate was registered in one constituency. In the second round the number of contenders went up to thirty-four in one constituency.

In 1,257 constituencies candidates were registered immediately upon nomination without district electoral meetings. In the rest of the constituencies such meetings were held, a total of 832 of them. Of 4,875 candidates considered at the district electoral meetings, 1,720 were registered.

In the first round of voting, 1,226 deputies were elected. In three constituencies elections were deemed null and void as less than half of the eligible voters had participated. In 274 constituencies a second round of voting had to be conducted.

There were 880 contenders for 750 mandates allotted to public organizations, so the selections were far less competitive. In all, 120 national public organizations nominated candidates; thirty-two of them held autonomous elections while the remaining eighty-eight formed seven groups. Nine of the organizations had no alternative candidates at all. The voting was held according to a multi-mandate system: in a few cases two rounds of voting were necessary.

Importantly, the elections resulted in a serious change of the social composition of the supreme representative authority. The new system of elections and the abolition of mandatory quotas for workers and peasants led to a dramatic drop in their representation (from 45.9 to 22.1 percent). The number of women dropped no less dramatically (from 32.8 to 17.1 percent). At the same time the share of intellectuals became considerably larger. The proportion of highly skilled white-collar employees reached 10.2 percent (as compared to 6 percent before). The share of middle management (i.e., heads of laboratories, workshops, sections, etc.) rose from 6.6 percent to 25.3 percent. There were only seven journalists in the parliament before (0.5 percent), now they number 60 (3 percent).

This tendency toward a new social composition of representative bodies was even more evident in the republican and local elections in spring 1990. For example, out of the sixty-five deputies of the Russian Federation representing Moscow, 70 percent are scholars or journalists while there is only one worker. A very similar picture was typical of municipal elections in Moscow, Leningrad, and many other major cities. This tendency is likely to continue. Professionals have an advantage in competitive political campaigns.

Thus was breached the fundamental principle of representation in the Stalin and Brezhnev period: in a workers' state, workers should have an overwhelming representation in the parliament. This principle has a fundamental flaw: to defend the interests of, say, the working class in a consistent fashion one need not be a member of that group; moreover, a professional politician is likely to be a more effective representative than, say, a metal worker or a miner.

The parliament's social structure thus ceased to be a mirror image of the social structure of society. But what was abolished was a mechanical preservation of artificially maintained proportions. The parliament now reflects the real level of political activity of various social groups and categories. In this sense, it moved closer to society and became more representative. For example, this was the first time that the retired received deputy mandates (37 people); they represent an important stratum of the population. It was also for the first time that the parliament included peasants working on lease (13), heads of enterprises and cooperatives working on lease (6), advocates (2), and even the clergy (5), something totally unthinkable before *perestroika*.

Yet another positive aspect is that the above changes resulted in a considerable growth of the parliament's intellectual capacity. The deputies have become stronger and more independent, thus raising the efficiency of the parliament in carrying out all of its functions and, in particular, radically changing its relationship to the executive branch.

The new fundamental premise in electing the parliament is to choose the most politically committed, educated, and professional people ready and qualified to assume this responsibility. Of course, these qualities are not equally shared among the deputies, but the very transition to a new principle of electing the parliament on the basis of personal skills rather than social representation opens up the prospect of gradually forming a powerful independent and truly professional legislature capable of fulfilling the role it should play in the political structure of a consistent democracy.

Another important result of the elections is that the apparatus still managed to hold its ground in the supreme legislature. This is of particular importance in analyzing the national balance of forces and forecasting the future activities and political outlook of the parliament.

The direct representation of the national top political leadership in the parliament was reduced by about half: there are now fifteen members and alternate members of the Politburo and secretaries of the Central Committee of the CPSU in the parliament (0.5 percent as compared to 1.5 percent before). However, there are significantly more party, government, and trade union officials from the republican and regional level, who in fact replaced members of the national and republican governments, formerly well represented in the Supreme Soviet of the USSR. This was because, according to the new legislation, one cannot hold both a ministerial post and a deputy mandate. The overall representation of upper-level civil servants actually remained unchanged (39.8 percent as compared to 40 percent before the elections) despite all the changes brought in by *perestroika*. This fact may provide a valuable insight into the dialectics of Soviet domestic politics in the late 1980s. It goes without saying that these people are a conservative force not interested in radical transformations that would threaten their social status and privileges.

In statistical terms, the parliament includes 155 (7.6 percent) first and second secretaries of republican Communist Party central committees and first secretaries of regional and district party committees and party committees of major cities. There are fourteen high-ranking officials of the CPSU Central Committee (0.7 percent). One national minister was elected. He was joined by thirteen chairmen of republican councils of ministers (excluding Latvia and Lithuania) and forty republican ministers; of course, all of them resigned upon election. There are thirteen top military commanders among the deputies, or 3.1 percent. In contrast to the past, there is not a single official of the KGB central administration, but there are ten KGB employees (0.5 percent), including nine republican KGB chiefs.

The Changing Role of the Communist Party

One of the significant sensations of the electoral campaign was the defeat of many high-ranking party officials, i.e., secretaries of republican Communist Party central committees and of regional, district, and city committees, including the first secretaries of Moscow and Leningrad. Thirty-eight such candidates lost in the elections (191 candidates at this level had run for mandates, 126 of them with no competition). This fact deserves some particular attention.

First, it is an indication of a qualitative change in the national political situation. Getting elected had never before presented a problem for such people: their *nomenklatura* position alone guaranteed 100 percent success. The first public electoral defeat of a number of leading party officials shattered the system of *nomenklatura* and undermined its previously unlimited authority, although it has not been eliminated altogether.

Second, it is evidence of the changing role of the party in society. The party did not fail--such a conclusion would oversimplify the situation. Elections were lost by individual party officials who had no sense of the times and no desire or ability to work and think in a new way. But due to their high-ranking positions, their defeat could not but affect the party at large. The party lost its sacred nature and was pulled down from its pedestal. It appeared that one could disagree with the party and express a lack of confidence in some of its leaders. (In many cases, even in noncompetitive races voters had made their choice by striking out the name of a secretary who was the only candidate on the ballot.) This is a sizable step toward democratizing the party's role in society as just one of many competing political forces rather than a mighty dictator. This is what a political party should be in a civilized society.

Summarizing the above, it should be pointed out that the overall results of the elections are an important step promoting the process of *perestroika*. Basically, this was a referendum in favor of the policy of *perestroika* and demonstrating firm popular support for it. The nation now has a qualitatively new supreme representative body. Although not ideal, it is very different from its predecessor. This body is new in terms of its structure, working procedures, the substance of its work, and most important, in its potential actually to live up to its constitutional and legal definition of being "supreme." From the very outset this body firmly and resolutely declared its readiness to assume responsibility for the future of *perestroika* and of the whole nation.

Note

1. The Estonian leadership took another bold democratic initiative during the republican and local elections in the spring of 1990. Instead of holding local community meetings it collected voters' signatures on petitions. To be nominated to the republican Supreme Soviet a candidate has to collect at least 75 signatures. About 40 percent of deputies were nominated this way.

4

THE NEW SOVIET LEGISLATIVE BRANCH

Stuart Goldman

Of the many changes made in the Soviet political system since 1985, one of the most important is the restructuring and upgrading of the legislative branch of government. The legislative branch has been transformed from a largely ceremonial entity into a system of popularly elected assemblies with real legislative authority. This legislative system is at the center of much of the democratization in the Soviet Union that is considered most praiseworthy by the West and may be the strongest protection against a reversal of those reforms. The success and sustainability of Soviet democratization, free market economic reform, and the abandonment of an ideologically driven anti-Western foreign policy may hinge in substantial part on the effectiveness of popularly elected representative government, i.e., the legislative branch.

Russia's Limited Parliamentary Experience

The Russian historical tradition is overwhelmingly authoritarian. The tsars ruled as absolute monarchs without constitutional restraint until 1905. There was, however, some limited parliamentary experience. In 1864, following the emancipation of the serfs, Tsar Alexander II began a system of popularly elected local and provincial legislatures, called zemstvos, which concerned themselves primarily with social and economic affairs. The zemstvos became an arena for political activists seeking to further democratize Russia and nascent political parties emerged. The reactionary Alexander III did his best to truncate the zemstvos toward the end of the century. But as a result of the Revolution of 1905, Tsar Nicholas II was forced to abandon autocracy, grant a constitution, and accept a popularly elected national legislature called the

Duma. Four dumas were elected between 1905 and 1914, providing a stage for national political parties of right, center, and left. Even the Bolsheviks were represented for a time. The Duma was swept away by war and revolution in 1917.

The Old Supreme Soviet

The word *sovet* is an old Russian word meaning council. During the revolutions of 1905 and 1917, councils (soviets) of workers' and soldiers' deputies sprang up and became key elements of the revolutionary process. In 1917, the Bolsheviks and their allies eventually gained a majority in the soviets and overthrew the Provisional Government using the slogan "All power to the soviets." They renamed the country Soviet Russia, later the Union of Soviet Socialist Republics. The national legislature, nominally the highest organ of state power, they called the Supreme Soviet. The recently restructured and upgraded Supreme Soviet of 1989 bears some structural resemblance to its predecessor, but the differences are far greater than the similarities.

The old Supreme Soviet (as restructured by Joseph Stalin in 1936 and Leonid Brezhnev in 1977-79) was a bicameral legislature of 1,500 deputies divided evenly between two chambers, the Soviet of the Union, representing electoral districts nationwide of roughly equal numbers of citizens, and the Soviet of Nationalities, representing the USSR's diverse ethnic and national groups. Deputies were elected to five-year terms on the basis of universal suffrage. The elections, however, were a sham. Candidates were selected by the Communist Party leadership and ran unopposed. Elections became public rituals in which party workers endeavored to persuade, cajole, or coerce virtually every eligible citizen to participate. The predetermined election-day "victories" by margins of 98-99 percent were trumpeted by the media as evidence of the overwhelming popularity and legitimacy of the regime. The Supreme Soviet itself was a ceremonial rubber stamp. It routinely met twice each year for several days and unanimously passed all legislation brought before it by government and party leaders.[1] This pattern was replicated throughout the federal structure at the republic, regional (oblast), and local levels.

Laws were made by party and government officials, or "apparatchiks." Experts from government ministries, the party apparatus, or an institute of the Academy of Sciences would prepare a first draft. This would be sent to government bureaucrats who might alter it beyond recognition. What conflict there was in the legislative process involved arguments behind closed doors between officials defending their institutional interests. Eventually an approved draft emerged to be rubber-stamped by the Supreme Soviet.

Beyond the undemocratic character of this whole process, the laws themselves had only limited authority and scope. There was little effort, for example, to write organic laws codifying the organization and role of government agencies. From its inception the Soviet political system was dualistic, with power divided unequally between the party, which made policy, and the government, which implemented it. The undisputed locus of political power was the Communist Party. The party's policy-making Central Committee and its ruling Politburo were the citadels of power, and the party's general secretary was the acknowledged national leader. Parallel and subordinate to the party were the government ministries, forming a huge administrative bureaucracy. The national legislature (the old Supreme Soviet), ostensibly the highest political organ of state, was a sham. The Soviet Union was ruled not by laws but by men--the leaders of the Communist Party. When it suited them, they, as well as government agencies, could act outside the law with impunity. Even the Constitution of the USSR posed no real obstacle to the rulers when they chose to flout it.

Gorbachev Proposes a New Legislative System

In mid-1988, at the extraordinary nineteenth party conference, Communist Party General Secretary Mikhail Gorbachev presented an elaborate set of radical proposals to restructure and upgrade the legislative system. The main thrust of the proposals was to create a democratically elected legislature vested with real legislative authority. Election laws would be changed to encourage multiple candidates for each seat and to ensure a secret ballot and honest vote count. The legislature would become in fact the supreme organ of state. A streamlined Supreme Soviet would be in session six to eight months per year, empowered to draft and enact laws to reshape the political, economic, and social landscape and vested with authority to oversee and overrule government agencies. This pattern was supposed to be replicated at the republic, regional, and local levels, where legislatures were to be provided with a revenue base derived from the economic enterprises operating within their respective administrative borders.

What motivated Gorbachev's initiative? When he assumed power in 1985, Gorbachev's top priority was to revitalize the Soviet Union's stagnant economy. Indeed, one of the criticisms of Gorbachev's leadership from today's perspective (early 1991) is that his economic reform policy was ineffective and failed to keep pace with the far more dynamic political reforms. Nevertheless, political reforms, including legislative restructuring, can be seen as means to help achieve economic goals as well as ends in themselves.

Gorbachev sought to transform the Soviet people from subjects who grudgingly did what they were told into citizens who believed they had a stake in the system and were at least partially responsible for its success. *Glasnost'*, democratization, and legislative reform signaled to the Soviet public that the regime trusted them and wanted them to participate meaningfully in government, thus enhancing the regime's political legitimacy. Gorbachev probably also planned to have the popularly elected legislature take responsibility--and some of the political heat--for painful dislocations that would undoubtedly accompany the transition to a market economy. The political reforms were also potent weapons in Gorbachev's struggle against conservative opposition forces within the party and government apparatus. In addition, Gorbachev, trained as a lawyer, saw democratization and legislative reform as desirable and perhaps necessary ends in themselves, helping to transform the Soviet Union into a civil society, fully accepted in the community of "civilized nations."

Adoption of the Reforms

Gorbachev dominated the proceedings of the extraordinary nineteenth party conference (June 29-July 1, 1988). Prior to the conference it was widely believed that he planned to use that gathering to purge the party's Central Committee and Politburo of conservative opponents. Conservative party leaders rallied and succeeded in getting many of their supporters elected as delegates to the conference. But instead of making a direct assault on the conservative cadres, Gorbachev proposed restructuring and democratizing the legislature. Despite vocal opposition from party conservatives, who saw in the proposal a threat to the party's supremacy and their own power, Gorbachev used his authority as presiding officer to orchestrate the meeting to his ends. He controlled the selection of speakers and interjected his own comments at will. He took the unprecedented step of having the proceedings televised live, thus putting the conservatives on the defensive by forcing them either publicly to come out against democratization or to acquiesce. In one of the more controversial features of the reform package, seen at the time as a concession to the conservatives, Gorbachev included the proviso that each soviet be headed by the party leader at the corresponding level.[2] Reformers protested that conservative party bosses would use their chairmanship of the fledgling legislatures to throttle or neutralize them. Gorbachev's supporters argued that the concession was necessary and pointed out, presciently, that in order to chair a soviet, a party leader would have to win election as a deputy. In the end, the conference obediently endorsed the concept of the reforms. Formal enactment required that specific measures be put forward for public debate and be approved by a party Central Committee plenum and by the Supreme Soviet.

In October 1988, draft constitutional amendments and election laws embodying the proposed reforms were prominently published and subjected to widespread public discussion and debate. Many conservatives undoubtedly remained dubious about the reforms, but it was difficult for them publicly to attack proposals that promised to make Soviet government more democratic, and in any case the tenets of party discipline inhibited their opposing the decision of the party conference. Some Baltic leaders, pro-democracy reformers, and dissidents pointed out that the effective combination of the posts of Communist Party general secretary and chairman of the upgraded Supreme Soviet would result in too great a concentration of power in the hands of one man. Andrei Sakharov, the prominent human rights advocate and Nobel Laureate, criticized Gorbachev for pursuing democratic ends through undemocratic means and warned that even if Gorbachev's intentions were honest, he had provided the means for a successor to recreate a dictatorship. Despite this opposition, the reforms appeared to enjoy broad popular support.

On November 29, 1988, a Central Committee plenum approved the proposed constitutional amendments and new election laws. On December 1, a special session of the Supreme Soviet--the last session of the old legislature --gave its formal approval, thereby making them the law of the land.

Structure and Functions of the Legislative System

At the time of this writing, the legislative branch again faces the prospect of major restructuring. In March 1991, the draft of a new Treaty of the Union was provisionally approved by eight of the union republics. This treaty, if adopted, would become the most fundamental legal document of the USSR, superseding even the Constitution. It provides guidelines for a new constitution and envisions major changes in the legislative branch. Most notably: the Congress of People's Deputies would be abolished; the Supreme Soviet would be directly elected; and the Soviet of Nationalities of the Supreme Soviet would be restructured. The adoption of the treaty and a new constitution, however, is uncertain. This section, accordingly, describes the legislative system as it evolved from 1989 through March 1991.

The Congress of People's Deputies

The legislature at the national level is an unusual and complex two-tier system with what amounts to four legislative fora. At the top of this structure is the new paramount organ of state power, the Congress of People's Deputies. The Congress has 2,250 deputies elected by universal suffrage for a term of five years. Deputies are limited to no more than two consecutive five-year terms. They are elected by three different types of constituencies. One bloc of 750 deputies is elected on the basis of equal electoral districts.[3] A second bloc consists of 750 deputies elected by national-territorial election districts, according to a set formula.[4] A third bloc of 750 deputies is elected from nationwide "public organizations" enumerated in the election law (and including, notably, the Communist Party).[5]

The Congress has full legislative authority, but because of its size and the infrequency of its sessions it was neither intended nor expected to function as an effective legislature. It was originally to meet regularly only once each year for a few days, but at its first session the deputies expanded its schedule to two sessions per year, up to two weeks each. The Congress is empowered to set basic guidelines for domestic and foreign policy and to amend the constitution. It elects from among its ranks a regular working legislature of 542 deputies, the new Supreme Soviet. It issues a list of agenda items for the next session of the Supreme Soviet, and can overrule any law the Supreme Soviet passes. The Congress was also empowered to elect the chairman of the Supreme Soviet, the legislature's presiding officer, who, as the head of state (president), combined executive and legislative functions. This arrangement was completely changed in March 1990, when the Constitution was amended again to create an executive presidency outside the legislature.

The New Supreme Soviet

The restructured Supreme Soviet is the center of most legislative activity. It is a bicameral legislature of 542 deputies, divided equally between a Soviet of the Union and a Soviet of Nationalities. It is normally supposed to hold two sessions annually, lasting three to four months each. Legislation, to be adopted, must be approved by a majority of each chamber or by both chambers in joint session, and then signed by the president. The president has veto power, which requires a two-thirds majority in each chamber to override. The Supreme Soviet is empowered to interpret USSR laws, ratify international treaties, and declare war. It must approve any use of the armed forces abroad. The Supreme Soviet has the right to call and question any government official. It can repeal orders of the Council of Ministers. Its own acts can be repealed only by the Congress of People's Deputies. Up to one-fifth of the membership of the Supreme Soviet is to be "renewed" each year by the Congress.[6]

The Chairman of the Supreme Soviet

As noted above, the constitutional amendments enacted in 1988 stipulated that the chairman of the Supreme Soviet be elected by the Congress of People's Deputies and serve as presiding officer of the Supreme Soviet and as head of state, combining executive and legislative functions. In March 1990, the Constitution was amended again to create an executive presidency outside the legislature (see below). The chairman of the Supreme Soviet is now strictly a legislative official, elected by the Supreme Soviet as its chief presiding officer. Following his inauguration as president of the USSR on March 15, 1990, Gorbachev resigned as chairman of the Supreme Soviet. His deputy, Anatolii Luk'ianov, was then elevated to the chairmanship.[7]

The Presidium of the Supreme Soviet

The Presidium of the Supreme Soviet is a leadership body of the legislature to which there is no precise analogue in the U.S. Congress. It is headed by the chairman of the Supreme Soviet and includes the chairmen of the Soviet of the Union and the Soviet of Nationalities, their deputies, the chairmen of the standing commissions and committees of the Supreme Soviet, and eighteen other deputies, one from each of the fifteen union republics, two from autonomous republics, and one representing autonomous provinces (oblasts) and districts (okrugs).

Both directly and through the secretariat that it directs, the presidium exercises great influence over legislative activities and over deputies, individually and collectively. The presidium prepares the agenda and organizes the work of the Congress and the Supreme Soviet. It coordinates the activities of the commissions and committees. It determines which committee has primary jurisdiction over a bill. It is also empowered to organize and conduct nationwide referenda and discussions of major draft laws and other key national issues, and is charged with responsibility to ensure the publication of all laws and other acts adopted by the Congress, the Supreme Soviet, and the president.

While Gorbachev was chairman of the Supreme Soviet he dominated and controlled the presidium. Since March 1990 the presidium has been run by Gorbachev's former deputy, Luk'ianov. It is widely believed that the presidium continues to serve and represent Gorbachev's interests in the legislature.

There appear to be few formal rules governing the presidium's actions and procedures. Its meetings are often closed and the record of its proceedings is not published. Some deputies cite the presidium's power, arbitrariness, and secretiveness as major flaws to be remedied.[8] The Supreme Soviet can vote to overrule its presidium, but as of this writing has done so only once. On September 10, 1990, the Supreme Soviet rejected the agenda for its fall 1990 session presented by chairman Luk'ianov on behalf of the presidium.[9]

The Secretariat of the Supreme Soviet

The Supreme Soviet secretariat, an administrative and service organ of the legislature, exercises a great deal of power behind the scenes. The secretariat, under the supervision of the presidium, performs administrative and staff support functions for the Congress, the Supreme Soviet, the presidium, all the legislative committees, and the individual deputies.[10] The secretariat currently provides all of the permanent staff support for the Supreme Soviet on administrative and financial matters and most of the staff support available on legislative and policy matters as well. The Supreme Soviet's committees have no salaried staff of their own, and individual deputies receive only 300 rubles per month (the average Soviet monthly wage) to pay personal staff.[11]

In contrast to the U.S. Congress, control of legislative staff in the Supreme Soviet is largely centralized in the secretariat and its leaders, who in turn are appointed by the presidium. Although specific departments and sections of the secretariat are assigned to assist particular Supreme Soviet committees and to respond to requests for information from individual deputies, the secretariat staff is directly accountable to their superiors in that organization and, through them, to the presidium.

The secretariat is headed by Nikolai Rubtsov, who has been a senior administrator in that organization for many years, as have most of his principal department heads. The secretariat includes departments of economic development, social and cultural development, legislation and legality, interethnic relations, international relations, work of people's deputies, financial management, personnel, general affairs, and others. It also has a separate information service for the legislature.

Each Supreme Soviet committee is served by one of these departments, but there are far more legislative committees than there are secretariat departments. The two largest departments, economic development and social and cultural development, for example, with a combined professional and clerical staff of seventy-eight, provide all the full-time staff support for nine Supreme Soviet committees. These two departments of the secretariat have created nine sections, one associated with each of the legislative committees served.

The secretariat's financial department deals with the legislature's own budget and salaries. According to the head of that department, the Supreme Soviet committees submit their annual budget request to the financial department and then he--a non-elected staff official--decides how much money they will receive. The Supreme Soviet has the legal authority to change this arrangement, and may do so in the future.

Before the restructuring of the Supreme Soviet in 1988-89, the secretariat had a staff of about 400 to serve a legislature that met infrequently and did little. In approximately one year the secretariat doubled in size. Its workload grew exponentially. According to the leadership of the secretariat, the staff is too small and many lack the experience and expertise needed for their duties. Furthermore, the senior officials of the secretariat are mostly veterans of the old regime. They are accustomed to directing and controlling the work of the legislature.

The secretariat performs essential duties for the Supreme Soviet for which there are no adequate substitutes at present. Yet, because of the secretariat's centralized control of staff and information resources, which is ultimately controlled by the leaders in the presidium, some deputies view this organization as a major obstacle to the realization of the full democratic and legislative potential of the Supreme Soviet. If something resembling a multiparty system does develop in the Supreme Soviet, deputies aligned with different parties or factions are sure to press for a system of staff and information support that is more nonpartisan than the present arrangement in which all the administrators and nearly all the professional staff of the secretariat are Communist Party members.[12]

The New Executive Presidency

Analysis of the legislative system requires some discussion of the new executive presidency and the role of executive-legislative relations in the legislative process. At a special plenum of the Communist Party Central Committee in February 1990, General Secretary Gorbachev issued a set of proposals to transform radically the structure of the government and the Communist Party. The centerpiece of these proposals was the creation of a powerful executive presidency. Gorbachev also called for reducing the power and authority of the Communist Party apparatus and separating party from state functions, abolishing the once all-powerful Politburo, and opening the way for a multiparty system by eliminating the Communist Party's constitutionally guaranteed "leading and guiding role."[13]

Despite outspoken opposition from conservative members, the Central Committee endorsed these proposals, whose principal effect appears to be the transfer of power from a self-perpetuating party elite to an elected president. Although the party appears to be the big loser, some of the expanded presidential power came at the expense of the legislative branch. The proposed changes in the structure of government involved extensive amendment of the Constitution, requiring approval by two-thirds of the Congress of People's Deputies. On March 13, the Congress approved most of the changes sought by Gorbachev. In several key areas, however, it modified the proposals so as to limit presidential and preserve legislative power.

The Constitution, as amended, stipulates that the president of the USSR is elected to a five-year term and can serve no more than two terms. Although Gorbachev was elected president by the Congress on March 14, 1990, the new amendments provide for direct popular election of the president in the future.[14] The successful candidate must receive a majority of all votes cast nationwide as well as in a majority of the fifteen union republics.[15]

The president nominates (and recommends removal of) the premier and other top government officials, subject to election by the Supreme Soviet and approval by the Congress.[16] The president signs laws and may, within two weeks of its passage, veto legislation of the Supreme Soviet. His veto can be overridden by a two-thirds majority in each chamber of the Supreme Soviet. He cannot veto acts of the Congress of People's Deputies. In the event of an impasse between the two chambers of the Supreme Soviet that cannot be resolved and that poses "a real threat of disruption to the normal activity of the USSR's supreme organs of state power and management," the president can request the Congress to elect a new Supreme Soviet (the Congress is not required to comply).[17] The president has no authority to dissolve, suspend, or remove the Congress of People's Deputies. The president can be removed from office by a two-thirds vote of the Congress if he is found to have violated the Constitution or a law.

On the basis of the Constitution and laws of the USSR, the president can issue decrees with "mandatory legal force." The president can, with the approval of two-thirds of the Supreme Soviet, declare martial law or a state of emergency and introduce temporary presidential rule in particular localities.

The president is the commander-in-chief of the armed forces and appoints the military high command. He can mobilize the armed forces and, in the event of a military attack upon the USSR, declare a state of war, which must immediately be referred to the Supreme Soviet. He negotiates and signs international treaties. He confers top military and diplomatic ranks and state awards, rules on questions of citizenship, and grants pardons.

Constitutional amendments of March 1990 created two new bodies to serve the president: a Presidential Council appointed by the president and responsible for assisting in implementing domestic and foreign policies; and a Council of the Federation chaired by the president and consisting of the "supreme state official"[18] from each of the union republics, an advisory body on issues of federalism, nationalities policy, and interethnic relations. However, the constitutional amendments of December 1990 that streamlined the executive branch changed these two bodies. With the transformation of the Council of Ministers into a smaller Cabinet of Ministers subordinated to the president, the Presidential Council became redundant and was abolished. The Federation Council, on the other hand, was upgraded to a policy-making body to help deal with the crisis of the Union.

The constitutional amendments enacted in March 1990 created a powerful, but not an unlimited, presidency. In three key areas the Congress made changes that limited Gorbachev's proposed presidential powers. The Congress made the Supreme Soviet's override of a presidential veto final, eliminating a proposed provision allowing the president to appeal an override to the Congress. The Congress subjected a presidential declaration of martial law or state of emergency to approval by a two-thirds vote of the Supreme Soviet (the original proposal required only consultation with the Supreme Soviet). Finally, the president does not, as was originally proposed, appoint the members of the Committee on Constitutional Supervision, whose responsibilities include reviewing the legality and constitutionality of presidential acts.[19] The guidelines in the March 1991 draft Union Treaty would transform the Committee on Constitutional Supervision into a more formal Constitutional Court.

Bicameralism in Theory and Practice

The Supreme Soviet is a bicameral legislature, but it does a substantial amount of its work in joint session.

The Supreme Soviet's two chambers are equal in size (271 deputies) and power. The Soviet of the Union is drawn from two of the three blocs of 750 deputies--those elected to the Congress from equal-sized electoral districts and those representing the all-union[20] level of certain public organizations. The Soviet of the Union is supposed to take the lead on issues affecting the entire nation such as national economic and social policy.

The Soviet of Nationalities[21] is drawn from the bloc of 750 deputies representing national territories and from those deputies elected to the Congress by the republic and regional branches of certain public organizations (e.g., the Ukrainian Communist Party). The representational formula in the Soviet of Nationalities gives disproportionate weight to the less populous units, in much the same way the U.S. Senate gives disproportionate weight to the smaller states. The Soviet of Nationalities is supposed to take the lead on matters relating to federalism and relations among ethnic and national groups.

Each chamber elects its own chairman as presiding officer and each chamber has standing commissions reflecting its distinctive role. The Constitution stipulates that legislation is enacted when approved by a majority in each chamber. There is a mechanism for reconciling different versions of a bill passed by the two chambers. The chambers meet separately to discuss issues clearly falling within the purview of one or the other. Often, however, they meet together. Most major legislation has been adopted in joint session on the basis of a majority of those present. Joint sessions are chaired by Supreme Soviet chairman Luk'ianov or the chairman of one of the two chambers (on an alternating basis).

Committee Structure

The Supreme Soviet has a powerful committee system that is the focus of most legislative work. The commissions and committees draft legislation, exercise oversight, and conduct investigations. Subunits of either of the two chambers of the Supreme Soviet are called commissions. Each of the two chambers currently has four standing commissions. Subunits of the Supreme Soviet as a whole are called committees.[22] The Supreme Soviet now has sixteen joint standing committees. In addition there are two joint commissions and various special investigating committees. The number and character of joint standing committees compared to the commissions of the two chambers reflects the fact that the Supreme Soviet does a good deal of work in joint session.

Membership on all commissions and committees is divided evenly

CONGRESS OF PEOPLE'S DEPUTIES (CPD)

2,250 members elected by popular vote every 5 years: 750 from population-based electoral districts; 750 from administrative districts; 750 from national public organizations. The CPD elects the Supreme Soviet and its Chairman, and approves the state plan and budget and constitutional amendments.

USSR SUPREME SOVIET
Chairman, Anatolii Luk'ianov

542 members elected from the CPD by secret ballot. Divided into two Councils, scheduled to meet in the spring and fall for sessions of 3-4 months. Supreme Soviet enacts legislation, approves top government appointments, adopts national budget and state economic plans, ratifies treaties, approves declaration of internal emergency situations, authorizes use of armed forces abroad, declares war. Up to one-fifth of members can be replaced annually.

PRESIDIUM OF THE USSR SUPREME SOVIET

Composed of the Supreme Soviet leadership (Chairman, chairmen and deputy chairmen of both Councils; committee/commission chairmen; representatives from each of the 15 union republics plus 3 representatives of autonomous republics, oblasts, and okrugs. Prepares agenda and organizes work of CPD & Supreme Soviet, coordinates commissions and committees, and organizes nationwide discussion of USSR draft laws.

SECRETARIAT

Council of the Union
Chairman, Ivan Laptev. 271 members based on equal population districts. Responsible for national issues: economy, legal rights, foreign policy, and national security.

Commissions

Industry, Energy, Machinery, and Technology Development
Labor, Prices, and Social Policy
Planning, Budget and Finance
Transportation, Communications and Information Technology

Council of Nationalities
Chairman, Rafik Nishanov. 271 members based on administrative regions. Responsible for federal and interethnic issues.

Commissions

Consumer Goods; Trade; Municipal, Consumer, and Other Services
Culture, Language, National and International Traditions, and Protection of Historical Heritage
Nationalities Policy and Interethnic Relations
Social and Economic Developments of Union and Autonomous Republics, Oblasts, Okrugs

Ethics Commission

Procedures Commission

JOINT COMMITTEES OF THE USSR SUPREME SOVIET

Responsible for oversight of ministries, initial confirmation of top appointments. Half of members are drawn from the Supreme Soviet, half from other CPD members.

Agrarian and Food
Construction and Architecture
Defense and State Security
Ecology and the Rational Use of Natural Resources
Economic Reform
Glasnost and Citizens Rights and Appeals
Health
International Affairs
Internationalist Servicemen's Affairs

Law and Order and Battle Against Crime
Legislation
Science, Education, Culture and Upbringing
Soviet of People's Deputies and Management and Self-management Development
Veteran and Invalid Affairs
Women's Affairs and Family, Mother, and Child Protection
Youth Affairs

THE SOVIET LEGISLATURE

between Supreme Soviet deputies and Congress deputies who are not deputies of the Supreme Soviet. The latter have full voting rights in committee and may participate in floor debate, but cannot vote on the floor of the Supreme Soviet. Their committee role is the most important of several provisions that draw deputies from the Congress into the work of the Supreme Soviet. The number of Supreme Soviet deputies on the joint standing committees is evenly divided between members of the two chambers.

The committee system was considered to have started *de novo* in 1989. Unlike the practice in most other legislatures, neither seniority nor party membership is a determining factor in committee membership. Committee assignments have been made by the secretariat of the Supreme Soviet, based on deputies' experience, expertise, and expressed interests, elicited by questionnaire during the first session of the Congress. Committee chairmen and membership were then decided by the Congress and the two chambers of the Supreme Soviet.

How a Bill Becomes a Law

The list of officials and institutions authorized to initiate legislation in the Congress of People's Deputies and the Supreme Soviet is quite long: Congress deputies, either chamber of the Supreme Soviet, its chairman, any of its standing commissions or committees, the Committee on Constitutional Supervision, the legislature of any of the union republics, the president of the USSR, the Cabinet of Ministers, the Supreme Court, the Committee for People's Control, the General Prosecutor, the Chief State Arbiter, the Academy of Sciences, and certain all-union public organizations.[23]

The presidium of the Supreme Soviet exercises broad power in determining how draft legislation is handled, setting the calendar and procedures for bills. The Congress can enact legislation, but, because of its size and the infrequency of its meetings, the presidium sends most legislation to the Supreme Soviet. A bill can be brought directly to the Supreme Soviet for action and be debated and voted upon in joint session or successively in the two chambers. As noted above, in its first year the Supreme Soviet did most of its legislative work in joint session. In its second year, however, separate sessions of the two chambers became more common. Major legislation is commonly brought to the floor for a first reading and then referred to committee.[24] The presidium decides to which committee or committees to assign the bill. Several committees can examine a bill simultaneously.

Committee work is a vital part of the process. Committees can amend and reshape a bill. Committees send bills back to the presidium when they have completed their work. On complex and controversial issues, committees can send several competing variants of a bill forward. The presidium and the chairmen of the two chambers can then schedule floor debate and an up or down vote. It can also have a second reading of the bill and return it to committee for more work. On issues of the greatest importance, it can organize nationwide public discussion of a bill and a referendum before taking final action.

The Supreme Soviet approves a bill by a simple majority in joint session or in each chamber separately. In the event that the two chambers pass different versions of a bill, a conciliation commission (conference committee) is formed by the leadership of each chamber, representing the two chambers equally. If agreement is not reached, the matter can be referred to the Congress. If the two chambers become deadlocked in a way that threatens to disrupt vital government activity, the president of the USSR can request the Congress to dissolve the Supreme Soviet and elect a new one.

The president signs legislation passed by the Supreme Soviet. He can, within two weeks of passage, veto a bill. A veto can be overridden by a two-thirds majority of each chamber of the Supreme Soviet. The Congress can overrule any action of the Supreme Soviet. The president cannot veto acts of the Congress.

In its first two years the legislature achieved impressive results in providing the legal basis for a pluralistic and more just political system. It did not have much success in addressing fundamental issues of economic reform --on which there was not a clear consensus.

Character and Political Complexion of the Legislature

The new Supreme Soviet deputies are overwhelmingly Communist Party members (87 percent), but they are communists of varying political hues. Despite the high percentage of party members, one of the most striking features of this Supreme Soviet is its lack of political experience.[25] Over 53 percent of the deputies are lower-level managers or laborers with little relevant prior political experience. Only 10 percent were members of the previous Supreme Soviet and fewer than 20 percent had any prior legislative experience. Although both Gorbachev and Luk'ianov have formal legal training, there are relatively few lawyers, jurists, or political scientists among the deputies.[26]

Deputies face difficult career decisions. They have the choice of maintaining their prior career and receiving a 200-rubles-per-month stipend for their added duties, or becoming full-time legislators on a 700-ruble-per-month salary. In either case they are provided with hotel or apartment accommodations and office space in Moscow. However, the constitutional limit of no more than two consecutive five-year terms makes it difficult to contemplate a career as a legislator. Many are torn between their sense of civic responsibility (or political ambition) and reluctance to surrender an established career for an uncertain political future. For many younger professionals living far from Moscow this is a particularly difficult choice.

The general lack of experience of the majority of deputies has many consequences. Especially at the outset, the work of the Supreme Soviet was chaotic. There were few useful rules and procedures to be carried over from the old rubber-stamp legislature, and few deputies had the parliamentary experience to help establish and implement new ones. This lack of experience coupled with traditional Soviet political culture creates an environment that undervalues the rule of law and due process. As a result, the Supreme Soviet is, by Western parliamentary standards, not only highly disorganized and imprecise, but often surprisingly casual about contradictions between law and action. Many legislators are tolerant of extralegal or even unconstitutional means if the ends are agreeable. This is not necessarily an attitude of lawlessness or cynicism, but a lack of appreciation of the tradition of legal process and rule of law. It extends to the deputies' own political status.

For example, the constitutional amendments of December 1988 provide for the Congress to "renew" one-fifth of the membership of the Supreme Soviet each year.[27] How this was to be done was not specified. In December 1989 the deputies decided that a 20 percent annual turnover rate would make the Supreme Soviet even more disorganized and unmanageable, so they amended the Constitution again to the effect that "up to 20 percent" of the Supreme Soviet deputies would be "renewed" each year. This constitutional provision was violated in two different ways the first time it was applied. The first "renewal" of deputies occurred in December 1990, eighteen months after the Congress elected the Supreme Soviet rather than the one year stipulated by the Constitution. The renewal was done on the basis of voluntary resignations from the Supreme Soviet. In the event, 36 percent of the deputies (196 of 542) chose to relinquish their seats. New deputies were elected from the ranks of the Congress.

Another manifestation of the deputies' lack of experience is that legislation is sometimes drafted imprecisely, using subjective and normative language. This makes implementation of such laws difficult and provides the executive branch with opportunities to circumvent the will of the legislature. In his closing speech at the end of the third session of the Supreme Soviet on June 15, 1990, chairman Luk'ianov cited inadequate oversight of the implementation of legislation as one of the legislature's greatest shortcomings.

Some observers criticized the legislature for lack of independence, especially in its first session. The radical deputy Iurii Afanas'ev criticized the "silent majority" of inexperienced deputies as a "Stalinist-Brezhnevite" (i.e., subservient) group.[28] This exaggerated the case but called attention to the fact that many deputies are susceptible to being led and manipulated. Gorbachev used this situation masterfully. He would make clear from the chair what position he favored on an important matter and was usually able to influence a majority of deputies to support that position. But deputies followed leadership from other quarters as well. Some politically astute pro-democracy reformers exercised influence far beyond their numbers on the basis of their political expertise. The size of the "silent majority" shrank as deputies gained experience and the Supreme Soviet developed institutional identity and greater independence.[29] When Gorbachev left the legislature for the newly created Presidency in March 1990, the Supreme Soviet became more independent, since its new chairman, Luk'ianov, was unable to exercise the same influence and leadership as his predecessor. But on most critically important votes, President Gorbachev continues to be able to get his way in the legislature.

Another factor that is changing the character of the Supreme Soviet is a newly discovered phenomenon--constituent pressure. Until 1989 Soviet citizens had little reason to appeal to their legislators since the latter had no authority. The new Supreme Soviet is different and "advertises" its authority nationwide on television. Many Western analysts assumed that the deputies would be slow to recognize the need for constituent service and that Soviet citizens would be slow to seek it. The deputies claim that the opposite is the case. Because citizens perceive the Communist Party and the rest of the government to be unresponsive to their needs, because local officials have little authority, and because many elements of the socioeconomic structure are failing, Supreme Soviet deputies are being overwhelmed by constituent requests.[30] This has a transforming effect on the Supreme Soviet as deputies are pressed to respond to constituencies with specific interests that do not necessarily coincide with the interests of the leadership. This pushes those deputies who want to be reelected toward more independent positions and makes the Supreme Soviet more truly representative.[31]

Deputies complain about what they see as a high degree of absenteeism. Rafik Nishanov, chairman of the Soviet of Nationalities, said at the end of the Supreme Soviet's second session that about 120 deputies were "regularly absent" and that seventy deputies had missed half its sessions. One-third of the deputies were also reported to be frequently absent from commission and committee meetings.[32] Part of the reason for this absenteeism is that despite the rhetoric of democratization, many of the candidates may have believed, as Viktor Astaf'ev said he did, that "we would just raise our hands and vote and nothing more--and vote 'yes,' of course, as is customary."[33] But because of the flood of legislation demanding attention, the lack of staff, and the level of disorganization, many deputies complain of having to work ten to fourteen hours per day. Some, especially "old thinkers" among the deputies, may simply be unwilling to put in those hours. This may help explain why the Supreme Soviet acted more liberally than many had anticipated immediately after it was elected by the Congress: a disproportionately large number of the absentees are probably traditionalists unwilling to accept the new work style.[34]

In late June 1989 the Supreme Soviet accepted the leadership's proposal to end live gavel-to-gavel television broadcast of their proceedings, on the grounds that the broadcasts were disrupting economic output. Instead, when the Congress or Supreme Soviet was in plenary session, TV channel 2 would broadcast a complete (except for procedural matters) time-delayed version of the session beginning at 6:00 p.m.

Organizational and Procedural Matters

The Supreme Soviet is struggling to create rules and procedures to make its work more orderly, but initially it was beset by such a succession of major political issues and crises that it was not able to focus effectively on procedural matters. The result was a good deal of improvisation and *ad hoc* decision making. A few characteristics are listed below to give at least a sense of the proceedings.

One rule limits deputies to no more than two speeches on the floor per day. The chair initially had virtually unlimited discretion in recognizing speakers and sometimes used this power to "steer" debate. More recently a rule was established whereby deputies send a written note to the chair when they want to speak and the chair is required to honor those requests in the order received.[35] The chair (especially under Gorbachev) has also exercised wide latitude in interjecting comments and arguments during debate and interrupting and cutting off speakers at will.

An important early procedural decision was to divide the time during Supreme Soviet sessions in half: two days per week for committee work, two days for full sessions.[36]

A major bill is typically submitted to a committee for drafting, goes to the floor for a first reading, then back to committee for refinement prior to final action. Yet many deputies continued to offer fundamental amendments to major bills when they were presumably in final form. In December 1989 the Congress stipulated that any amendment to a bill after the first reading would have to be submitted to the relevant committee for consideration.[37] In May 1990 the Supreme Soviet established a new joint Commission on Procedures.

Staff

One of the most frequent complaints one hears from Supreme Soviet deputies concerns the inadequacy of staff. Deputies have small budgets to hire one or two personal staffers. The committees do not have their own dedicated staff but are staffed instead from the secretariat of the Supreme Soviet, which has a corps of over 800 people. The Defense and State Security Committee, for example, draws a staff of seven from the secretariat. Its three subcommittees have no separate staff.[38] When Supreme Soviet deputies visit a U.S. Congressmember's office, they are overwhelmed by the size and sophistication of the staff. The size of the staff of a typical U.S. senator surpasses comprehension. Then they hear about district offices, and eyes begin to glaze over.

In addition to inadequate numbers, questions have been raised about the competence and political loyalty of some of the secretariat's staff. Many of them are holdovers from the old regime. A large contingent (perhaps eighty people) was transferred from the staff of the CPSU Central Committee after that organization was sharply reduced in size in 1988-89. Some of this contingent might be suspected of divided loyalty in political struggles between the legislature and the party apparatus.

Helping to partially offset these staff limitations is the fact that the legislative branch gained rapidly in political stature and attracted some very capable professionals from government ministries, research institutes, and universities, who saw it as an exciting and important new political arena in which to build a career and render significant public service. Volunteers, especially from among the Moscow intelligentsia, supplement the limited staff.

Legislative research services for the Supreme Soviet are provided in part by the Information Section of the secretariat. In addition, the Institute for State Structure and Legislation (ISSL) was transferred in 1989 from the Ministry of Justice to the Supreme Soviet for this purpose. Elements of the Lenin State Library are also dedicated to parliamentary service. The largest of these units is the ISSL. According to its director, however, its professional staff devotes about 90 percent of its time to drafting legislation, leaving little time for research and policy analysis.[39]

Weaknesses of the Legislature

The most important weaknesses of the new legislature derive from its newness and inexperience. This contributes to the disorganized, "unprofessional," and often *ad hoc* character of the proceedings, as noted above. A number of deputies have said they thought many of these problems would be overcome when the present crop of inexperienced deputies was replaced in future years by "professional politicians." The shortage of staff is also a major problem.

Another area of weakness apparent to Western observers concerns budgetary matters. The Supreme Soviet does not exercise effective control over either the state budget or the budget for its own legislative activities. Some deputies know theoretically that the "power of the purse" is the fundamental source of parliamentary power. But it will be difficult for the Supreme Soviet to establish this in practice until, as economists say, the Soviet economy is "monetized." The Soviet ruble is not only artificial, unconvertible, and highly inflated, it is not the real basis of economic exchange. The Soviet macro-economy resembles a barter system in which goods and services are exchanged directly. The state *assigns* prices.

Accounting and budgetary practices are, at best, nonuniform. Some Western analysts now believe that Soviet officials may in fact not know, for example, what their own real level of defense spending is. Under these circumstances, exercising control over the state budget is one of the most daunting challenges facing the Supreme Soviet. Its importance is compounded by the revelation, made public for the first time in reports to the Supreme Soviet, that the Soviet Union faces a massive budget deficit problem. Responsible Soviet officials differ on the size of the deficit, but as a percentage of GNP the deficit is authoritatively reported to be proportionally at least two to three times larger than that of the United States. The Supreme Soviet lacks the technical expertise to attack this problem aggressively and appears to be at the stage of groping to discover actual levels of government spending.

Surprisingly, the Congress and the Supreme Soviet do not have independent budgets that they control. They are funded as a part of the overall state budget. According to one deputy, the Supreme Soviet has been allocated approximately 40 million rubles per year--up from 7 million per year for its rubber-stamp predecessor. This gives rise to an anomaly. Supreme Soviet committees have begun the process of overseeing the budgets of various government ministries. But those committees must apply for operating funds to the Supreme Soviet secretariat, which then consults with those very government ministries to secure the funds. For example, the Supreme Soviet Defense and State Security Committee's February 1990 trip to the United States was funded by the Ministry of Defense.[40]

The Future Implications of the New Legislative System

Separation of Powers

The political system that Gorbachev inherited was a one-party dictatorship in which the undisputed locus of power was the Communist Party. The party was run by a relatively small circle of mostly like-minded men,[41] a self-perpetuating elite operating in a system described as "the circular flow of power." One of its defining characteristics was an extraordinary concentration of power at the center. The new legislative system changes this decisively, providing the basis for a separation of powers.

By creating a popularly elected legislature defined as the paramount political organ of state and imbued with genuine legislative authority, Gorbachev broke the power monopoly of the Communist Party's central apparatus. He may have intended an institutional separation of powers, with the party and the Supreme Soviet as the principal countervailing forces. That appeared to be the outcome in 1989. This did not necessarily imply a reduction of Gorbachev's power, since he held the leadership of both institutions in 1989.

By 1990, the opposition of the conservative central party apparatus to

Gorbachev's reforms and the decline of the party's prestige and popularity appeared irremediable, and Gorbachev moved against the party apparatus. Despite his emphatic rejection in 1989 of the idea of a multiparty system for the Soviet Union as "rubbish," he reversed himself and embraced the idea in early 1990. In endorsing the elimination of the Communist Party's constitutionally mandated "leading and guiding role" (Article 6 of the USSR Constitution), Gorbachev sided with the democratic reformers, and in March 1990 the Congress amended Article 6, thereby establishing the legal basis for a multi-party system. At the same time Gorbachev proposed and the Congress approved the creation of the executive presidency--a new power base for Gorbachev (as he apparently prepared to relinquish the leadership of the party) and a new countervailing institution juxtaposed against the legislature.

In 1989 and early 1990 the antidemocratic forces appeared to be on the defensive, fighting a delaying action. But the intensification of regime-threatening crises, especially the danger of fragmentation of the Union and of economic collapse, galvanized the reactionaries and strengthened their ranks inside the legislative branch as well as in the executive branch, the party, and the military and security forces.

The political situation in the Soviet Union is unstable at this time and the present institutional arrangements will probably be altered further. But the present constitutional arrangement, a separation of powers between a popularly elected legislature and a president who is also to be popularly elected, is far removed from the highly centralized circular flow of power exercised by the ruling party elite only a few years ago. This is a fundamental political change. A potential negative implication of the legislative reform is that competing power centers may increase confusion and impede effective decision making.

Democratization

The widespread enfranchisement, political mobilization, and empowerment that resulted from the recent legislative reforms and elections are unprecedented in Soviet history. The newly elected legislatures--not only the Congress of People's Deputies and the Supreme Soviet of the USSR, but the republic, regional, local, and municipal legislatures--are generally in the vanguard of democratization. The process of democratization is far from complete, and many significant undemocratic features remain. The forces of authoritarianism and reaction are seeking to reverse the democratic reforms. Yet at this point it appears that much of what in the West is regarded as positive change in the Soviet Union results, directly or indirectly, from legislative activity or the restructuring of the legislative branch of government. The vitality of the legislative branch and the continued growth of political pluralism, competing parties, and electoral politics associated with that branch appear to be keys to the further development of democracy in the USSR, its republics, and, perhaps, its successor.

Reversibility

The legislative system provides a substantial bulwark against the reversal of democratization. During Gorbachev's first years in power the great question in the West about *glasnost'* and *perestroika* was whether the reforms were real and whether it was in the West's interest for them to succeed. Now the main debate is over how far and in which directions the reforms will go--and whether they are reversible.

In the most literal sense, the reforms and events of 1985-1990 probably are not reversible. It would not seem possible to turn the clock back and recreate the conditions of Brezhnevism or Stalinism. But so narrow an answer begs the question. Is democratization reversible? It probably is. Few specialists maintain that the triumph of democracy in the Soviet Union is inevitable. The regime-threatening crises of economic collapse and dissolution of the Union exacerbate one another. Such conditions are not conducive to the transition to democracy. The reemergence of a highly authoritarian regime is viewed by many as quite possible. The weight of Russian history inclines against democratic institutions.

There is no guarantee that democratization in the Soviet Union will not be reversed--or deflected, or undermined, or marginalized. But the strongest protection against such negative outcomes appears to be the vitality of the legislative branch. Popular participation in electoral politics and the dynamics of pluralism and representative government are bulwarks against totalitarianism. The emergence of the Nazi regime from the democratic and parliamentary government of Weimar Germany reminds us that such bulwarks provide no absolute guarantee. But in the Soviet context it is the political life that has sprung up around the legislative branch that appears most likely and able to resist the forces that would reverse the democratic trends.

Notes

1. In October 1988, three deputies made headlines by actually voting against a piece of legislation proposed by the leadership.

2. The oblast party first secretary would be chairman of the oblast soviet; the republic party first secretary would be chairman of the republic supreme soviet; and the general secretary of the Communist Party of the Soviet Union (CPSU) would be chairman of the USSR Supreme Soviet.

3. Each of these 750 districts is supposed to be comprised of approximately 257,000 voters. The actual range is from 139,000 to 379,000.

4. Each of the fifteen union republics of the USSR, regardless of size, elects 32

deputies; autonomous republics 11 deputies; autonomous oblasts 5 deputies; and autonomous okrugs 1 deputy.

5. CPSU (100), cooperatives and consumer associations (100), Communist Youth League (75), women's organizations (75), veterans (75), scientific organizations (75), creative and artistic organizations (75), other nationwide organizations (75).

6. As originally adopted, this unusual provision required a 20 percent annual turnover rate of Supreme Soviet deputies. It was then amended to state that "up to 20 percent" of the Supreme Soviet deputies were to be "renewed" each year. The actual turnover rate in the first renewal (December 1990) was 36 percent (see below).

7. Luk'ianov's election was contested. Nineteen candidates were nominated, eleven of whom withdrew. Luk'ianov received 1,202 "yes" and 682 "no" votes. Konstantin Lubenchenko, a pro-democracy university professor, came in second with 377 votes. See *RFE/RL Daily Report*, 16 March 1990.

8. Supreme Soviet deputies and staff members visiting the U.S. Congress now almost invariably ask detailed questions about congressional procedures and frequently request copies of published rules and procedures.

9. The presidium's agenda had thirty-three items, some of which were dismissed as being of "secondary importance" by Anatolii Sobchak, a spokesman for the Interregional Group of Deputies (and, more recently, mayor of Leningrad). Sobchak suggested ten other items for inclusion, including a prompt vote of no confidence on the USSR government headed by Nikolai Ryzhkov, chairman of the Council of Ministers, a review of the lawfulness of certain presidential decrees, and an investigation of the KGB. The Supreme Soviet voted to form a special conciliation commission to draw up a compromise agenda.

10. In addition, the secretariat is supposed to assist the republic, regional, and local legislatures, of which there are 52,000--an immense and probably impossible task. This discussion will focus on the secretariat's work in support of the USSR Supreme Soviet.

11. Not surprisingly, officials of the secretariat complain of being highly overburdened while deputies complain of being very understaffed. See below for a fuller discussion of legislative staff.

12. Theoretically, another alternative would be for each party to have its own information and research service. But in view of the profusion of emergent parties and the meager resources of most of them, this does not seem practical.

13. Gorbachev argued that these radical changes were needed in order to deal decisively with a deepening economic crisis and the ethnic and national unrest threatening civil war and fragmentation of the USSR. Other important factors were the intensifying Kremlin power struggle, the sharp decline in the Communist Party's authority and prestige, and the influence of the East European revolutions of 1989.

14. The president at the time of election must be no less than thirty-five years old and no more than sixty-five. The latter restriction may be a reaction to the pattern of "gerontocracy" that weakened the Soviet leadership in the Brezhnev period.

15. This provision seems designed to prevent the election by a Russian or Slavic majority of a candidate who was opposed by voters in a majority of the other republics.

16. The executive branch was substantially restructured by constitutional amend-

ments in December 1990. The former Council of Ministers, renamed Cabinet of Ministers, was subordinated directly to the president and the number of ministries was sharply reduced.

17. This provision was misinterpreted in many Western press accounts to imply that the president had the power arbitrarily to dissolve the Supreme Soviet and then to rule by emergency decree. This is incorrect. Even if the Congress of People's Deputies agreed to dissolve the Supreme Soviet, it presumably would immediately elect a new Supreme Soviet from among its own members.

18. This phrase acknowledges that the title of the head of government may vary among republics.

19. On September 14, 1990, in its first constitutional ruling, the Committee on Constitutional Supervision declared illegal President Gorbachev's first presidential decree (April 1990), which authorized the USSR Council of Ministers to rule on applications for political rallies in Moscow. The Committee on Constitutional Supervision noted that the president is not empowered to amend laws, and that the law leaves decisions on rallies to local authorities. *RFE/RL Daily Report*, no. 177 (17 September 1990), p. 4.

20. The Soviet Union is a federal system. The term that they use to refer to the highest level of government (which corresponds in the U.S. system to the national or federal level) is "all-union." Since many of the administrative subdivisions in the USSR such as union republics and autonomous republics are designated as nations, the term national-level would be ambiguous.

21. See note 4, above.

22. The number of standing commissions and committees is not fixed. Initially there were 22 (4, 4, and 14 respectively). Four more were added in the first year.

23. So far, most draft laws have been introduced by the Cabinet (formerly Council) of Ministers. The legislature, however, has often flatly rejected or greatly modified these drafts.

24. In this discussion, the term committee is used to denote both commissions and committees of the Supreme Soviet.

25. Alexander V. Mishkin, "Toward a Law-Governed Society," *New Outlook,* Spring 1990, p. 16.

26. Lenin, himself a lawyer, despised the legal profession. (See Adam B. Ulam, *The Bolsheviks* [New York: Macmillan, 1965], pp 211-12.) The Bolsheviks created a political system in which the rule of law and legal adjudication played but a minor role, hence the low regard for and relatively small number of lawyers.

27. I.e., approximately 100 new deputies each year would be cycled from the Congress of People's Deputies into the Supreme Soviet and vice versa. Commission and committee chairmen were to be exempted from this rotation system.

28. *FBIS*, CPD and New Supreme Soviet, p. 9. Afanas'ev, a historian, is Rector of the Soviet State Archival Institute. Despite the staid-sounding career, he is one of the most outspoken and iconoclastic deputies. In a public talk at the Library of Congress in October 1988, he astonished his audience with his candor.

29. Mishkin, "Toward a Law-Governed Society," p. 16.

30. Interviews with deputies, August 1989 to March 1991.

31. Louise Shelley, Testimony before the Commission on Security and Cooperation in Europe, November 28, 1980.

32. *RFE/RL Daily Report*, 19 December 1980.

33. Astaf'ev's comments at the Kennan Institute for Advanced Russian Studies, October 26, 1989.

34. Another major cause of absenteeism is the unresolved question of whether Supreme Soviet deputies are to be professional legislators or retain their "primary" jobs away from the legislature.

35. Marat Abullayev, "USSR People's Deputies' Privileges, Problems," *SOIUZ* (Moscow, in Russian), 29 January-4 February 1990. Translated in Joint Publications Research Service (JPRS), USSR Political Affairs, UPA-90-014, p. 1.

36. "Making the Soviet Supreme," *The Economist*, 30 September 1989, p. 45.

37. Mishkin, "Toward a Law-Governed Society," p. 17.

38. Interviews with delegation of deputies from the Defense and State Security Committee, February 1990. See U.S. Congress, House of Representatives, Committee on Armed Services, *The New Soviet Legislature: Committee on Defense and State Security*, 11 April 1990 (101st Congress, 2d sess.), p. 7.

39. The leaders of these research services visited Capitol Hill from January 31 to February 7, 1990, studying the Congress and congressional procedures, the Congressional Research Service, and other congressional support agencies.

40. February 17-19, 1990, at the invitation of the House Armed Services Committee, U.S. Congress, Committee on Armed Services, *The New Soviet Legislature: Committee on Defense and State Security*, p. 8.

41. In the early 1980s, the party's highest organs (Politburo, Secretariat, and Central Committee) numbered about 300, mostly old men.

THE FORMATION OF
NEW PARTIES AND
POLITICAL GROUPINGS

5

GORBACHEV'S REFORMS AND THE FACTIONALIZATION OF SOVIET POLITICS
Can the New System Cope with Pluralism?

Donald R. Kelley

The New Pluralism of Soviet Politics

One of the most remarkable consequences of the sweeping reforms initiated by Mikhail S. Gorbachev is the rapidly growing pluralism of Soviet politics. As the number of political actors grows seemingly without limit, and as the new legislative institutions and the presidency strive to define their respective roles, it becomes increasingly apparent that the new Soviet political system faces a challenge common to any would-be democracy: to provide mechanisms that effectively represent the diversity of political views but that also permit, and hopefully foster, the emergence of some form of consensus building and coalition formation. While the former might be termed the *representational aspects* of the system, which focus on the articulation of newly organized political interests, the latter can be thought of as the *aggregational aspects*, which provide either organizational or other consensus-building mechanisms that bring seeming order out of apparent chaos.

For obvious reasons, the attention of Western analysts has focused primarily on the representational aspects of the Soviet Union's new democracy. The proliferation of political parties, the clash of personalities and programs, and the ubiquitous presence of "street politics" in most major Soviet cities have riveted the attention of Western observers, as have the bitter and sometimes violent clashes between central authorities and the restive provinces.

There is no question that it is now possible to speak of a *behavioral, if not yet fully institutionalized, pluralism* in Soviet politics, a pluralism going well beyond that envisioned in the first years of Gorbachev's tenure in office, when hopeful reformers spoke of the possibility of greater flexibility within the framework of a modified one-party system. The rules have changed, and although the concatenation of events is familiar to anyone who has followed Soviet politics over the last several years, it bears at least quick repetition because of the cumulative impact of events: the Communist Party of the Soviet Union, once the "leading core" of the system, has shattered into squabbling factions, some representing various ethnic territories through a *de facto* federalization of the party, some reflecting the now-admitted ideological diversity of a party desperately trying to find a role in society, some attempting to cling to former, institutionalized mechanisms of rule, and some simply following real or would-be charismatic leaders; new political parties running the gamut from monarchists to "true" Marxists have formed as a consequence of the revocation of Article 6 of the constitution and the passage of a new law sanctioning the creation of political organizations; informal political organizations, now numbering well over 60,000, have sprung into existence, sometimes dealing with single issues such as local concerns or the environment and sometimes forming broader coalitions with other parties and organizations; loosely united coalitions of parties and informal groups have emerged in the form of popular fronts; and factions have formed within the newly created two-level legislature, with coalitions such as the Interregional Group of Deputies or Soiuz representing proreform or conservative elements within the Congress of People's Deputies and the Supreme Soviet.

But to acknowledge the existence of such pluralism is not accurately to portray the Soviet Union as a true multiparty system--at least inasmuch as that description commonly implies that the party structures channel political conflict, accurately reflect the views of and speak for particular constituencies, and take part in the functioning of government or opposition. In many ways, the evolution of the party and group structures has not reached that level of maturity. Having stressed the politically easier task of articulating the views of constituencies, which in many cases they hope to activate, parties and groups have placed less emphasis on their own internal organization and the creation of effective campaigning and electoral mechanisms. One might argue that they function more as what we might term "pre-parties," or, perhaps better yet, as what early analysts of Soviet interest groups under the old regime called "tendencies of articulation" whose rhetorical abilities far exceeded their organizational successes.[1]

The new pluralism of Soviet politics must also be explained, at least in part, in terms of the purposeful devolution of real political power throughout the system. While always *de jure* a federal system, the Soviet Union under the old order was *de facto* a highly centralized political-administrative structure. Both the CPSU's monopoly of political power and the dominance of the all-union government reduced the number of effective decision-making locations, at least for politically significant issues, to one: the center itself.

Moreover, the dominance of the party over the Supreme Soviet or its local counterparts meant that on most issues the former's policies were merely given *pro forma* attention as they were transformed into formal acts. While the republican-level and local soviets exercised some power over local issues, they operated within tightly constricted parameters.

That too has changed. Both the geographic devolution of power and authority *downward* to republican and local-level bodies (both party and state) and the *lateral* dispersal of power at the all-union and lower levels through the creation of more powerful legislatures and presidential offices have created what Western students of democracy have termed *multiple points of access* to decision makers. The formation of such new institutions and the empowerment of what were rubberstamp bodies have had the predictable effect of animating political forces whose activities are targeted at these newly powerful entities. The situation is further complicated by the widespread uncertainty about who decides what: is economic or social policy made at the all-union level as before, or do each of the republican governments and the major cities decide their own priorities in consultation with, or in complete isolation from, Moscow? The tendency to shift the focus of political agitation away from the inherently more conservative (or perhaps merely more distant) central institutions in Moscow to the republican or local levels has been strengthened by the relative ease with which local coalitions have dislodged the formerly entrenched party and state establishments; whether through the use of ethnic or nationality issues, as in the Baltic, through the strong appeal of greater local autonomy, or through the strength of reformist coalitions such as those that captured control of city governments in Moscow and Leningrad, such locally based forces have created an entirely new level of political activism in the Soviet system.

Consideration must also be given to the role of *glasnost'*, or openness, in the transformation of the body politic. While it is not the purpose of this essay to chart the shifting parameters of *glasnost'*, there are several ways in which Gorbachev's policies of greater candor and freer access to information have facilitated the emergence of Soviet pluralism. First, the new truthfulness of the Soviet media and official willingness to fill in the so-called "blank pages" have affected the issue-formation and agenda-setting processes in Soviet politics. No longer does the party, through its control of the communications process and its gatekeeper function within the institutional structure, filter, selectively interpret, or outright prohibit the discussion of controversial issues. To be sure, Gorbachev *initiated* the discussion of certain questions to raise embarrassing issues as political weapons against his conservative opponents. But any hopes that *glasnost'* could be contained within the parameters of the party's or the reformers' control have been dashed by the proliferation of media sources and by the radicalization of the audience itself. *Glasnost'* has permitted the generation and legitimation of issues *from below*, that is, from the politically competitive activity of new parties and informal groups, each hoping to win its moment on the television screen or carve its niche in the political firmament.

It is far more doubtful that *glasnost'* has improved the *aggregational performance* of the system, at least insofar as the new political order has failed to generate effective and broadly popular parties or coalitions of parties that pull together disparate groups. To be sure, communication among them has improved markedly, and in special circumstances, such as the creation of popular fronts in the Baltics or broad coalitions uniting around procedural as opposed to distributional issues (e.g., the revocation of Article 6 of the Constitution or the endorsement of the creation of a multiparty system), broad coalitions have emerged. But on other issues, better communication and more open discussion have resulted as much in the discovery of *differences* as in the recognition of similarities, and so have fostered the resuscitation of ethnic or political rivalries that had been suppressed in a kind of pax Sovietica.

The emergence of a stable balance between the representational and aggregational aspects of Soviet democracy has been retarded by the fluid nature of the new institutions and the changing civic culture within which they must operate. Indeed, one cannot speak of a single civic culture at the all-union level; the devolution of political power has led to the emergence of distinct and coherent regional cultures--again, the Baltic republics offer the best example--but there is no widespread agreement on the norms, both formal and informal, governing national political life. One can simply conclude that the *party culture* formerly imposed by the CPSU, which was the true meaning of *partiinost'*, has been shattered, and nothing substantively has arisen to take its place.

The institutional arrangements are similarly muddled, with no agreement over the proper devolution of political power from the all-union to the republican or local levels, no consensus over the relationship between the executive and legislative branches, and no common understanding of the role of the party system, now including the CPSU itself. In other, more stable democratic systems, such creative tension has performed the dual function of providing viable checks and balances and spurring each branch or party to guard zealously its prerogatives. But in the Soviet context, the result so far has been quite the opposite; the creation of a *de facto* system of checks and balances has tended to polarize the legislative and the executive branches, resulting either in a pattern of immobilism or in the strengthening of the powers of the presidency through the grudging acquiescence of the legislature, which has come to doubt its own ability to govern. The same has been true of the evolution of the CPSU itself. The hopes of early reformers either that the party would be transformed into an umbrella-like coalition of moderate-to-progressive reformers or that the new parties and groups would form into identifiable coalitions and thus impose some order and organization on the political spectrum have been in vain; the proliferation and dispersal of political forces have been the rule of the day.

The Politics of Representation: Many Speakers, Many Voices

If Mikhail Gorbachev's political reforms are to be assessed in terms of mobilizing new political actors and broadening the range of political discourse, then they must be judged an unbridled, if cacophonous, success. The floodgates have been opened, at least for a while, and what has poured forth has been combination of demands for the righting of past wrongs, the recognition of (frequently self-proclaimed) privilege and entitlement, and--at a more sophisticated level--the acceptance and legal formalization of the institutional and philosophical pluralism of contemporary Soviet society. To be sure, such demands have been made in the past. As a self-proclaimed child of the twentieth party congress, Gorbachev himself witnessed the first round of reforms under Khrushchev, whose tenure in office accepted the reality of *de facto* institutional pluralism even if it did nothing to formalize the arrangement.[2] That at least some like-minded elements would organize in some fashion to press their demands on political authority has been an accepted part of Soviet political reality, as the studies of interest groups that were first undertaken in the 1960s convincingly demonstrated.[3] Party control was maintained, however, and the CPSU performed the dual function of gatekeeper and legitimator; neither new issues nor new political groups could take the stage without its approval, and that power of control was only grudgingly surrendered, even under Gorbachev. At first change came slowly, with the caveat that the party would preserve a special role, if not its old "leading role," in the political process. It was to transform itself into a broader political coalition, leading nonparty elements by example and coopting, as it always had, the best and the brightest of the new politics; it was to lead through its role in popular fronts, which would link the CPSU to other parties and to the growing array of informal groups; and finally, it was to win its leadership role through the ballot box, transforming itself into a parliamentary party both in the sense that it won popular approval through the electoral process and in the sense that it formed a coherent working parliamentary bloc within the legislature. According to the February 1990 Central Committee plenum, the party was to continue to perform a "unifying" and "consolidating" role within the new pluralistic political environment, functioning "strictly within the framework of the democratic process."[4]

The twenty-eighth party congress further confirmed the party's attempt to transform itself along parliamentary lines. In an act of rhetorical juggling, Gorbachev asserted that it would remain as a "vanguard" and be "active in all spheres of life" while eschewing its "exclusive position" as once defined in Article 6. Finding what were termed "new political methods," the party would "implement its policies and struggle to retain the mandate of a ruling party within the confines of the democratic process," seeking its goals by "working through Communists, especially Communists holding leading positions," and cooperating with all other parties having a "progressive orientation."[5]

But Gorbachev's and the party's best laid plans went astray. Careful and controlled pluralization quickly gave way to a less well defined and guided process. At times, the general secretary himself accelerated the pace of change as a weapon against his opponents, especially within the conservative apparatus. What had begun as a campaign to transform the party quickly became a process of supplanting it, in part with the mechanisms of elected democratic institutions and in part with the creation of a strong presidency. The party, and eventually the new presidency itself, lost control of the two key elements that had preserved order in the past--control over the political agenda and veto power over the creation of alternative political institutions.

Adding to the disorder has been the factionalization of the CPSU itself along regional and ideological lines. National party leaders have been compelled to accept the de facto federalization of the party. The growing assertiveness of non-Russian republics has led to the creation of nativist and pro-Moscow wings of once unified local communist party organizations, themselves either replaced at the helm by noncommunist popular fronts or put under severe pressure by such entities to chart a course different from that dictated by the center. The creation of executive presidencies in each of the republics patterned after Gorbachev's office has further complicated the party's dilemma; of the fifteen presidents, six are political independents with ties to nationalist popular fronts or noncommunist political groups, three are titular party leaders who work closely with such fronts or parties, and only six can be considered pro-Moscow.[6]

The creation of a separate communist party for the Russian republic has also complicated Moscow's task; except for a brief period under Khrushchev, the Russian republic party organizations were administered directly by the central party apparatus, a mechanism that ensured their loyalty. The initial call for the creation of a separate organization came from conservatives in Leningrad who hoped that it might provide a counterweight to Gorbachev's more liberal leanings. Gorbachev countered with a proposal to create a separate Bureau for the Russian Republic (the Khrushchev ploy), but by September 1989, pressures for the formation of a separate republic-level party organization had grown.[7] The formal creation of the separate party organization occurred in June 1990, and a conservative party leader, Ivan Polozkov, was elected first secretary. The program of the CP RSFSR predictably stresses Russian nationalist themes (and admits to the misdeeds of central party leaders against the Russian people), calls for the preservation of the USSR as an integrated state, and--most importantly--articulates conservative positions opposing full marketization of the economy and the elimination of the privileged role of the party itself.[8]

Other factions abound within the CPSU, including: (1) the Leningrad Initiative Group, founded in the spring of 1990 and advocating a defense of Russian economic interests within the Union, a vanguard role (the old definition, we must presume) for the Communist Party, and opposition to market reforms of the economy; (2) the Democratic Platform of the Communist Party of the Soviet Union, created in January 1990 as an alliance of democratic forces in opposition to party conservatives, and advocating a two-stage transition to democratic socialism, beginning with the transfer of party power to the soviets, the democratization of the party, the renunciation of dogmatic Marxism, the admission of the party's responsibility for the creation of a totalitarian system, and the transformation of the CPSU into a parliamentary party working within a multiparty system; (3) the Marxist Platform of the CPSU, founded in April 1990, seeking to restore public confidence in the party through the dismantling of the party apparatus, the development of self-management, and the transformation of the many informal political organizations that have sprung into existence into important participants in government and administration; (4) the Union of Constitutional Communist Democrats, founded in the summer of 1990 and arguing for the reunification of party and society through the creation of a government based on the rule of law, the creation of separate branches of government, freedom of expression, and the creation of a multiparty system within which the Communist Democrats would form the leadership of coalition governments within the soviets at all levels; and (5) the Moscow Party Club, founded in June 1990 as an informal association of party members at the center advocating democratic reform within the party, political pluralism and a multiparty system, an end to democratic centralism (that is, internal party discipline), and the development of a market economy.[9]

The abolition of the CPSU's constitutionally mandated status as the only legitimate political party opened the door for the creation of a plethora of new organizations. In the first six months after the revocation of Article 6, more than one hundred political parties and other organizations were formed, with over twenty claiming to be active at the all-union level.[10] Since other contributions to this book deal at length with these new parties, it will not be our purpose to go into detail concerning either the rapid proliferation of such entities or the details of their programs. Suffice it to say that such parties run the full political spectrum from left to right and focus on a great variety of particular issues or constituencies. From the representational point of view, their creation has both broadened the scope of political debate and mobilized a seemingly ever greater number of new participants in the political process.

But it is also important to understand what these new parties are not and what they cannot do. For the most part, they remain small organizations without organized and mobilized constituencies. With the exception of a few (such as the Democratic Party in the Russian republic), they lack electoral mechanisms designed to communicate with voters, select candidates, and conduct campaigns. Fewer still offer coherent and specific platforms on a wide assortment of issues; to the extent that such platforms exist, they focus on a narrow range of issues of concern to a particular constituency (for example, environmental issues, workers' rights, etc.), the problems of a particular region, or general philosophical statements. Eloquent about the general state of affairs they wish to see created (or, conversely, avoided), such platforms usually offer few specifics. Symbolic issues--democratization, freedom of speech, and the like--are the common mainstay, and difficult economic issues are avoided or are handled only through general reference pro or con on the question of marketization.

The leadership of these parties also leaves much to be desired. To be sure, there is no reason to expect that skilled political leaders would emerge to guide this new assortment of parties; democratization has become a learn-by-doing process in the Soviet Union. But even with such allowances, it remains apparent that the parties frequently are merely extensions of a particular leader or group of leaders. Personalities as much as platforms govern the ebb and flow of party cohesion and factionalism, and questions of building broad coalitions and a viable electoral base of support seem to occupy lower priority than the dominance of a particular party leader.

While the creation of political parties has fundamentally altered the landscape of Soviet politics and contributed to the expansion of the representational aspects of the system, the formation and growth of informal political associations--simply termed "informals" by supporters and critics alike--has further led to the proliferation of political actors. Such "informals" are best conceptualized, at least by Western audiences, as functioning much as interest groups, political action committees, and the plethora of single-issue groups that have changed the political process in most democracies. Even before their legalization in 1990, they grew like the proverbial mushrooms after the rain, responding to the new freedom for political discussion created by *glasnost'* and filling the void that existed in a political culture in which there had been few organizations to mediate between the individual and political institutions. Given added impetus by democratization, they raised new issues, in many instances fielded candidates for election, joined in usually loosely united coalitions on questions of national or local importance, and--perhaps most importantly--served as the first introduction to the new democracy for many formerly inactive citizens. By the end of 1989, over 60,000 such groups were estimated to be functioning, ranging from single-issue groups concerned with questions of the environment, historical preservation, the rehabilitation of the victims of political repression, and the like, to broader orientations dealing with more sweeping reform issues. Even more importantly, their rapid growth was marked both by a process of politicization and subsequent radicalization and by halting attempts to form ties among themselves to create viable popular fronts or political parties. While the latter efforts have been less than successful, except under special circumstances in which local issues such as regional independence have created a common ground, these groups have stretched the boundaries of the political system, legitimating new issues and adding both to the level of true representation and to the decibel level of the debate.[11]

At first Soviet leaders encouraged the emergence of such groups--before they created viable regional popular fronts opposed to central rule or sought to form broader party-like coalitions--and sought to channel their efforts along acceptable lines. At least as they were first conceived in 1986 and 1987, they were to provide a structure for the involvement of the average citizen in the new political life of Soviet democracy; they were to raise "safe" issues and to be controlled through the Komsomol and the party itself and through the formation of popular fronts linking like-minded groups. By 1988, however, the informals had transformed themselves from a collection of relatively apolitical debating societies into increasingly militant and vocal political action committees. By 1990 the leadership's attitude had changed, and the informals found themselves unambiguously labeled by more conservative forces as narrow in focus and interested only in obtaining power through the new political process. Policy shifted from support and amazed tolerance to scrutiny and closer supervision, especially by the party itself, whose grassroots organizations were instructed to infiltrate and guide informal associations.[12]

Official encouragement for the formation of popular fronts also added to the growing pluralism of Soviet democracy. Initially thought of as umbrella groups whose coalition-building activities would mediate the impact of the growing number of informal groups and lead, it was hoped, to a sense of compromise and moderation, the popular fronts were to form broad alliances linked by the acceptance of common themes and policies. Among the first were a series of proreform or pro-*perestroika* groups that united fledgling democratic forces. Such fronts were to provide public sounding boards for Gorbachev's reforms, playing the dual role of cheerleader and Greek chorus and demonstrating broad public support for the reform agenda. And at first (until 1988-1989), the fronts performed their assigned tasks; not yet full-fledged political parties, they bridged the gap between the new informals and the general public searching for an outlet for political expression.

By the end of the decade, the role of popular fronts changed, in part as a consequence of the growing radicalization of Soviet political life and the polarization of conservative and proreform forces, and in part because the most successful fronts coalesced around disruptive issues, especially nationalism and the question of national self-determination and independence. While the most notable--and potentially powerful--fronts have emerged in the Baltic states, similar developments have occurred throughout the Soviet Union. In part because of the inherent volatility of questions of national self-identity, autonomy, and independence, and in part because local political leaders, including the republic-level party organizations, purposely used appeals to nationalism to win support and to deflect attention away from Moscow's emphasis on economic and political reform--issues that could cost local elites their power within party and state--the popular fronts focused on the always sensitive question of center-periphery relations. Finding their source of unity in real and imagined mistreatment by central authorities and in the growing desire for a redefinition of the Treaty of Union, the fronts formed viable coalitions at the regional level, bridging the differences that separated local political forces, but in the process raising extremely disruptive issues at the national level.[13]

Although they had already established a firm *de facto* presence, the new parties, informals, and popular fronts lacked a formal legal basis for their existence and activities. While Gorbachev had promised the passage of a new law on political associations since 1987, conflicts over the actual content of the legislation and whether informal groups and political parties should be treated differently delayed action. No fewer than four drafts were presented from 1987 to 1990, with the earlier versions drawing criticism from democratic forces for their restrictive content. Each subsequent draft seemingly loosened restrictions, providing greater acceptance of the growing pluralism of Soviet society.[14]

Final passage of the Law on Public Organizations came in October 1990, and the preamble paid due respect to Gorbachev's desire to create a "civil society" of competent political activists. The law broadly defines such associations as including "political parties, mass movements, trade unions, women's and veterans' organizations, organizations of disabled persons, young people's and children's organizations, scientific, technical, cultural-enlightenment, physical culture/sports and other voluntary societies, creative unions, organizations of people from the same area, [and] foundations and other associations. . . ."[15] Broadly mandated to act "for purposes of the exercise and protection of civil, political, economic, social and cultural rights and liberties," they are authorized to carry out any activities "not prohibited by law." However, such associations may not have as their goal the "overthrow of or violent change in the constitutional system or the forcible violation of the unity of the USSR," nor may they conduct "propaganda for war," stir up "social discord," or advocate the "commission of other criminally punishable acts." Prohibited also are activities that "infringe on the health and morality of the population" and on the "rights and legally protected interests" of citizens.

The law further guarantees that all such associations will stand legally equal before the state; government will eschew interference in the legal activities of these new entities, just as it will be prohibited from providing financial and other material support, except for the public funding of campaigns for the Congress of People's Deputies. While associations and parties are required to register with public officials and to submit information about their internal organization and sources of financial support, the regulations are not onerous or oppressive.

Public organizations are accorded the right to distribute information to the general public, to operate printing houses, to "participate in the formation of bodies of state power and administration," that is, to hold executive positions in the new democratically elected government, and to initiate legislation. Political parties are given the explicit right to nominate candidates, campaign, and form groups of deputies within the legislature itself.

Aggregational Aspects: Finding Order Amidst Disorder

While the foregoing analysis leads to the conclusion that Gorbachev's political reforms score high marks in terms of expanding and institutionalizing the *representational aspects* of the system--that is, broadening the boundaries of political debate and institutionalizing mechanisms through which such discourse occurs--it is far less certain that *demokratizatsiia* has as successfully provided processes and mechanisms through which the *aggregational aspects* of the political process may be accomplished. In one sense, of course, any movement away from a single-party toward a multiparty system complicates the task of aggregation. Whatever its other liabilities--and they were legion--the "old" CPSU was the ultimate aggregator; it legitimated political issues, formulated questions and shaped debates along lines acceptable to the party leadership, and, most importantly, performed a significant, if highly restrictive, gatekeeping function.

The question now arises whether the new mechanisms of Soviet political life--the political parties, the "informals," the popular fronts, and the legislative bodies themselves--can perform that aggregationai function. Despite the admittedly fluid nature of Soviet politics, there are at least some potential sources of such activity. As in any political system, such order will emerge when some mechanism or mechanisms are created through which consensus building may occur. There is no requirement--and no guarantee-- that any single mechanism or any combination of mechanisms will solve the pressing substantive questions facing decision makers; rather our concern lies with the creation of a *process* through which political demands are filtered, mediated, and eventually processed through the existing institutions in ways that permit the creation of effective agreement. In short, we are concerned with the creation and maintenance of a balance between what we have termed the representational aspects of the new political order and the system's ability to contain, channel, and eventually manage conflict. There are four possible sources of such mediational activity: (1) a reformed Communist Party will lead democratically through the new political institutions; (2) the new political parties, informal groups, and popular fronts will find mechanisms for bridging the gaps that separate them either in the pre-electoral phase or through the formation of effective coalition governments within the legislature; (3) the legislature itself will provide effective internal mechanisms leading to the emergence of such consensus or, failing to do so, will provide alternative sources of stability independent of the party structures; and (4) *de facto* coordination will emerge through the growing strength of the presidency, coupled with the self-realization on the part of the legislature itself that its internal divisions have produced immobilism. Let us examine each of these possibilities in turn.

A reformed Communist Party will lead through the new institutions. In its most optimistic form, this scenario holds forth the possibility that the CPSU will transform itself into a parliamentary party along the lines suggested by Gorbachev at the February 1990 Central Committee plenum.[16] Although stripped of its constitutionally mandated lock hold on power, the party would remain the nation's leading political force because of its ability to mobilize public support for further reform. It would legitimate its leadership both through the ballot box and--as it had always claimed in the past--through the indispensable guidance provided by the party's best and bright cadres who continued to hold important decision-making positions at all levels of the system. Formally separated from the day-to-day concerns of governance, the party would be free, as it had never been in the past, to offer overall leadership on important questions of policy. It would form a broad coalition at all levels, linking reform elements within the party itself to a broader grassroots proreform constituency, which it could mobilize against conservative forces.

The success of such a scenario would depend on two conditions. First, the party itself would have to accept the proreform mandate offered by Gorbachev, setting aside, at least temporarily, the short-term concerns of institutional prerogatives and personal power and recasting the party's role in society. Second, the broader grassroots constituency upon which the party would depend, through the ballot box, for its continuance in power would have to respond to the proffered leadership; it would have to accept both the validity of the party's changing role in society as a genuine long-term transformation of the CPSU and the short-term economic and social difficulties that would accompany such reforms.

Even a cursory examination of the party's fate under Gorbachev indicates that this scenario has failed to materialize, at least in terms of rallying the party to take the lead in a reform-oriented coalition of party and grassroots elements. While Gorbachev must be given high marks for attempting to transform the party along these lines, the present reality--and especially the transfer of important decision-making powers to the presidency, the

Federation Council, and the Security Council--confirms that the party's actual influence over events has waned. Serious and perhaps insurmountable problems exist both within the party itself and in its relationship to the broader constituency to which it hoped to appeal.

At all levels, the party is now internally divided not only over the basic orientation to *perestroika* and the other aspects of Gorbachev's reforms but also over the increasingly strident question of local autonomy or independence. As an all-union political force, the party has lost both its sense of unified direction and the political clout of a tightly disciplined political machine operating through the apparatus and the control of the *nomenklatura*, or appointment, process.

In part because of Gorbachev's sweeping personnel changes within higher party bodies and his politically motivated restructuring of virtually all command structures (the Politburo and the Secretariat have lost virtually all of their ability to shape events on a day-to-day basis, and the Central Committee has been reduced to a hollow debating forum), and in part because the party itself has bitterly split over the issue of reform (narrowly avoiding an open rupture at the recent twenty-eighth party congress only because disaffected elements chose to abandon the party rather than split it openly), the CPSU has not responded to the general secretary's attempts to recast it as a parliamentary party leading a wide coalition of reform forces. Even where it has sought to embrace the reform agenda, as in the Baltic states, where significant portions of the existing party leadership attempted to place themselves at the head of proreform forces, the party has been seriously challenged and in most instances deprived of its majority in republic and local elected bodies by nonparty popular fronts and newly created political parties.

The grassroots public support that Gorbachev had hoped to mobilize in tandem with reforms within the party itself has also failed to materialize or has abandoned the CPSU in favor of more radical parties or leaders. What had begun as a hopeful balance between admitting the party's past errors and filling in the "blank pages" of Soviet history on the one hand and the reconstruction of a viable and attractive "new" parliamentary party on the other has become an orgy of rejection and incrimination, in part because of the general secretary's own strident criticism of the conservative forces still lodged within the party apparatus and in part because of the Pandora's box effect of *glasnost'*. Once the party admitted its institutional fallibility as opposed to the misdeeds of past individual leaders, the door was open to a rejection of the legacy of the past seventy years. Few long-standing democracies, and probably even fewer new ones can resist the temptation to use the political process for punitive as well as constructive purposes, and the rallying cry of "throw the rascals out" served as an across-the-board indictment of the legacy as well as the current reality of party rule.

Yet despite the attacks of its opponents and its own factionalism and self-doubt, the CPSU remains the best-organized political force in the country, led by a charismatic, if controversial, general secretary whose boldness and political skill have averted a formal split in the face of mounting internal divisions. In many ways, the *de facto* federalization of the party and the challenges it faces at the city and local levels at least suggest that the regional and local leaders will now be freer to respond to constituency issues; if the first round of public elections in 1989 and 1990 were a sobering experience in terms of pointing out the pitfalls of democracy to once secure party officials, then we must also assume that they were also something of a learning experience for a relatively pragmatic apparatus, which, for opportunistic if not for ideological or programmatic reasons, will adapt to the new rules of the game. Such adaptation will be made all the easier by the survival of the party's apparatus, albeit in attenuated form; whatever else one may conclude about the CPSU's network of organizations and operatives, one must admit that it remains the best political machine in the USSR. As people grow less sanguine about the prospects that their new democratically elected legislatures will solve vexing problems, and as those legislatures themselves begin to operate on a more routinized basis, the discipline and solidarity of party organizations and the scope and depth of their extraparliamentary organizations will become ever more important elements of political power.

At present, the CPSU constitutes the largest voting bloc within the Congress of People's Deputies. Responding to a recent poll measuring the deputies' association with the various blocs and groups that have emerged within the legislature, 730 deputies, or nearly a third of the total membership, identified themselves as belonging first and foremost to the CPSU bloc. The importance of such a voting bloc and its counterpart in the smaller Supreme Soviet cannot be underestimated, especially in a political climate in which other forces are disorganized or constitute much smaller and poorly disciplined legislative blocs. Within the Congress of People's Deputies, the loosely organized conservative bloc Soiuz numbered only 561 members, while the equally poorly disciplined Interregional Group of Deputies found support among only 229 legislators.[17]

A second, alternative scenario is also possible that would preserve an important role for the party, albeit a party that assumed the mantle of a conservative bastion against social and economic disorder, the anti-egalitarian implications of the marketplace, and the disintegration of the nation. Even if one allows for the obvious disaffection within the apparatus and party leadership at virtually all levels, pondering their own fate and that of their party as Gorbachev became an ever more radical proponent of *perestroika* and *demokratizatsiia*, it is still possible that the party, damaged and demoralized as it is, would respond to more conservative guidance, whether from a general secretary whose own views have grown more cautious or from other leaders. The seeming defeat of the conservative elements of the party, including Egor Ligachev, at the twenty-eighth party congress should not be read as extirpating the view that the pace of change should be slowed and perhaps reversed; the questions of social disorder, the creation of a competitive market, and the growing restiveness of non-Russian peoples have deep resonance within the party and society as a whole. Gorbachev's own more conservative approach to economic and social questions since November 1990, and his strengthening of the presidency with emergency powers, should be understood only in part as an attempt to enhance his own personal control of events; they also offer at least *prima facie* evidence of the growing self-awareness of conservative forces and the general secretary's willingness to bend to political pressures from the right. It is indeed paradoxical that, for the foreseeable future, the party's major political role may lie in its identity as the centerpiece of a conservative coalition of forces within the legislature and the society as a whole, a role it may be able to sustain through the ballot box despite its current understandable unpopularity if more radical democratic forces divide into squabbling factions and if the process of democracy itself seems incapable of providing solutions to the nation's economic and social problems.

Newly formed political parties, informal groups, and popular fronts will coordinate policy. This second scenario holds forth the possibility that the newly formed political parties, informal groups, and popular fronts will find the political will and the mechanisms through which to broker their divergent interests. Such compromise could occur either in the pre-electoral environment through the formation of permanent or floating coalitions or within the legislative environment through coalition governments. Several preconditions would need to be met before such mechanisms could channel political conflict. First, the parties themselves would have to develop a clearer sense of self-identity and purpose. At present, party platforms typically remain vague generalities, dealing more with procedural issues or general strategies of economic reform rather than spelling out specific allocational and distributive priorities.

Second, the parties themselves would have to evidence greater willingness to compromise their differences both over policy and over the more immediate questions of leadership. If the first two years of Soviet democracy are an accurate predictor, we may expect the continued proliferation of smaller and specialized parties and the splintering of existing parties because of factional disputes over policy or leadership issues.

Third, successful brokerage in the pre-electoral phase would require that existing parties form formal or tacit alliances or offer common platforms and slates of candidates. Yet to date, efforts to create such alliances have largely proven futile, breaking down over predictable issues of leadership and policy.

Reviewing the recent formation of such small and disunited parties, one commentator, quoting a Soviet sociologist, has noted that the current state of affairs in Russian politics should be described not as *partiinost'*, the development of genuine parties, but as *portsialnost'*, the battle of ideological groupings lacking a "real social base."[18]

Citing the characterization by Soviet sociologists of such parties as "protoparties," he observed they have been formed on

the basis of populist, ideological, or charismatic impulses common to their members; their numbers are small, their organizations are weak and prone to internal splitting; and their programs are undeveloped and show only rudimentary ideological differences, with a marked opposition to the current state of affairs their most common feature.[19]

The formation of such coalitions seems most difficult among the democratic parties; while they share common agreement about the need to preserve democracy, they divide on the nature of the threat to the preservation of the new order--whether the greater danger comes from surviving authoritarianism and the creation of a strong presidency, or from the social disorder and the possible break up of the USSR that might come from too rapid a shift to unbridled democratic rule--and on the inevitable question of who would lead such a coalition.

Attempts to form an alliance of democratic forces have floundered, even in light of Gorbachev's seeming shift to a more conservative stance in the late fall of 1990. A conference of all "generally democratic" forces held in Kharkov in late January 1991 to create a Congress of Democratic Forces produced only partial agreement. Participants represented democratic forces in ten union republics, including the Russian Republic, Ukraine, Belorussia, the Baltic republics, Transcaucasia, and Central Asia. Only thirty of the forty-six parties attending signed the final conference documents, with the major point of division remaining the question of whether democratic forces should unquestioningly endorse national and ethnic independence movements or back the creation of a reformed and looser all-union government.[20] Other attempts to bond together nascent democratic forces have also yielded only marginal results. Within the Russian republic itself, three of the major democratic parties--the Democratic Party of Russia, the Social Democratic Party of Russia, and the Democratic Platform--have participated in the creation of a Democratic Russia front, which is attempting to create branches in the major cities of the RSFSR. But despite general agreement that unity is desirable, no concrete steps were taken to move toward a formal consolidation of the movement or to integrate the parties into a single organization.[21]

While the parties *per se* seem ill-prepared to perform such brokerage activity, the popular fronts that have typically emerged in the non-Russian areas have fared far better. Such popular fronts exist in virtually all union republics and in the majority of autonomous republics and provinces. Within the Russian republic, an estimated 140 such fronts have been set up in cities and regions, with some winning control of local elected bodies.[22] Because of their very nature as broad-based coalitions that place the question of national identity and greater autonomy or independence ahead of other considerations, they have bridged gaps and survived internal leadership squabbles that would have split more conventional parties. But in one sense, their strength is also their weakness, at least in terms of brokerage; because of their single-minded concern with local issues, such popular fronts have deemphasized other critically important issues such as economic reform, except where such issues could be turned against Moscow's erstwhile control, as in the case of the center's exploitation of local resources. When popular fronts have emerged as ruling coalitions, as in the Baltic states, they have either tended to avoid difficult political and economic issues that would divide their natural base of support or attempted to redefine them as center-periphery issues.

The attempts by political parties and popular fronts to move toward some clear definition of political forces have been made more difficult by the parties' own declining sense of effectiveness within the legislature and by the growing disaffection of the average citizen with a democratic process that seems unable to confront the nation's problems. At the all-union level, recent legislative sessions paradoxically have been marked by the increasing militancy of democratic forces that oppose Gorbachev's purposeful or unwitting shift to the right and by the legislature's willingness to vote even greater powers to the presidency he created.[23] And at the local level, if the Moscow City Soviet is to be regarded as a good example, legislative bodies have substituted debate for meaningful action; during the first four weeks of the fall 1990 session, that body took only four decisions, and even in those cases adopted only general principles of legislation rather than creating specific policy directives and the appropriate administrative measures.[24]

The possibility also exists that the so-called "informals" will coalesce into working coalitions. Clearly among the most rapidly proliferating of new political entities, such groups could enjoy several distinct advantages. First, because of their typical single-issue focus, they can exploit the image of being "above politics," at least insofar as that perception would distance them from the growing criticism with the larger (and less disciplined) political parties and popular fronts. Second, they at least have the potential of mobilizing political forces that would be beyond the reach of the existing political process, especially if they are able to present themselves as concerned with issues and policy outcomes rather than the mere struggle for power. And third--and this may be an important advantage--they represent a wholly new form of political organization within the Soviet context; their very uniqueness may be one of their greatest strengths, at least in terms of mobilizing public support.

Despite these features, and perhaps in the long run because of them, the informals may find it difficult to have an organized and lasting impact on the political system and may serve to divide an already factionalized political milieu rather than to foster unity. In terms of both their political identity and their tactics, the informals are much like the single-issue groups that rapidly proliferated in American politics beginning in the 1970s. Disappointed with the unresponsiveness of otherwise democratic institutions and cognizant of their own ability to mobilize a dedicated if numerically small constituency that could have impact far out of proportion to its actual size, these groups have fundamentally altered the nature of the political process in the United States and other democracies.

Yet by their very nature, such groups will tend to further subdivide the political spectrum, especially insofar as their single-minded focus on a particular issue, no matter how significant and laudable in its own right, makes it difficult to create more broadly based coalitions. If the American experience with such groups is any indication, we may anticipate that the proliferation of informals will contribute to the rejection of a shared substantive consensus except on the most general procedural issues such as a defense of democratization and *glasnost'*. Increasing activity by such groups will lead to the creation of multiple intensely committed constituencies with few overlapping interests or memberships. Single-issue politics will introduce a punitive orientation--if you do not support a particular group on its issue of choice, then it will oppose you no matter what positions you have taken on other issues--making the task of political calculation a competitive assessment of the power of intensely motivated advocacy and veto groups.

The militancy of single-issue informals is likely to intensify as the political agenda shifts from symbolic and participational issues--that is, issues on which such groups can more easily find agreement in defense of democratic institutions, open discussion, and the like--to distributional and allocational issues, which will bitterly divide the community as the costs and benefits of political and economic reform are meted out throughout the society. While it is easy to agree, at least in principle, about the desirability of democracy or *glasnost' per se*, it is far more difficult to find accord on exactly which groups or which regions will pay the costs or reap the benefits of reforms. The likely increase in what may be termed "entitlement issues" will also complicate the task of finding compromise; such issues might deal with many different substantive questions--one's "right" to national self-determination, or a clean environment, or a decent standard of living--but they would have in common their growing militancy and inflexibility in terms of finding balance among competing interests.

Coordinating mechanisms will emerge within the legislature itself. It is also possible that mechanisms will emerge within the legislature to bring order to the growing factionalization of Soviet politics. Coordination might emerge through three mechanisms typical of other multiparty parliamentary systems: (1) the emergence of coalition governments in the post-electoral phase, especially to the degree that the creation of a legislative majority (however shifting and temporary) becomes the key to power within the legislature; (2) the creation of parliamentary blocs falling short of formal coalition governments; and (3) the formation of procedural mechanisms, most likely through the creation of a viable and depoliticized committee structure, that produce *de facto* agreements.

In the first instance, the creation of *bona fide* coalition governments seems unlikely, although the existing mechanisms by which deputies to the Congress of People's Deputies are selected in the first round of the election/selection process were intended to produce what was presumed to be a stable core of representatives of the existing establishment. As long as one-third of the Congress deputies--that is, 750 of the total 2,250--are chosen by the public organizations rather than by direct popular election, there is a strong likelihood that they will respond less willingly to popular pressures. This is not to argue, of course, that such institutions might not select representatives who are themselves as reformist or even more radical than those selected from normal geographic constituencies; the results of the first round of such institutionally based elections produced mixed results, with organizations such as the Communist Party selecting centrist and conservative elements, while other institutions such as the Academy of Sciences eventually returned a reformist slate. But it is to observe that this form of indirect election insulates up to a third of the Congress itself from direct popular pressures. It is likely that there will be strong pressures to change the electoral procedures to provide for the direct constituency-based election of all delegates, and the results of such efforts will be an important bellwether for the stability or further radicalization of the Congress.

The process through which deputies to the Congress of People's Deputies are chosen for membership in the Supreme Soviet was also intended to slow and filter the direct exercise of popular will. From among their own number-- including the 750 delegates representing public organizations rather than geographic and ethnic constituencies--the deputies choose 542 delegates for membership in the bicameral Supreme Soviet. Even if it is assumed that the legislators chosen for membership in the higher body will faithfully mirror the political divisions of the lower house, the overall effect will tend toward the selection of less radical delegates.

While the legislature holds the ultimate power of confirmation over the president's nominees to the premiership and the cabinet, to date it has only sparingly used its prerogatives to limit the chief executive's power. Although on occasion legislative opposition in the confirmation process has applied sufficient pressure to force a premier to withdraw cabinet submissions, there is little prospect that the legislature could force the resignation of the premier himself; Nikolai Ryzhkov's political demise stemmed from

Gorbachev's lack of confidence and his availability as a convenient, if not very credible, scapegoat, rather than his vulnerability to direct legislative intercession. The same is true of the new post of vice president; while legislative approval is required for the appointment, the reality is that strong executives will almost certainly be able to secure the appointment of their chosen candidate.

In the second instance, the creation of parliamentary blocs has already begun to occur, with some, such as the Interregional Group of Deputies, the principal liberal coalition, and Soiuz, its conservative counterpart, playing an important role in structuring the debate if not the flow of legislation. The Interregional Group is an instructive example of both the strengths and the weaknesses of such formations. Founded in July 1989, at the first session of the Congress of People's Deputies, the Interregional Group was designed to gather together into one faction all of the deputies who advocated democratic reform. Its original leadership included notables such as Boris Yeltsin, Andrei Sakharov, and Iurii Afanas'ev, and it quickly became the major spokesman for the democratic opposition to Gorbachev's "aggressively obedient majority" within the legislature. It took the lead in the organization of Democratic Russia, its counterpart group within the Russian republic which became the dominant faction in the republic's legislature. Despite these accomplishments, the Interregional Group has failed to emerge as a full-fledged parliamentary opposition. It remains internally divided over key questions of economic reform, the fate of the all-union government, and-- most importantly--the powers to be granted to Gorbachev's strengthened presidency. Key leaders--especially Yeltsin since his break with the CPSU-- have remained aloof from complete identification with the group, using it instead as a sounding board for their personal positions and attacks on Gorbachev. Moreover, the Interregional Group has failed to develop extraparliamentary mechanisms through the formation of grassroots political organizations. While it has counterparts at virtually all levels of republican and local legislative bodies, little has been done to unite such groups into a viable national political force.[25]

Similar intraparliamentary groups exist at the national level. Within the Congress of People's Deputies, membership in such groups is widespread, with deputies officially registered as members of eighteen factions. As noted above, the largest group remains the bloc of CPSU loyalists, who constitute 730 members. The conservative Soiuz faction is second, claiming 561 members, and other large groups include an agricultural bloc at 431 members, workers numbering 400 deputies, and the Interregional Group of Deputies at 229 members. Other groups include ecologists at 220 members, a women's interest group at 216 deputies, self-proclaimed "centrists" at 153 members, young deputies at 125 members, and Afghan war veterans at 52 delegates (deputies were permitted to register with more than one group).[26]

In the third instance, it is also possible that the Supreme Soviet's committee structure could provide a series of fora through which consensus could emerge on day-to-day legislative matters, especially if the committees avoid internal divisions along party or parliamentary factional lines. Twenty-two committees exist within the new structure. Four separate committees exist within each house of the Supreme Soviet, with the Soviet of the Union forming committees in planning, budget, and finance; industry and technology; transportation, communications, and information science; and labor, prices, and social policy. The Soviet of Nationalities has separate committees dealing with relations among nationalities; economic and social development; consumer goods and other public services; and culture, language, and historical legacies. Fourteen joint committees also exist linking both houses; these include committees on international affairs; defense and state security; law; local soviets; economic reform; agrarian questions and food policy; construction and architecture; science, education, and culture; public health; women's and family affairs; veterans; youth affairs; ecology; and *glasnost'* and civil rights.[27]

The committees quickly attempted to assert their prerogatives by carefully cross-examining and eventually rejecting nine (thirteen percent) of Premier Ryzhkov's initial cabinet nominees, although some of the rejectees were subsequently approved on a floor vote. On several other critical issues the committees refused to approve draft legislation requested by Gorbachev and his compliant premier. But committee powers have remained essentially negative: the ability to conduct investigations, cross-examine and eventually reject cabinet nominees, and block desired legislation. The committees have shown far less success in forging consensus within a divided legislature or in taking the initiative in the legislative process.

But on the other hand, the composition of the committees suggests that they could play a consensus-building role because of their apolitical membership. Membership in each committee is evenly divided between deputies of the Supreme Soviet and the larger Congress of People's Deputies, providing at least a possible mechanism for bridging the gap between the two layers of the legislative system. More importantly, committee members are chosen more for their knowledge and experience in the particular subject area than for their ability to represent the proportional strength of parties and parliamentary factions. For example, of the twenty-one deputies from the Supreme Soviet serving on the Council of the Union's Industrial Development Committee, six are factory heads and twelve are industrial workers. In similar fashion, the Committee on Culture contains artists and teachers, and the joint Defense and State Security Committee's twenty-one members include seven military officers and five specialists in the defense industry. Similar relevant specializations are found within the other committees, suggesting that these bodies possess at least the potential to emerge as respected commentators on proposed legislation and that they could avoid association with the most divisive aspects of partisan and factional politics.[28]

Leadership will come from the newly created presidency. A fourth scenario holds forth the possibility that effective leadership within the legislature will come through the newly created presidency, with the chief executive providing policy leadership, initiating important legislation, and winning support (albeit sometimes grudging support) within the legislature to secure the passage of key enactments. Within this context, both leadership and coordination will transcend the partisan divisions of parties and groups noted above; presidents will be "above politics," at least in the sense that their popularity, national mandate (once directly elected, to be sure), and real or potential independent powers as president will make them a force to be reckoned with, especially by the leadership of a divided and self-immobilized legislature.

Many of the powers of the new presidency seem intended both to set it apart from the day-to-day fray of the legislature and to provide mechanisms through which the chief executive can guide or intervene in the workings of a divided Supreme Soviet and Congress of People's Deputies.[29] While the list of such powers is long and the implications of their real or threatened use still not fully known, a brief summary will suggest the potential for effective leadership:

--Although legislative confirmation is required, the president has *de facto* control over the identity of the premier and significant and probably controlling influence over the selection of the cabinet if he chooses to exercise it; moreover, the legislature has grudgingly complied with Gorbachev's request to strengthen the president's direct control over the cabinet in the administration of the day-to-day affairs of government.

--The president undoubtedly will take the lead in calling upon the legislature to hold public referenda on significant policy issues and enjoys important if not exclusive advantages in terms of shaping the definition of the issue and mobilizing public opinion; the referendum on the preservation of the Union provides an instructive example of both the importance of such presidential initiative and the liabilities of growing presidential unpopularity.

--The president can issue presidential decrees that have the power of legislation, although their faithful implementation by federal and local officials remains in doubt.

--The president can impose--or threaten to impose--states of emergency or direct presidential rule, although legislative approval is eventually required.

--The president can mediate significant political differences between the two houses of the Supreme Soviet and, in the event such mediation fails, propose to the Congress of People's Deputies the selection of a new Supreme Soviet from among their membership.

--The president can create (and seemingly change at will) his own executive cabinet(s), although political realities suggest that close attention be given, as in the Federation Council, to the increasing salience of ethnic representation; such cabinets can and have emerged as important policy-making bodies operating independently of the Council of Ministers.

--Once popularly elected, the president will speak with a national mandate, both because of the nature of the electoral mechanism itself (a successful candidate must receive over fifty percent of the total votes cast in the country as a whole and also over fifty percent in a majority of the union republics) and because of the likelihood of continuing factionalism within the legislature.

But despite advantages, successful leadership of the legislature would depend upon the president's, or his premier's, ability to translate a national mandate into effective pressures on what is likely to remain a legislative body divided by partisan, group, and regional loyalties. The current state of affairs suggests that attaining such influence will be difficult, at best.

First, at least to date, the threatened use of referenda and presidential decrees to bypass the legislature has had little impact in terms of pulling a recalcitrant Supreme Soviet or Congress of People's Deputies into line. The mechanism for referenda can be employed sparingly, at best, and the use of presidential decrees to impose direct control has proven ineffective as both federal and local authorities largely ignore Gorbachev's directives. The more drastic powers of direct presidential rule or the declaration of a state of emergency have so far proven politically impossible because of the threat of widespread public opposition, especially in the non-Russian areas. To the extent that Gorbachev has imposed his will on the dual levels of the legislature, it has been either through the voting strength of the party's parliamentary bloc and its informal allies (the so-called "aggressively obedient majority") or through the legislature's own willingness to give greater powers to the presidency because of its own self-proclaimed ineffectiveness and immobilism. Yet the continued numerical dominance of the Communist Party bloc will come under increasingly serious challenge with each new round of popular elections to the Congress of People's Deputies. For obvious political and historical reasons, the party will bear the stigma of past failures, and it is likely both that its popular support will decline and that pressures for a formal split in party ranks between pro- and antireform forces will resurface.

Second, much of the current political challenge to Gorbachev's continued rule is largely extraparliamentary in nature. It is important to recall that his most strident critics have largely remained outside the existing party structures, although from time to time they have spoken of the creation of mass-based parties. Most visible, of course, is Boris Yeltsin, who has avoided formal affiliation with any party since his dramatic resignation from the CPSU at the twenty-eighth party congress. Much as in American politics, where the presidential party organization is separate from and frequently at odds with the congressional party leadership, Soviet politics seems to be developing a dual-track political life. While in one sense such dualism insulates the chief executive from the problems of day-to-day legislative affairs, it also diminishes his ability to exercise leadership at this level except through the indirect mechanisms of allied party structures and de facto floor leaders, and dependent on the nature of his office as a bully pulpit, neither of which may be effective.

Conclusion

We began this examination of the new pluralism in Soviet politics with a simple but important question: Does there currently exist, or is there likely to exist in the future, a working balance between the increasing proliferation of new parties, informal groups, and popular fronts and the creation of mechanisms within the party system, the legislature, or the presidency that will mediate and find consensus within this growing universe of political actors? The question is hardly an exercise in academic speculation; no system that fails to create such a balance will survive in reasonably democratic form, for if there is no equilibrium between the forces that pull the society apart and those that attempt to find common ground, there can emerge no widespread consensus on the purposes and procedures of government.

At least in the short term, the existence of such a balance seems seriously in doubt in Gorbachev's Soviet Union, or whatever may be left of it. The proliferation of new parties and groups, the growing defiance of regional and local governments, and the radicalization of political life in general suggest that what we have analytically termed the representational aspects of the new political order have come into being more quickly than those which would bring order from such chaos. Simply put, the new Soviet democracy seems better able to articulate demands, spawn new political entities that zealously set themselves apart from others in the political spectrum, and press for solutions to real and imagined grievances than to generate mechanisms that produce political consensus, working coalitions within the legislature, and plausible national leadership. With little immediate likelihood that such agreement can be expected to emerge from the parties and groups themselves or from the internal procedures of the legislature, it is probable that voters increasingly will turn to the presidency in search of such leadership. But while that office exercises significant powers, it also faces striking liabilities, including its limited control over the legislature, the absence of strong party organizations led by viable presidential candidates, and the inability of any chief executive to focus on more than a few chosen issues. Yet in the absence of other viable organizational alternatives, it is likely that voters increasingly will focus both their hopes and their frustrations on the nation's highest post, leaving Soviet presidents, like their American counterparts, to lament the gap that separates public expectations from presidential power.

Notes

1. H. Gordon Skilling and Franklyn Griffiths, eds., *Interest Groups in Soviet Politics* (Princeton: Princeton University Press, 1971).

2. Donald R. Kelley and Shannon G. Davis, eds., *Khrushchev and Gorbachev as Reformers* (New York: Praeger, in press).

3. Skilling and Griffiths, *Interest Groups*.

4. *Pravda*, 6 February 1990.

5. Dawn Mann, "Gorbachev's Report to the Twenty-eighth Party Congress: Reform of the CPSU," *Radio Liberty Report on the USSR* (hereafter *Radio Liberty*), 2, no. 28 (13 July 1990), pp. 10-13.

6. *The Economist*, 24 November 1990.

7. *Pravda*, 21 June 1990; Elizabeth Teague and Vera Tolz, "Moves to Create a Russian Communist Party," *Radio Liberty*, 2, no. 19 (11 May 1990), pp. 1-3.

8. Anne M. Gruber, "Political Parties and Groups in the USSR," *New Outlook*, 1, no. 4 (Fall 1990), pp. 29-38.

9. Ibid.

10. Aleksandr Meerovich, "The Emergence of Russian Multiparty Politics," *Radio Liberty*, 2, no. 34 (24 August 1990), pp. 8-16.

11. Vera Tolz, "Informal Groups in Soviet Politics in 1989," *Radio Liberty*, 1, no. 47 (24 November 1989), pp. 4-7.

12. Vera Tolz, "Informal Groups Hold First Officially Sanctioned Conference," *Radio Liberty*, 23 September 1987; idem, "Informal Groups in the USSR in 1988," *Radio Liberty*, 30 October 1988; idem, "A New Approach to Informal Groups," *Radio Liberty*, 2, no. 10 (9 March 1990), pp. 1-3; Vladimir Brovkin, "Revolution from Below: Informal Political Associations in Russia 1988-1989," *Soviet Studies*, 42, no. 2 (April 1990), pp. 233-57.

13. For a brief history of the formation and radicalization of such a popular front, see Stanley Vardys, "Lithuanian National Politics," *Problems of Communism*, 38, no. 4 (July-August 1989), and Alfred Erich Senn, *Lithuania Awakening* (Berkeley: University of California Press, 1990).

14. Aleksandr Meerovich, "Soviet Draft Law on Public Associations Makes Slow Progress," *Radio Liberty*, 2, no. 28 (13 July 1990), pp. 6-8.

15. *Pravda*, 16 October 1990.

16. *Pravda*, 6 February 1990.

17. The poll was reported on "Vremia" on 24 December 1990, and summarized in "The USSR This Week," *Radio Liberty*, 3, no. 4 (24 January 1991), p. 61.

18. Meerovich, "Emergence."

19. Ibid.

20. Vera Tolz, "The Congress of Democratic Forces: Soviet Democrats Make Another Attempt to Unite," *Radio Liberty*, 3, no. 6 (8 February 1991), pp. 6-8.

21. Michael McFaul, "The Social Democrats and Republicans Attempt to Merge," *Radio Liberty*, 3, no. 3 (18 January 1991), pp. 6-9.

22. Vera Tolz, "The Emergence of a Multiparty System in the USSR," *Radio*

Liberty, 2, no. 17 (27 April 1990), pp. 4-6.

23. *Pravda*, 16 March 1990; see also Dawn Mann, "Gorbachev Sworn In as President," *Radio Liberty*, 2, no. 12 (23 March 1990), pp. 1-4; and Elizabeth Teague, "The Powers of the Soviet Presidency," *Radio Liberty*, 2, no. 12 (23 March 1990), pp. 4-7.

24. McFaul, "Social Democrats."

25. Alexander Rahr, "Inside the Interregional Group," *Radio Liberty*, 2, no. 43 (26 October 1990), pp. 1-4.

26. "Vremia," 24 December 1990.

27. *Izvestiia*, 5 June 1989.

28. Stephen Foye, "U.S. Congressional Report on Soviet Committee for Defense and State Security," *Radio Liberty*, 2, no. 19 (11 May 1990), pp. 6-8; and Mikhail Tsypkin, "The Committee for Defense and State Security of the USSR Supreme Soviet," *Radio Liberty*, 2, no. 19 (11 May 1990), pp. 8-11.

29. *Pravda*, 16 March 1990.

6

THE CHALLENGE TO SOVIET DEMOCRACY FROM THE POLITICAL RIGHT

Joel C. Moses

The Soviet Political Right in a Multiparty System

With the removal of Article 6 from the Soviet Constitution in March 1990, the monopoly of the Communist Party was formally ended. By August of the same year over a hundred political parties, popular fronts, and other quasi-parties had been formed.[1] Some of these are at best legislative coalitions or ideological factions of like-minded Supreme Soviet deputies that grew out of policy conflicts during the first session of the Congress of People's Deputies in the summer of 1989. By 1990 these legislative coalitions/parties had organized voters' clubs to mobilize electoral support for their candidates in the republic and local elections held in the winter and early spring of 1989-90. In some cases, especially in the Baltic republics and Ukraine, they competed with ethnic popular fronts organized since 1987 by so-called "informal" interest groups, whose candidates typically were committed to secession from the Soviet Union and independent statehood for their republics.

In many respects, the party divisions evolving in the new Soviet democracy are a throwback to those of the tsarist Duma period of 1906-17 when ideological conflicts between Westernizers and Slavophiles were prevalent. In other ways the new democratic socialist parties and movements resurrect political conflicts within the Communist Party of 1921-28, and the platforms of the "Left and Right Deviationists" and the Democratic Centralists and Workers' Opposition. They also mirror the new political movements and party alignments in Western Europe--and Eastern Europe since the revolution of 1989. All of the parties represent ideological reactions to the Soviet experience since 1917, now almost universally repudiated in the liberal

Soviet media, and various degrees of support for or opposition to Gorbachev's democratic reforms of Soviet society since 1987.

On the Soviet democratic left are various social democratic parties whose political philosophies seem inspired by parties of the same name in Western and Eastern Europe. Counterparts of the European Green parties have organized in many Soviet cities and republics to oppose environmental pollution, nuclear energy, and military spending. The Democratic Platform originated in early 1990 as a liberal faction within the Communist Party, pushing democratic reforms for delegate selection to the twenty-eighth party congress and the devolution of real political power in the party to the rank-and-file party membership at the local level. At the congress, held in July 1990, prominent leaders of the Democratic Platform, such as Anatolii Sobchak, Gavriil Popov, and Boris Yeltsin, resigned from the party. The Democratic Platform's criticism of authoritarianism within the party and defense of grass-roots party democracy revive conflicts last openly stirred by the Democratic Centralists six decades ago, at the tenth party congress in 1921. Today's Marxist Platform and Boris Kagarlitskii's Socialist Party recall the Workers' Opposition at the same tenth party congress; they advocate a decentralized rather than capitalist economy and worker self-management rather than private enterprise.[2] In their view, state-owned industrial enterprises should be owned and managed by the enterprise workers rather than transferred to a new class of Soviet capitalists, and wholesale and retail markets should be controlled and owned by citizen-based consumer cooperatives in competition with a private sector.

In the Soviet center are political parties identical in name and political philosophy to the European Christian Democrats and Liberal Democrats. Yet the political center retains a distinctively Soviet shading. Like a ghost out of the Duma past, the Soviet center includes at least two newly formed parties claiming the name and goals of the Constitutional Democrats (Kadets) of 1906-17. And by the end of 1990 the Democratic Platform had split into two contending groups--one remaining within the Communist Party in coalition with reformist communists and the Marxist Platform, the other forming an independent Republican Party to compete with social democrats and Greens on the Soviet left.[3]

On the Soviet political right in the early 1990s are movements and parties that recall the Russian nationalism, Slavophilism, racist populism, militarism, and anti-Semitism of the late tsarist era. The old Russian right united strange political bedfellows--influential members of the regime and hangers-on along with powerless citizens themselves victimized by that same regime. The new Soviet right attracts hard-line defenders of the communist autocracy and a strong unified state from elites in the party-state bureaucracy, the military, and the intelligentsia. In appealing to the Soviet working class it equates reform with an anti-worker authoritarian conspiracy of Jews, political liberals, and organized crime. The common defining features of the old

Russian right of 1906-17 and the Soviet right of the 1990s are an ideology of racist nationalism; a visceral fear of democracy and economic liberalization; a conspiratorial mindset; and a politics of hate.

The movements and parties of the Soviet right actually overlap to a great extent. The most recognized national figures on the Soviet right tend to reappear in the leadership roles, rallies, conferences, letters to the editor, and organizing sessions of otherwise different groups or parties.[4] Broadly defined, the Soviet political right also can be clearly identified with certain Soviet newspapers and journals.

At the same time, important differences of background, personality, and tactics do appear to exist within each of the movements and parties of the Soviet right. "Moderate" and "radical" wings can be distinguished. The "moderates" oppose violent political tactics; disassociate themselves from the more rabid anti-Semites; gain their principal following among writers and scientists; and denounce the Communist Party establishment while openly identifying with the political views of anti-Gorbachev conservative party leaders. In their primary concern with Russian problems and the negative consequences of communism for Russia, the "moderates" share views not totally dissimilar from those of more popular and respected figures such as Solzhenitsyn.

"Radicals" on the Soviet right sanction violent tactics in their demonstrations and protests; primarily target Jews and an alleged Jewish conspiracy; enlist their most enthusiastic followers from the urban working class; and despise communist officials while admiring the strong integrating role of the Communist Party for the nation. In their racist populism, the "radicals" share a vision of the world not totally unlike that of certain nationalist parties in Eastern Europe, the National Front parties in Western Europe, and the Ku Klux Klan in the United States.

Differences between "moderates" and "radicals" aside, the most identifiable movements and parties of the new Soviet right in the early 1990s include as many as seven different organizations in Moscow alone claiming the name Pamiat' (Memory), as well as Nina Andreeva's Edinstvo (Unity for Leninism and Communist Ideals Society), Veniamin Iarin's Ob"edinnenyi Front Trudiashchikhsia or OFT (United Workers' Front), Soiuz (Union), sympathizers within the Communist Party leadership of several republics and the national trade-union officialdom, and numerous literary-cultural organizations. Various shadings of "moderates" and "radicals" can be found within each of these movements and parties.

Pamiat', closely linked in philosophy to party-movements calling themselves the Union for Spiritual Revival of the Fatherland and the Russian National Patriotic Center, blames all the ills of Soviet society over the past seven decades on a worldwide Jewish-Masonic conspiracy.[5] Notorious for its militaristic uniforms, aggressive anti-Semitism, and Russian racist nationalism seemingly inspired by the ideology of Adolf Hitler, Pamiat' has recruited several hundred members from the intelligentsia as well as the working class and has staged noisy rallies in Leningrad and Moscow. But although Pamiat' has attempted to identify itself with the anticommunism and antiestablishment populism of the Soviet electorate, its violent tactics have repulsed most of its potential supporters. Continuous questions about hidden sources of support have shaken Pamiat's credibility as an antiestablishment force. One high-ranking former KGB official has openly charged on Soviet national television that the KGB organized and funds Pamiat' to undermine democratic changes; and links have been suggested in the Soviet media between Pamiat' and sympathetic local party officials, who have allowed their buildings to be used by Pamiat' organizers.[6] In October 1990 one prominent leader of Pamiat' was convicted and sentenced to two years in a labor camp for breaking into a meeting of Moscow writers in January 1990 and verbally assaulting them with anti-Semitic insults. During the trial circumstantial evidence of ledgers and photographs was introduced implicating local Moscow communist officials with the defendant's organization.[7]

Edinstvo suffers from an equally negative public image as a political party dedicated to reinstilling "Bolshevik principles" and organized by the notorious Nina Andreeva.[8] Edinstvo reveres Stalin as the last true defender of the Soviet working class and vilifies party leaders from Khrushchev to Gorbachev for having reintroduced "exploitative capitalism" into the Soviet Union in league with a corrupt Jewish-dominated party establishment. Andreeva is the Leningrad teacher and author of the lengthy anti-Semitic and Stalinist denunciation of Gorbachev's liberal democratic reforms published in *Sovetskaia Rossiia* in March 1988. At the time, it was widely rumored in the Soviet Union that highly ranked party officials (such as Egor Ligachev) who opposed the reforms and wanted to retain the communist autocracy had conspired to use Andreeva and the letter to mobilize public sentiment in their favor. Despite her persistent denials in interviews since 1988, Andreeva has been unable to alter a general public image of herself as an agent of party apparatchiki and has openly admitted that her association with Edinstvo was a liability in recruitment.[9]

Distinct in certain philosophical points of departure, Pamiat', Edinstvo, and their most conspicuous leaders are typically rated as the least-admired public organizations and politicians in Soviet public-opinion polls and are usually lumped together by both Soviet and Western critics. Observers conventionally term the leaders and activists of Pamiat' "national fascists" and those of Edinstvo "national Bolsheviks." Indeed, the views of both party-movements seem almost indistinguishable in the articles and editorials that appear monthly in the Komsomol journal *Molodaia gvardiia*. Typical articles in the journal extol the virtues of Stalin as a working-class hero and the spiritual superiority of the Russian nation, while condemning corrupt Jewish influences in the Communist Party and liberal media.[10]

The United Workers' Front (OFT) was organized in the fall of 1989 as a self-defined conservative working-class organization to counter the majority liberal working-class movement and the Confederation of Labor, which had evolved from the national coal-miners' strike in the summer of 1989.[11] OFT has been most closely identified with one of its founders, Veniamin Iarin, a steel worker from Sverdlovsk and deputy to the USSR Supreme Soviet, who was appointed to the Presidential Council by Gorbachev in the spring of 1990. Iarin and other workers allegedly formed OFT to protect working-class interests in the new democratically elected legislatures, which Iarin and conservative trade-union officials claim are unnaturally biased in favor of intellectuals and liberal economic views.

OFT adamantly opposes a free market economy in the Soviet Union and equates Western investment with "foreign enslavement" of the Soviet working class. It defends the unity of the Soviet state, the Soviet armed forces, the KGB, and the Communist Party against an alleged antiworker conspiracy on the part of the democratic left secretly bankrolled by the Soviet mafia. In the 1990 Russian republic and local elections, OFT allied with a number of right-wing Russian nationalist groups in forming the United Council of Russia and Rossiia to coordinate their electoral campaigns and mobilize sympathetic voters in precincts.

Soiuz originated as a response in early 1990 to the possibility of secession by the Baltic republics and to a perceived threat against the Soviet armed forces and Russian ethnic minorities in the Baltic and other Soviet republics.[12] Soiuz brings together high-ranking Soviet officers elected to deputy positions in the union and republic soviets with officers commanding certain military districts or leading conservative veterans' organizations, such as the All-Union Council of War, Labor, and Armed Forces Veterans, chaired by the former Soviet chief-of-staff, N.V. Ogarkov. Soiuz extols militaristic values, advocates Russian as the official state language of the country, and adamantly opposes independent statehood for the republics.

Soiuz blames Gorbachev and the democratic left for the disintegration of political authority in Soviet society and the alleged loss of national security for the country since the toppling of communist regimes in Eastern Europe in 1989. Soiuz's critical views of alleged failures in Soviet foreign policy closely echo those expressed by top conservative party officials including Egor Ligachev.[13] Following his retirement from the Politburo in July 1990, Ligachev hinted that he intended to remain active in national politics by joining the Soiuz deputies in the Supreme Soviet. Highly flattering interviews with Soiuz leaders and positive evaluations of their attempt to reinstill military patriotism have predictably appeared in *Krasnaia zvezda*, the daily newspaper of the Soviet armed forces, and *Sovetskaia Rossiia*, the daily newspaper of the Russian Republic Communist Party, strongly biased toward the political right.

By the end of 1990 Soiuz deputies in the Supreme Soviet led the opposition attacking Foreign Minister Shevardnadze and President Gorbachev for cooperating so closely with the United States against Iraq's occupation of Kuwait, criticism that echoed Soiuz's repeatedly stated opposition to Shevardnadze and Gorbachev for having abandoned so-called "international principles" of solidarity with pro-Soviet regimes in Soviet foreign policy. Nationally, Soiuz has begun to form links with the conservative Russian Intermovements in the Baltic region, which oppose the secession of Estonia, Latvia, and Lithuania from the Soviet Union.

By December 1990, prominent legislative leaders in Soiuz were threatening to introduce a vote of no confidence against Gorbachev in the Congress of People's Deputies and force him out as Soviet president unless he declared a national state of emergency, formed a Committee of National Salvation, temporarily dissolved all republic governments and political parties, and reinstituted authoritarian political controls over the entire country. Soiuz's criticism of Shevardnadze personally and its challenge to Gorbachev almost certainly led to Shevardnadze's dramatic speech before the Soviet parliament in December 1990 announcing his resignation as foreign minister and warning against the threat of a "coming dictatorship" instigated by those in military uniforms.

The Russian nationalists on the right benefit from both an institutional base of support and a certain degree of respectability for their policy views in the Russian Republic. Antidemocratic and conservative Communist Party officials prevail in the leadership of both the All-Union Central Council of Trade Unions and the Russian Communist Party. Under the leadership of Ivan Polozkov, the Russian Republic Communist Party was established in June 1990 in a clear attempt of conservative party officials in Russian locales to organize themselves against Gorbachev in the central government and against the democratic left of Yeltsin and the Democratic Russia bloc now in control of the parliament and ruling government of the Russian Republic.[14] Activists in OFT and Edinstvo rather than rank-and-file party members were among the earliest and most enthusiastic supporters of a separate Russian Communist Party.

The Russian Communist Party leaders and union officials defend their positions and berate democracy and economic liberalization, citing concern over the loss of working-class political power and the threat to jobs for millions of average workers in the Soviet Union.[15] Democracy is equated with the removal of many working-class deputies from legislative soviets; economic liberalization, with the enrichment of so-called "speculators" in the cooperatives and the threatened unemployment of millions of Soviet workers. This same core of conservative officials controls the editorial board of the Russian Republic Communist Party's daily newspaper, *Sovetskaia Rossiia*, which predictably echoes their views in slanting negative stories on democratic changes and market reforms in Soviet society.

The conservatives who control the leadership of the Russian Writers'

Union and the editorial boards of literary publications such as *Literaturnaia Rossiia, Nash sovremennik*, and *Moskva* provide the Soviet right and Russian nationalists with a certain degree of intellectual respectability and visibility. The writers and periodicals maintain a constant ideological litany bordering on an outright persecution mania. They blame the liberal democratic changes in Soviet society since 1987 and the immoral Western influence of the political left and Jews in the Soviet media and arts for the environmental pollution of Russia, the falling birthrates of ethnic Russians (an alleged Russian "ethnocide"), pornography, increasing violent crime, contempt for patriotism among Soviet youth, the imminent collapse of the country into civil war, and a growing tide of hatred against Russians and Russian cultural values (an alleged "Russophobia").[16]

Turning Points

All political leaders and parties in the Soviet Union today concede that the country is both in a serious crisis and at a critical "turning point" in its evolution. They disagree over the reasons for the crisis and the point at which things began to go wrong and a course of actions was taken that led to the present impasse threatening the very survival of the nation. The solution is to return Soviet politics spiritually to the correct "turning point" and this time to avoid repeating those mistakes.

The oft-stated goal of Gorbachev and other centrist party reformers is to revive or renew socialism. The turning point to which they would return the Soviet Union is March 1921 and the adoption of the New Economic Policy (NEP) by the tenth party congress.[17] In essence, Gorbachev reasons that Stalin's ending of the NEP in 1928 represented the lost opportunity to realize the "democratic socialist" potential of Leninism. Gorbachev contends that returning to the spirit of the NEP, with a Western-type democracy and a mixed market economy, can realize the opportunity lost in 1928 and that, if this program succeeds, the many ethnic minorities will want to remain in the Soviet state as sovereign republics of a federation.

For others, including the noncommunist left parties and former Communist Party members and Gorbachev supporters such as Anatolii Sobchak and Gavriil Popov, February 1917 is the turning point to which the Soviet Union must be returned, for it was the Bolshevik Revolution itself that doomed any potential for political democracy. The tragic course of Soviet history since 1917, leading to the current crisis, inevitably stemmed from the overthrow of the Provisional Government and the imposition of the communist autocracy. To prevent the return of Bolshevism it is necessary to avoid the political mistakes of the Provisional Government and to counter the threats to today's fledgling Soviet democracy. These threats come from the Soviet political right, the modern version of the Bolsheviks in 1917, and a growing wave of working-class populist resentment against all politicians, in an atmosphere of uncertainty and economic collapse not unlike the condition in 1917.[18]

Nothing more clearly distinguishes the Soviet political right from the center and the left than its quite different interpretations of the "turning point." Those associated with Pamiat' reject the entire history of the Soviet Union back to 1917. They blame Jewish "nihilists" who supposedly infiltrated positions of authority in the Communist Party and are now propagating false Western models for the current political and economic crises of the country. Invoking an idealized image of the tsarist past, Pamiat' would seem to want to return the country to the era of 1881-82, when Alexander III encouraged pogroms against Jews to eliminate their allegedly alien influence in Russian culture and society. Not totally opposed to the secession of non-Slavic ethnic groups, Pamiat' members want to restore an "undefiled" Russian nation.

Gorbachev's renewed socialism has very little in common with the kind of socialist restoration envisaged by Nina Andreeva and Edinstvo. Andreeva would return the Soviet Union to the era of the first two five-year plans of 1928-37, and not coincidentally the Great Terror of 1937-38. In this view the early five-year plans under Stalin epitomized true socialism, mobilizing the nation and empowering the proletariat to develop the economy and defeat the exploiting classes. The Great Terror was an unfortunate but objectively necessary effort by Stalin to eliminate corrupt antiproletarian influences and internal enemies.

At a minimum, Andreeva and Edinstvo would return the Soviet Union to some point prior to February 1956 and Khrushchev's commission of the "original sin" in his "secret speech" at the twentieth party congress. By condemning Stalin and calling into question Stalinist institutions and values, Khrushchev ushered in the return of exploitative capitalism into the Soviet Union over the next three decades. Andreeva and Edinstvo consider the Communist Party reformers "right-wing revisionist-opportunists" if not outright "counterrevolutionaries" who have committed the ultimate apostasy. Party reformers have repudiated the Bolshevik Revolution and have reduced the nation to a state of political-economic crisis and imminent civil war like that of February-October 1917. With her political rallying-cry of "socialism or death!" Andreeva seems to call for another Bolshevik Revolution.

The conservative working-class populists in OFT would return the Soviet Union to October 1917, when the Bolshevik Revolution made equality and justice for the working class an obtainable goal, later somehow perverted and undermined by evil and corrupt bureaucrats. The working-class control of factories during War Communism (1918-20) seems to represent their ideal model and reference-point in Soviet history.

For conservative Communist Party and trade-union elites, the goal is to return the Soviet Union to April 1985. At that time, Gorbachev's agenda was to crack down on corruption and to institute moderate economic reforms that would have preserved party-state control of the economy and society.

For the conservative military officers in Soiuz, the turning point to which the country must refer is May 1945, when the Soviet Union emerged from World War II victorious and with newly incorporated territories along its borders. At a minimum they can agree with conservative officials on a return to the unified Soviet state of April 1985, before the threat of full-scale conversion of military to civilian production and the elimination of central control of the national economy.

For Russian cultural nationalists affiliated with the Russian Writers' Union and certain literary journals, everything has been wrong since the forced abdication of the tsar in February 1917. Russian nationalists invoke an idealized image of 1612, when the Russian nation allegedly came together with the Russian Orthodox Church to form the Romanov dynasty. They view the Russian empire as a civilizing force of salvation and assimilation for the many non-Slavic ethnic groups incorporated into the empire after 1612. Russian nationalists repudiate the "Western" democratic reforms of Alexander II as well as the entire twentieth century of Soviet history as betrayals of Russia's moral-religious grandeur epitomized by Romanov absolutism from 1612 until the 1860s.

Multiparty Political Systems

That the Soviet Union has quickly evolved into a multiparty rather than a two-party system is important in itself in projecting any real threat to Soviet democracy from the antidemocratic right. The nature of the party system in any democracy directly affects the prospects for political stability and the responsiveness of governments to social problems and interest groups.[19] Under certain societal-cultural conditions, a multiparty system promotes moderation and consensus in a society by balancing effective political authority with broad political participation and democratic pluralism. Under other realities, a multiparty system can destabilize a democracy by polarizing society and immobilizing government.

Since World War II the multiparty systems of Western Europe have offered a positive model showing how the presence of several political parties can contribute significantly to the relative adaptability and stability of liberal democracies.[20] Elections in Western European multiparty democracies, unlike two-party systems, rarely produce a majority of seats for one party. With a wide choice on the ballot, the voters can find a party ideologically positioned to champion their cause or needs and can reasonably anticipate that their party will win at least a few seats in the parliament. All other things being equal, multiparty systems will tend to have higher voter turnouts than two-party systems because the electorate has a greater incentive to vote. Although one party will generally win a plurality, several others will gain a sufficient number of parliamentary seats to necessitate a balancing of group interests in the government. In most cases the winning party will have to broker coalitions with some of the other parliamentary parties to form a government and will compromise the language of its most important policy proposals in order to gain their passage with the largest parliamentary majority possible. The appearance of a majority consensus among the parties and strong parliamentary support are especially important in gaining national public acceptance of the government's economic policies. Arend Lijphart has coined the term "consociational democracy" to characterize the interaction among the parliamentary parties in the small European countries since World War II.[21] The parties cooperate in working out a consensual national economic policy while they retain their distinct ideological and programmatic differences over all other issues.

The characteristics of the multiparty systems in Western Europe have served to enhance the legitimacy of the decisions of their governments, even when those decisions seem contrary to the immediate felt interests of many groups in the electorate. The systems moderate political passions by granting all parties some influence nationally but requiring them to compromise their differences. The emergence and "political domesticization" of the environmental movement through the Green parties represented in all of the European parliaments well illustrate this strength of the multiparty system in incorporating and adapting to new demands and interests.

In a two-party system like the United States, many issues are ignored by both parties because of their allegedly controversial nature. Certain groups outside the political mainstream, such as the homeless or the black underclass, are effectively excluded from the political process and fail to vote. Unable to form an effective alternative party and win public offices, the only hope for excluded groups is to gain support and advocates within one of the two established parties. Thus the appearance of great stability and continuity in a two-party system may be achieved at a long-term political cost. Social problems are left to fester and polarize a society, unaddressed by the increasingly ineffectual two political parties. The excluded become potential recruits for movements hostile to the system, often led by authoritarian, charismatic leaders.

The Western European model of a multiparty system is not readily applicable to the quite different political realities and cultural pluralism of the Soviet Union and many other Eastern European countries. The model only works under certain societal and cultural conditions: (1) a relatively narrow range of differences of basic political values and principles, (2) long-term economic growth over decades coincidental with the multiparty system, (3) a strong overriding sense of national identity, (4) the relative absence of sectarian ethnic-religious pluralism and communal conflicts in the country, and (5) party divisions that cut across rather than reinforce any sectarian conflicts in the country. Indeed, a multiparty system in a society with intense sectarian conflicts can either sublimate tensions or hasten a country's descent into a Lebanon-style civil war, the difference depending on the relation between party alignment and sectarian divisions, the nature of interaction among parties, and the parties' conduct of campaigns and the nature of their appeals for support.

Belgium, with its Flemish-Walloon division, has tended to illustrate the positive, sublimating effect of a multiparty system in resolving political differences between opposing religious-language communities.[22] One reason is that in Belgium party membership and electoral support for the traditionally dominant Liberal, Catholic, and Socialist parties cut across rather than reinforce differences by language-group or social class. As a consequence, the parties play a "peace-making" role across the two communities by mediating their political conflicts. In other ways, too, Belgium has been the exception that proves the rule about the conditions necessary for a multiparty system to promote stability and adaptation. Belgium has experienced relatively continuous economic growth as a member of the European Economic Community; it is surrounded by countries with stable political democracies; and the main political parties essentially support the existence of the state and have learned to accommodate each other and the conflicts that have arisen between the Dutch- and the French-speaking communities over several decades.

In general, however, if such conditions are absent, a multiparty system tends to polarize a society. Each of the many political parties has less incentive to seek coalitions with others and more incentive to position itself in the public mind by emphasizing its ideological differences from all other parties--particularly those parties on the same side of the political spectrum that might be able to siphon off potential votes. When consensus is lacking on basic political values and principles, and when there are long-term economic problems and widescale sectarian conflict, political parties in multiparty systems tend to factionalize. Leader cults and sectarian groups increase their political leverage to blackmail parties with which they are temporarily allied and can readily form new political parties with enough support to win a few seats in local or national legislatures.

The factionalization of parties makes stable coalition governments impossible. Ruling governments become more accountable to sectarian groups or nationally charismatic leaders than to the public at large. Ineffective governments cannot institute long-term policies to resolve the societal, cultural, and economic problems that are being manipulated for political advantage by numerous small parties. The most extreme views indirectly dictate the temper of political debate, forcing moderate political parties on the right and left to exaggerate their differences in order not to lose potential votes to radicals. Political corruption tends to increase as governments are reluctant to press criminal charges against the leaders of fringe groups and small sectarian parties whose support is needed at any price to hold together the unstable majority of the ruling party coalition.

Perhaps no democracy better typifies these negative attributes of a multiparty system in polarizing politics and making ruling governments captives of extremist fringe groups than Israel, especially since 1977 under the conservative Likud party coalition.[23] Under a system of proportional representation in the Israeli parliament (Knesset), Israelis vote for party lists rather than candidates. Parties win parliamentary seats proportionate to their national vote above the minimum cut-off of one percent. No single party (or party coalition) has ever won more than 50 of the 120 Knesset seats. With no party able to win an absolute majority of seats, the number of political parties elected to the Knesset has never fallen below ten. The last decade has actually witnessed an increase in the number represented, due to factionalization within the dominant religious and conservative party bloc. Since 1949 all ruling governments in Israel have been coalitions of several political parties, the small and especially the Orthodox religious parties holding the ultimate balance of power in every coalition. Their threatened pull-out from the government magnifies their political leverage and forces Israeli prime ministers to placate them by adopting their ideological views as government policy and giving them free rein over their ministries without any real cabinet accountability.

Since Likud came to power the lack of any real consensus on basic political values between the Israeli right and left has only intensified. In turn, Likud has been factionalized and captured by a number of right-wing fringe parties formed among settlers in the occupied territories of Gaza and the West Bank led by extreme Jewish nationalists and among Orthodox Jewish hasidic sects led by charismatic rabbis. These fringe parties can easily gain the support of at least one percent of the Israeli electorate to win some seats in the Knesset and together block any attempt by the majority of the Knesset to change the electoral system. To neutralize the electoral appeal of these parties Likud leaders have increasingly adopted their policies. To attract their participation in government coalitions, Likud leaders have tolerated both the corruption of these fringe leaders and the violence perpetrated by their paramilitary organizations against Palestinians in the occupied territories and against liberal Israeli Jews.

Israel has also suffered severe economic problems of inflation, stagnation, and unemployment almost continuously since 1977, and the extremist parties have been the chief political beneficiaries of these conditions. They have been able to increase their electoral support among the non-European Jewish working class most directly affected by the economic downturn and more susceptible to the rabid Arab-baiting and nationalism propagated by the right. In this sense the conflict between left and right in Israeli politics has been transformed into a sectarian struggle between the Jewish communities of European Azhkenazim and Oriental Sephardim.

Indeed, a certain perverse irony attends the emigration of hundreds of thousands of Soviet Jews to Israel since 1989. Fleeing the Soviet Union because they fear the anti-Semitism now inflamed by the Soviet right, Soviet

Jews are moving to a country where right-wing Jewish nationalism and antidemocratic extremism have polarized politics and threaten Israeli democracy. The very presence of the Soviet Jews only worsens the prospects for Israeli democracy. In opinion polls two-thirds of the Soviet Jews have stated their intention to vote for Likud or right-wing fringe parties.

Given the already desperate shortage of affordable housing in Israel, the influx of Soviet Jews will also have a destabilizing effect on the standard of living. Like all Jewish immigrants, Soviet Jews receive subsidies and first preference in housing allocated by the government. This will increase the pressure for Jewish settlement in the occupied territories, enhancing the political power of the extremist groups that dominate the governing councils in the territories and increasing their leverage on Likud.

Back to the Future?

Like the Israeli electorate over the past decade, the Soviet voter in the republic and local elections of 1989-90 had a wide range of choice, from the social democratic left to the ultranationalist right, but for the most part Soviet voters supported center-left political parties and candidates. In the Russian Republic the Democratic Russia coalition won a plurality of seats in the Russian Congress and majorities in the Leningrad and Moscow soviets. The Patriotic Bloc of right-wing Russian nationalists was resoundingly defeated, winning only two seats in the Russian Congress and failing to win a single seat in Leningrad or Moscow. The elections of Boris Yeltsin to chair the Russian Republic Supreme Soviet and of Gavriil Popov and Anatolii Sobchak to chair the Moscow and Leningrad city soviets were resounding victories for the noncommunist democratic left. In their public actions and conduct with their legislatures, the three popular leaders symbolize a new breed of democratically committed politicians emerging in republics and locales throughout the Soviet Union.

Any conclusion that democracy has triumphed irreversibly over the antidemocratic right, however, would be extremely premature. The problem is not a lack of popular leaders, but the weakness of the political parties. With a multiparty system that virtually precludes large electoral pluralities for the candidates of any one party, Soviet democracy may be doomed to suffer Israel's fate of factious coalition governments dominated by political extremists. Indeed, the numerous Soviet political parties and ethnic popular fronts have been noteworthy for their ideological extremism, appeals to the basest fears and irrational prejudices of the Soviet electorate, a prevalent identification with their newly popular national leaders, and their common denunciations of conspiracies and the "totalitarian" Communist Party establishment.

The center-left political parties and popular fronts have been especially conspicuous for their failures.[24] Because party organization and discipline are identified with the notorious "democratic centralism" of the Communist Party, party leaders are reluctant to organize at the grass-roots level and hesitate to take clearly defined positions on the issues without a lengthy process of internal discussion and consensual decision making. As a consequence, the new center-left parties resemble debating clubs more than responsible competitors for political power. To the same extent, they have been either unable or unwilling to recruit members and to mobilize a wide base of national support for themselves among the many diverse social and ethnic groups in the Soviet electorate. Reluctant to forge coalitions with like-minded parties in the parliaments, they have been evasive and even irresponsible in not educating the Soviet public on the hard choices and the real tradeoffs and uncertainties that will be involved if market reforms are to be implemented successfully in the 1990s.

In 1917 the end of tsarism brought with it a breakdown of central political authority and an intense struggle for political power between the Provisional Government and numerous legislative soviets, political parties, and secessionist ethnic regions. The divisiveness, vacillation, and ineffectiveness of the Provisional Government only contributed to already widespread societal polarization, economic breakdown, and public cynicism toward any political authority. The radical antidemocratic Bolshevik Party under Lenin took advantage of the malaise to seize power and institute authoritarian rule and a reunified state by 1921, under the pretext of saving the revolution and the people from counterrevolution.

In the 1990s the dissolution of communist authoritarianism has given way to a democracy in a political vacuum. Majority sentiment may support political democracy, the devolution of power to the republics, and the institution of wide-ranging market reforms, but groups and political parties in the democratic center and left squabble over timetables and the specifics to arrive at these goals. They seem unable to overcome their suspicions of each other's ulterior motives, their minuscule policy differences, and the personal ambitions of their leaders. Less in evidence are a demonstrated commitment to democratic norms or a willingness to compromise to form a majority coalition government that could deal with the economic crisis and the social and ethnic conflicts that are tearing the country apart.

Parties on the left accuse one another of collusion or collaboration with self-declared reformist communist officials who, it is alleged, covertly intend to preserve the Communist Party's monopolistic domination of Soviet society and to use privatization of the economy only to enrich themselves once more at the public expense. Several reasons are cited for these suspicions.[25] Newly elected noncommunist local governments have had to struggle, often unsuccessfully, to reclaim government buildings and printing presses that for decades were automatically leased for the Communist Party's sole use. Many former functionaries have left their state and party posts to take over ownership and management positions in the cooperatives and the newly denationalized sectors of the local economy. Accusations have been made that some of them channeled state funds into these same cooperatives and joint ventures prior to leaving their government offices.

Furthermore, left democratic parties warn that, despite the disintegration of the Communist Party's authority nationally, party loyalists who retain their dominance in the state bureaucracies will be able to frustrate the decisions of noncommunist majorities in local legislative soviets. In some regions such power struggles are already a fact, and there have been conflicts between local soviets and local Communist Party committees over the assignment of executive positions in the local government--a patronage right still claimed by party officials to fall under their powers of *nomenklatura*.

Anyone who has been a Communist Party member and particularly anyone who held an administrative position in the Soviet government before 1989 is potentially suspect of being an agent of this amorphous but allegedly still omnipotent Communist Party establishment that is manipulating events behind the scenes. Political morality has come to be associated with uncompromising hatred of the Communist Party and with suspicion of anyone previously affiliated with the party establishment. The Soviet electorate judges the political sincerity, honesty, and genuine commitment to democratic values of candidates for political office by the degree to which they were insulted, hounded, and persecuted in the past by the party establishment. Widespread popular support is almost assured for anyone once forced from high political office who is astute enough to capitalize on the fact, like the former Moscow party leader Boris Yeltsin or the former head of KGB counter-intelligence Oleg Kalugin. Conversely, anyone willing to compromise with reformist communists and to utilize the administrative experience of government officials is vulnerable to widespread public suspicion of collusion. Extremism and intolerance have been made into virtues, pragmatism and compromise into vices.

Linked to the reformist wing of the Communist Party leadership, the new centrist parties refute the allegation that they are less committed to democratic reform than the left parties or that they are front groups of the Communist Party establishment. They contend that the left parties, by their unwillingness to compromise on seizing all Communist Party property, outlawing the party, and dismembering the Soviet state, are playing into the hands of those hard-line conservatives in the party, the military, and the KGB who are secretly plotting to oust Gorbachev and return the Soviet Union to the autocratic status quo of 1985.

The same antidemocratic intolerance, paranoia, and extremism fuel internecine conflicts among factions within the ethnic popular fronts and political parties that have positioned themselves to assume political power in several republics and are pledged to gaining independent statehood. In the Baltic republics, factions within now ruling popular fronts have divided radicals and pragmatists.[26] The radicals demanding immediate secessions come very close to accusing the pragmatists of collusion with the Union officials in Moscow, evidenced by their willingness to negotiate the terms of secession through diplomacy and compromise.

In the elections to the Georgian republic legislature in 1990, open violence broke out between the two dominant factions of the anticommunist popular front comprised of seven political parties.[27] Each faction, led by well-known nationalists, accused the others of being less than totally committed to gaining immediate independence for Georgia, and implicitly, of collaborating with the Communist Party. The contending factions in the popular front together won a majority of the seats and control of the republic government; but their electoral victory gave an open-ended mandate to Zviad Gamsakhurdia, the newly elected president of the republic and one of the two charismatic nationalist leaders. A common fear was that he would use his mandate and authority to institute reprisals against his rivals in the other faction and plunge Georgia into open civil war.

Ominously, the one thing that the Georgian factions could agree upon in the electoral campaign was to endorse discrimination against ethnic minorities that do not share their goal of immediate Georgian independence. They supported a decree of the electoral commission that in essence banned from the ballot any candidates of political parties representing the Abkhazian and Ossetian minorities. The Abkhazians and Ossetians fear discrimination and violence, and in self-defense they intend to secede from Georgia and form sovereign republic governments remaining within the Soviet Union. Their fears are dismissed by the Georgian nationalists as ploys of the communist establishment in Moscow to undermine Georgian independence, and their parties are assumed to be creations secretly organized and funded by the Communist Party and the KGB in Moscow.

If common sense, realism, pragmatism, and tolerance are essential to a democracy, they have been ill-served by the extremism and jockeying for power among the contending center-left parties and ethnic popular fronts. Their extremism has only exacerbated the normal paranoia in Soviet political culture and the tendency to view policy conflicts as a "deviations" rather than as sincerely held differences of opinion over common principles, to regard opponents as "enemies" rather than as potential "allies" for similar goals, and to distrust all political authorities and political institutions.

Clear evidence of a political vacuum can be seen in the wave of protests, demonstrations, sit-ins, strikes, rallies, and marches so common throughout the Soviet Union since 1987, and unabated even after democratic elections were held. While the protests express a common rejection of communist authoritarianism, they also reflect the failure of the new parties to generate enough public confidence in themselves as effective institutions. In stable democracies, political parties mediate between society and the government. If they fairly represent the cross-section of all groups in a society, they can integrate public demands and limit the necessity of resorting to protests and demonstrations. Conflict in a democracy is normally resolved by political parties through their elected officials in legislatures, not by clashes among groups in the streets.

The political immaturity of the Soviet democratic center and left coincides with a general political trend. Having dismantled the most oppressive authoritarian system of the twentieth century, Soviet society has lurched to the opposite extreme and seems to be suffering from an excess of democratic pluralism. The new Soviet politicians in the popular fronts and center-left political parties act as leaders of mass movements rather than political parties. Otherwise they would form majority coalitions, pass laws in the parliaments, and assume a future public accountability for their policies at the polls. The popular fronts are more concerned to assert independence from Russian domination than to capitalize on their popularity to promote tolerance for minority rights. In many ways, these leaders still seem to regard themselves as powerless, as if no real political power over leadership selection and public policy making had been wrested away from communist officials.

There is little sense that these new leaders understand Western democracy in practice as opposed to theory. In practice, policy making in Western democracies evolves through compromise and bargaining. Politics is the highly imperfect art of the possible. Elections in Western democracies often turn on the volatile, irrational response of the electorate to events and to the personalities of the candidates. Winning parties rarely enter office with clearly defined majority mandates. In Western democracies, political programs are not miracle solutions to problems by heroic leaders, anointed by some unambiguous electoral general will to carry out clear priorities and rational public mandates.

The movement nature of the popular fronts and center-left political parties has transformed the Soviet Union into one of the most politicized and polarized societies in the world. National political authority is being challenged openly by all republic governments, which claim the supremacy of laws passed by their own republic parliaments over those of the Union. Within several republics, the national democratic revolution has turned into an orgy of ethnic self-determination and declarations of sovereignty.[28] Provinces and territories have declared independent statehood from their own republic governments and asserted their right to make laws, control their own economies, and assume ownership of all local resources. In turn, cities, boroughs, and even neighborhoods have declared their own independence from any higher authority or jurisdiction.

The historical legacy of Stalin's empire--rivalry over scarce resources in an economy near collapse, and the release of ethnic self-expression suppressed for decades under tsarist and Soviet rule--is the background to the volatile situation in the Soviet Union in the 1990s. Yet the popular fronts and the political parties of the center-left bear a not inconsiderable responsibility for the resurgence of ethnic nationalism and, particularly, for the open conflict between groups. Popular fronts and center-left parties have vied with each other to prove their commitment to regaining self-rule and dominant political authority for the titular ethnic majority in their republics. In particular, fronts and parties have stressed their support for laws making the titular ethnic language the official state language of a republic and restricting the right to vote and hold political office to members of the predominant nationality.

Few of the republic-level fronts or parties have made any concerted effort to expand their electoral base of support beyond a single ethnic group. None either institutionally or programmatically has attempted to create a truly Union-wide political party, actively seeking members among the many diverse ethnic nationalities residing within each of the republics. In the 1990 elections, their winning candidates overwhelmingly (85-95 percent in each republic) were members of the dominant, titular ethnic group in the republic.[29]

The emerging multiparty system has been both a cause and a symptom of the intensified and bitter conflicts between the ethnic majorities and minorities in several of the republics. The assertion of independent statehood and sovereignty by provinces and territories results from a worry that republic statehood will be achieved at their expense. A not unfounded fear is that the republic popular fronts will remain so committed to self-determination for ethnic majorities that ethnic minorities living in these provinces will be subjected to legal discrimination.

The immaturity of the democratic parties is easy to rationalize: they have only existed and been allowed to register and compete for political offices since 1990, in an environment where democratic values and norms had long been suppressed. But understandable as their immaturity may be, the actions of the new parties in 1990 contributed to the immobilization of the newly elected legislatures and failed to win them public confidence. And this has provided an opening for the antidemocratic political right.[30]

The Soviet public, despite general support for democratic reforms, has become disillusioned by the squabbling and inaction of the new, democratically elected legislatures. This is a Soviet public justifiably frightened by the threat of massive unemployment and a general economic breakdown, which they associate with a transition to private enterprise and a market economy. This is also a Soviet public affected by the political extremism and scapegoating characteristic of the rivalry among the various fronts and parties.[31]

Soviet and Western observers worry that the rivalry within the Soviet center-left has obscured the real danger to democracy and a real struggle for power whose outcome will set the course for the country in the immediate future. On one side stand most of the popular fronts and new political parties, reformist communist leaders, and a majority of the Soviet public committed to political and economic liberalization; on the other side stands a diffuse but inherently more cohesive political alliance of the right. The Soviet political right is drawn together by a common bond of fear of losing their dominance of Soviet society with a transition to democracy and a market economy and by a common visceral revulsion at the repudiation of communist values and ideology since 1987, rather than by any positive programmatic alternative.

Conclusion

Despite the low public support for candidates of the political right in the 1990 elections, and despite the low public ranking in national polls for its most identifiable political organizations and leaders, the challenge of the Soviet antidemocratic right cannot be dismissed. Without strong party identification, the Soviet electorate has a large and volatile "floating vote" that so far has gone predominantly to candidates of democratic parties, but is not bound to them. The democrats have been successful in tapping universal public hatred of the Communist Party and resentment at the disclosed corruption and elite privileges of communist officials. But if the newly elected officials fail to improve conditions, the same "floating vote" of hatred and resentment against those in power easily could be turned against them, for example by conservative populist-nationalists. An alarming omen was that, within weeks of assuming the leadership of the Moscow and Leningrad city governments, Popov and Sobchak confronted wild-cat strikes by their municipal workers.

Very few would question the assertion that Soviet democracy and democratic pluralism cannot survive without publicly influential and accountable political parties. But some would contend that one year is an unfairly short time-period in which to judge the nature and impact of Soviet political parties in the fledgling Soviet democracy. They would argue that the future Union, republic, and local elections in 1992-94 will be the real test for the Soviet multiparty system. By then Soviet political parties will have had sufficient time and experience to organize effectively, to articulate clear political choices, and to generate a strong voter party identification with their candidates and legislative platforms. The 1992-94 elections will test whether Soviet political parties have matured enough to translate electoral outcomes into responsible and stable ruling majority governments.

The problem is that time is unlikely to be an ally of the Soviet political parties. In contrast to the complete dissolution of the communist systems of Eastern Europe, the Soviet political system is still only in transition between autocracy and democracy. Influential leaders in the Communist Party, the military, and the KGB retain sufficient organizational capability and financial resources to lend their support either covertly or overtly to new political parties. Only the extremist parties of the right share their antipathy to democracy and economic liberalization and favor retaining a strong unified state.

Given projections by Soviet economists that as many as sixteen million jobs may be eliminated in this decade, it requires very little imagination to see unemployed Soviet workers rallying to the parties of the right. In this scenario, there is no reason to assume that the center-left political parties could win a majority of votes in the 1992-94 elections; the appeal of the political right cannot and should not be discounted. An even more extreme scenario would foresee the failure of center-left parties precipitating a revolution of the right. Like Lenin and the Bolsheviks in the fall of 1917, the Soviet right represents the antidemocratic and nonparty alternative. It appeals to public fears and promises political salvation and security through a reimposition of authoritarian rule. Thus the real choice in the Soviet Union in the 1990s is between political parties and a reconstituted police-state dictatorship.

Notes

1. For general overviews of the emerging Soviet party system, see Gleb Pavlovskii and Maxim Meyer, "Public Movements in the USSR," *Moscow News*, no. 7 (25 February-4 March 1990), p. 9; Valentin Davidov, "The Informal Movement: More Questions than Answers," *Soiuz*, no. 20 (May 1990), pp. 8-9 [translated in *Foreign Broadcast Information Service: Soviet Union* (hereafter *FBIS*), 12 June 1990, pp. 10-14]; and Aleksandr Meerovich, "The Emergence of Russian Multiparty Politics," *Report on the USSR*, 2, no. 34 (24 August 1990), pp. 8-16.

2. On the Marxist Platform and the Socialist Party, see "Vremia," 14 and 16 April 1990, transcribed in *FBIS*, 16 April 1990, pp. 48-50; "Marxist Platform for the 28th Congress," *Pravda*, 16 April 1990, p. 4; "Pertinent Question: How Many Platforms Do Marxists Need?" *Pravda*, 9 May 1990, p. 3; and Meerovich, "Emergence."

3. Radio Moscow, 17 November 1990. As summarized by Julia Wishnevsky, *Radio Free Europe/Radio Liberty Daily Report*, 19 November 1990, p. 61.

4. "Sem' dnei," Moscow Television, 28 January 1990 [transcribed in *FBIS*, 31 January 1990, pp. 68-69]; "Toward National Consensus: From the Election Platform of the Bloc of Russian Socio-Patriotic Movements," *Sovetskaia Rossiia*, 30 December 1989, p. 3, translated in *FBIS* (3 January 1990), pp. 77-79; " 'Edinenie' Association Founded," *Krasnaia zvezda*, 17 June 1990, p. 3 [translated in *FBIS*, 29 June 1990, p. 112]; and T. Khoroshilova, "Nina Andreeva Again?" *Komsomol'skaia pravda*, 23 February 1990, p. 1 [translated in *FBIS*, 28 February 1990, pp. 56-57].

5. Evgenii Ambartsumov, "Socialism or Stalinism?" *Sovetskaia kul'tura*, 19 September 1989, p. 2 [translated in *FBIS*, 29 September 1989, pp. 93-96]; "Unity Declares War Against Restructuring--Nina Andreeva: We Are Facing a Long and Difficult Struggle," *Magyar Hirlap*, 8 December 1989, p. 2 [translated in *FBIS*, 14 December 1989, pp. 104-8]; "Interview with Nina Andreeva," *Le Figaro*, 22 February 1990, p. 6 [translated in *FBIS*, 27 February 1990, pp. 57-59]; "Interview with Nina Andreeva," Hungarian Domestic Radio Service, April 1990 [transcribed in *FBIS*, 26 April 1990, pp. 64-66]; and Andrei Chernov, "Manifesto No. 2, or Nina Andreeva's April Theses,"

Moscow News, no. 20 (20 May 1990), p. 5.

6. Valentin Korolev, "Vzgliad," 19 October 1990 [as summarized by Alexander Rahr, *Radio Free Europe/Radio Liberty Daily Report*, 22 October 1990, p. 4]; and V. Potemkin, "How a Political Club Cheated a Party Raikom," *Sovetskaia kul'tura*, 16 September 1989, p. 1 [translated in *FBIS*, 6 October 1989, pp. 63-65].

7. A. Tarasov, "Sentence Pronounced," *Izvestiia*, 12 October 1990, p. 3.

8. Supra note 5.

9. "If We Come to Power--The Rightist Forces That Are Torpedoing Restructuring Are Consolidating," *Argumenty i fakty*, 2-8 June 1990, pp. 4-5 [translated in *FBIS*, 14 June 1990, pp. 66-68].

10. Pavel Gutiontov, "Recent Issues of Periodicals. Shameful . . . ," *Izvestiia*, 2 January 1990, p. 4 [translated in *FBIS*, 5 January 1990, pp. 91-92]; and Nikolai Proshunin, "Is *Molodaia gvardiia* Our Contemporary?" *Sovetskaia kul'tura*, no. 20 (19 May 1990), p. 3 [translated in *FBIS*, 12 June 1990, pp. 19-25]. The journal's murky ties to extreme Russian nationalists, Pamiat', and the Soviet KGB are personified by Sergei Bobkov on its editorial board. A former secretary of the Russian Republic Writers' Union, Sergei is the son of Filipp Bobkov, first deputy chairman of the KGB and head of its domestic counterintelligence directorate until his retirement in February 1990. Bobkov was accused by a former KGB official of having masterminded Pamiat' as a KGB secret branch. See Alexander Rahr, "The KGB's Gray Eminence Retires," *Report on the USSR*, 3, no. 9 (1 March 1991), p. 11.

11. "Standpoint--All Power to Working People," *Moskovskaia pravda*, 19 September 1989, p. 2 [translated in *FBIS*, 17 October 1989, pp. 92-95]; "We Are Protecting the Workers' Interests," *Trud*, 15 October 1989, p. 2 [translated in *FBIS*, 20 October 1989, pp. 71-73]; Pavel Gutiontov, "Moscow Holds Rallies," *Izvestiia*, 4 July 1990, p. 3.

12. "We Introduce a Deputies' Group: Soiuz Is . . . ," *Krasnaia zvezda*, 15 March 1990, p. 1 [translated in *FBIS*, 16 March 1990, pp. 71-72]; "Common Anxiety About the Future of the Union," *Sovetskaia Rossiia*, 22 March 1990, p. 2 [translated in *FBIS*, 30 March 1990, pp. 54-56]; Lt. Colonel V. Kharchenko, "We Share the 'Soiuz' Stance," *Krasnaia zvezda*, 5 April 1990, p. 1 [translated in *FBIS*, 16 April 1990, pp. 58-59].

13. See, for example, the interview with Ligachev and his speech to the Veterans' Council: "An Atmosphere of Creativity Is Necessary," *Veteran*, no. 5 (31 January-4 February 1990), pp. 2-4 [translated in *FBIS*, 8 March 1990, pp. 79-85]; and "For the Socialist Renewal of Society," *Veteran*, no. 13 (26 March-1 April 1990), pp. 2-3 [translated in *FBIS*, 17 April 1990, pp. 56-60].

14. Vitalii Potemkin, "Consolidation or Division?" *Sovetskaia kul'tura*, no. 17 (28 April 1990), pp. 1 and 8 [translated in *FBIS*, 3 May 1990, pp. 82-83]; and Otto Lacis, "Who Suffered Victory?" *Moskovskie novosti*, 16 September 1990, p. 3 [translated in *The Current Digest of the Soviet Press*, 42, no. 36 (10 October 1990), p. 13].

15. Anatolii Salutskii, "More Action--Interview with Ivan Polozkov," *Sovetskaia Rossiia*, 1 July 1990, pp. 1-2; A. Molokov, "In Search of an Alternative," *Sovetskaia Rossiia*, 25 October 1990, p. 2; "Interview with Gennadii Ianaev," TASS, 6 June 1990

[translated in *FBIS*, 7 June 1990, pp. 36-37]; "AUCCTU: Clear Position," *Trud*, 31 May 1990, p. 1 [translated in *FBIS*, 7 June 1990, pp. 37-38]; S. Chugaev, "Trade Unions Set Conditions," *Izvestiia*, 30 June 1990, p. 1; and A.A. Sergeev, "Speech to the 28th Party Congress," *Pravda*, 8 July 1990, p. 6.

16. Igor' Shafarevich, "Russophobia," *Nash sovremennik*, no. 6 (June 1989), pp. 167-92; Aleksandr Prokhanov, "Tragedy of Centralism," *Literaturnaia Rossiia*, no. 1 (5 January 1990), pp. 4-5 [translated in *FBIS*, 26 January 1990, pp. 93-98]; "Selected Excerpts from the Speeches of Writers at the Plenum of the Board of the RSFSR Writers' Union," *Nedelia*, no. 47 (20-26 November 1989), pp. 16-17 [translated in *FBIS*, 21 December 1989, pp. 95-99]; "Letter from the Writers of Russia," *Literaturnaia Rossiia*, no. 9 (2 March 1990), pp. 2-4; and "Who Is Using the Threat of Fascism?" *Sovetskaia Rossiia*, 7 March 1990, p. 4 [translated in *FBIS*, 13 April 1990, pp. 93-95].

17. Gorbachev continued to use the 1921 analogy as recently as his opening address to an October 1990 Central Committee plenum, drawing parallels to the crises and turning point confronting the Communist Party and the Soviet Union in the 1990s. See *Pravda*, 9 October 1990, pp. 1-2.

18. Gavriil Popov, "Dangers of Democracy," *The New York Review of Books*, 37, no. 13 (16 August 1990), pp. 27-28; "Anatolii Sobchak: 'It Will Be Difficult, But We Have to Try,' " *Literaturnaia gazeta*, no. 12 (30 May 1990), p. 2 [translated in *FBIS*, 5 June 1990, pp. 93-95]; and "Anatolii Sobchak: 'There Will Not Be Dual Power,' " *Moscow News*, no. 22 (3 June 1990), p. 5.

19. On party systems and democracies, see, for example, Giovanni Sartori, *Parties and Party Systems* (Cambridge: Cambridge University Press, 1976); G. Bingham Powell, Jr., *Contemporary Democracies: Participation, Stability, and Violence* (Cambridge, MA: Harvard University Press, 1982); and Kay Lawson and Peter W. Merkl, eds., *Why Parties Fail: Emerging Alternative Organizations* (Princeton, NJ: Princeton University Press, 1988).

20. See, for example, Steven B. Wolinetz, ed., *Parties and Party Systems in Liberal Democracies* (London: Routledge, 1988).

21. Arend Lijphart, *Democracy in Plural Societies* (New Haven, CT: Yale University Press, 1977).

22. Arend Lijphart, ed., *Conflict and Coexistence in Belgium: The Dynamics of a Culturally Divided Society* (Berkeley, CA: Institute of International Studies, University of California, 1981); and Maureen Covell, "Stability and Change in the Belgian Party System," in Wolinetz, *Parties and Party Systems*, pp. 105-29.

23. On the polarization of Israeli politics by religious-nationalistic groups, see, for example, Myron J. Aronoff, "The Failure of Israel's Labor Party and the Emergence of Gush Emunim," in Lawson and Merkl, *Why Parties Fail*, pp. 309-37; Ian Lustick, *For the Land and the Lord: Jewish Fundamentalism in Israel* (New York: Council on Foreign Relations, 1988); Avishai Margalit, "Israel: The Rise of the Ultra-Orthodox," *The New York Review of Books*, 36, no. 17 (9 November 1989), pp. 38-44; and Yoav Peled, "Retreat from Modernity: The Ascendance of Jewish Nationalism in the Jewish State," unpublished paper presented at the American Political Science Association

convention, 30 August-2 September 1990, San Francisco, CA.

24. A. Kiva, "Wealth Is Not a Vice--Thoughts about Whether Expropriation Could Happen Again," *Izvestiia*, 2 June 1990, p. 4 [translated in *FBIS*, 12 June 1990, pp. 30-33]; A. Kiva, "A 'Third Force'--In the Opinion of Political Scientists, It Exists on Our Political Scene, in Addition to Reformers and Conservatives," *Izvestiia*, 28 September 1990, p. 3 [translated in *The Current Digest of the Soviet Press*, 42, no. 39 (31 October 1990), pp. 8-9].

25. V. Kornev, "He Refused to Join the Bureau," *Izvestiia*, 27 May 1990, p. 2; V. Bogdanovskii, "Lvov--The Fuss About the Third Floor," *Krasnaia zvezda*, 8 July 1990, p. 1 [translated in *FBIS*, 27 July 1990, p. 85]; Andrei Chernov, "Who Wields Real Power in Leningrad?" *Moscow News*, no. 19 (20-27 May 1990), p. 5; Mikhail Chulaki, "Invasion and Invaders," *Moscow News*, no. 16 (17-23 April 1990), p. 3; and O. Gapanovich, "Legacy--Leningrad Is Broke," *Izvestiia*, 10 October 1990, p. 3.

26. Riina Kionka, Dzintra Bungs, and Saulius Girnius, "Political Disputes in the Baltic," *Report on the USSR*, 2, no. 44 (2 November 1990), pp. 26-29; Riina Kionka, "The Estonian Political Landscape," *Report on the USSR*, 2, no. 49 (7 December 1990), pp. 17-19.

27. Elizabeth Fuller, "Georgia on the Eve of the Supreme Soviet Elections," *Report on the USSR*, 2, no. 45 (9 November 1990), pp. 18-21; idem, "Round Table Coalition Wins Resounding Victory in Georgian Supreme Soviet Elections," *Report on the USSR*, 2, no. 46 (16 November 1990), pp. 13-16.

28. Ann Sheehy, "Fact Sheet on Declarations of Sovereignty," *Report on the USSR*, 2, no. 45 (9 November 1990), pp. 23-25.

29. Valerii Tishkov, Director of the Institute of Ethnography, USSR Academy of Science, at Stanford, CA, 7 December 1990.

30. German Diligenskii, "The Reformers and Conservatives: Who Will Tip the Scales?" *New Times*, no. 10 (6-12 March 1990), pp. 8-11; L. Gordon and E. Klopov, "Workers' Movement: Costs and Gains," *Pravda*, 18 January 1990, p. 4 [translated in *FBIS*, 24 January 1990, pp. 80-83]; Boris Bagariatskii and Mikhail Leont'ev, "Dramatis Personae of Restructuring: Who Finds Abalkin Bothersome," *Nedelia*, 14 (2-8 April 1990), pp. 2-3 [translated in *The Current Digest of the Soviet Press*, 42, no. 20 (20 June 1990), pp. 15-17]; L. Shevtsova, "He Who Is Not Against Us Is With Us--An Alliance Between the Democratic Forces and the President Could Effect Public Accord," *Izvestiia*, 8 October 1990, p. 3; Kiva, "Wealth Is Not a Vice."

31. Public attitudes favoring the Soviet right already exist as evidenced from a national mail survey and local surveys of the Gorky Province and Kalmyk Autonomous Republic taken after the March 1990 elections. One-third of all respondents identify themselves with positions advocated by the Soviet right, blame new Soviet interest groups for aggravating the economic crisis only to grab power for themselves, and resort to the same demagogic slogans in explaining the country's problems most closely associated with rightist extremists. V.O. Rukavishnikov, "The Peak of Social Tension under the Sign of the White Horse," *Sotsiologicheskie issledovaniia*, no. 10 (October 1990), pp. 22-24.

7

PARTY FORMATION AND DEFORMATION ON RUSSIA'S DEMOCRATIC LEFT

Michael E. Urban

Political Parties in Depoliticized Context

The rich variety of political species that have appeared in the course of Soviet society's reawakening plays havoc with many of our conventional categories. What are we to make, for instance, of a situation in which communists are regarded as "conservatives" and proponents of capitalism as "left-wing radicals"? How is it that monarchists are often enough numbered among the "democratic forces"? Moreover, in focusing our attention on the proper object of this chapter, namely, those organizations on the "democratic left" that have chosen to call themselves political parties, we immediately encounter a number of reasons for adopting a skeptical attitude toward this appellation itself. Programs regularly fail to distinguish one "party" from another, their memberships are usually small and fluid, they claim insignificant portions of electoral support, their leaders often spend inordinate amounts of time quarreling with one another, leading in turn to what have become all but predictable results--expulsions, walkouts, and the consequent founding of yet more "parties."

In order to come to grips with this baffling phenomenon of party formation on Russia's democratic left, we might begin by reminding ourselves that political parties are expressive institutions. Whether in one instance they articulate the concrete demands of a social group or, in another, the worldview of a social class or, in yet a third, the aspirations of a particular people, their common denominator consists in the fact that they are expressing something, (allegedly) on someone's behalf, to someone else. Parties, then, constitute a singularly important means by which a given society maintains a political dialogue with itself.

Our topic also forcefully recalls the fact that, in addition to being expressive institutions, political parties are themselves expressions of the society in which they have emerged. They reflect that society's history as stored in, and interpreted through, its culture; at any moment in time they manifest on the political level that society's structure of power and extant challenges to it; collectively, and with discordant voices, they disclose that society's visions of its own future. When viewed from this perspective, the Russian parties look less like discrete "things," bewildering in their odd array and strange behavior, and more like the recognizable products of a system undergoing deep and profound transformation. At the core of this transformation--and certainly the very emergence of political parties testifies to this fact--is the rebirth of political society in the Soviet Union. On one hand, this involves the idea of expression in the first sense mentioned above, the sense in which some seventy years of the Communist Party's political monologue is now giving way to a political dialogue in which different points of view contend. On the other hand, however, what is being expressed to, and on behalf of, whom is a matter determined by our second concept of expression, in which parties are themselves expressions of the social context in which they are rooted. What might appear to us on first inspection, since we are looking with our Western eyes, as something strange or even inexplicable, becomes easier to understand against this backdrop. For if we direct our attention to the context and exercise some care with respect to the concepts that we employ, it becomes clear that it makes no sense to speak, as we already have done, about the "Communist Party's political monologue." The notion of "political monologue" is as oxymoronic as that of a "single-party system." Accordingly, the context in which these parties function, often described by Western political scientists as "Soviet political culture," becomes especially problematic inasmuch as a salient feature of some seventy years of Communist Party rule has been the depolitization of Soviet society, the near complete erasure of its political life.[1] Speaking of a "political culture" under such circumstances hardly makes more sense than speaking about, say, agriculture among the Eskimos or aquaculture among nomadic peoples of the desert. The notion of "culture" without a corresponding practice is a hollow one that misleads rather than elucidates.[2]

Setting aside, then, any ready-made ideas about Soviet political culture, we might begin by inquiring into the concrete context in which Russia's new parties have emerged. From this vantage, we see them growing out of the as-yet-undead corpse of Soviet state socialism. And in this consists the anomaly of the parties on the democratic left. For these parties have all adopted the imperative that euthanasia should be performed on this creature as quickly as possible, while at the same time their own lives have been inextricably bound to it. Seen in this double-sided context, we have a basis for comprehending both the movement character of these parties, which continually blurs distinctions among them, as well as their tendencies to replicate within themselves many of the practices and attitudes of the old order which they outwardly detest.

The initial impetus toward party formation came from the democratic movement in Russia, which first began to organize itself as a myriad of "informal" political groups and clubs during the second and third years of Mikhail Gorbachev's *perestroika*. By the summer of 1988, two tendencies were already apparent within the movement, tendencies that it would continue to exhibit in one form or another throughout the various stages of its development. The first concerns the efforts of many of these groups to define their respective political orientations and, concomitantly, to unify their memberships around programmatic goals. The fact that these boundaries were often rather vague, and thus led to extended and at times pointless disputes, should not deflect our attention from the fact that numerous leaders in the informal movement were indeed attempting to draw them. Their efforts in this respect obviously anticipated a further stage of political development at which parties would be admitted to the arena of political activity. They were preparing for that moment.[3]

The second tendency moved in the opposite direction, toward amalgamation rather than differentiation. Inspired by the groundswell of political activity that emerged in the Baltic republics in spring 1988 and impressed by the success of the popular fronts that stimulated, organized, and directed these movements, many Russian "informals" adopted a similar strategy whereby their small and rather ineffective groups would combine forces within the framework of a popular front that would be large enough to represent a real challenge to the entrenched power of the Communist Party's ruling apparatus and capable, therefore, of establishing a political presence that would draw more people into their movement.

The dominant position of the Communist Party determined from the start, then, a critical aspect of party formation in Russia. In order to offer resistance to its dominion, political groups would draw together in a larger movement, thereby diluting their individual identities. This phenomenon, already apparent in the pre-party stage of development, would surface repeatedly once party formation proper was under way. As we shall see, the dominant presence of the Communist Party and this reaction to it have continued to reinforce the movement character of Russia's new parties and, by that measure, to impede the process of party formation.

A related influence of Communist Party dominance has been the fact that its opponents, in the course of their struggles against the CPSU, have themselves often taken on a number of its characteristics. This is perhaps above all evident in the case of the first group to announce itself a political party, the Democratic Union. This party was founded in early May 1988 by politically active intellectuals representing a number of discrete orientations: liberal, social-democratic, and Eurocommunist.[4] The Democratic Union has experienced repression from its inception and accordingly has maintained a defiant and provocative posture toward the regime. As a consequence, the first self-proclaimed party among Russia's new political forces has in fact remained at a pre-party stage of development. It boycotted the elections of 1989 and 1990, and those of its members interested in party activity for the most part have left to join other groups.[5] As one observer has remarked, the Democratic Union has become something of a mirror image of the CPSU. Neither organization is a party in the proper sense of the term and, whereas the CPSU represents a political "mafia," the Democratic Union appears purely as a form of protest against this mafia. Ironically, as the CPSU has begun to disintegrate, the Democratic Union has become rudderless and is disintegrating along with it.[6]

This particular relation between the Communist Party and the Democratic Union is perhaps symptomatic of a broader correspondence between the "old" and the "new." Irena Fomicheva, for instance, has pointed out how leaders of the democratic movement cloak their own positions on issues in inflated phrases such as "in the name of the people," or "in the name of the working class," precisely as communist rulers did in the pre-*perestroika* era.[7]   Aleksandr Verkhovskii has noticed a similar tendency whereby the democratic movement has defined itself almost exclusively in terms of its opponent, the totalitarian order that it seeks to bring down. Having defined itself in this way, however, it is as if the democratic movement has remained oblivious to its own success. Its discourse continues to pivot on the notion of resistance to this already moribund order, thereby sustaining and enhancing a rhetoric of uncompromising radicalism rather than the adoption of a practical attitude toward the concrete tasks of organizing popular constituencies to bring about the very transition celebrated in its rhetoric.[8]

Verkhovskii's characterization might be supplemented with another consideration. What is the audience to which this movement and its component political parties are addressing themselves? And relatedly: Which forms of communication are likely in the present context to receive a positive response? Here, the question of political culture or its relative absence can scarcely be avoided. As Fomicheva has put it, we would be wrong to mistake "five thousand people, [acting] as a choir, shouting 'no' at some meeting or other, for public opinion." In fact, she continues, public opinion does not exist in Russia today; in its stead we merely find uninformed preferences set out in black and white.[9] Similarly, Alexei Levinson of the All-Union Center for the Study of Public Opinion has shown that for Moscow, where political consciousness is arguably most advanced in Russia, those with this black-and-white political outlook, coupled with those who have no political consciousness whatsoever, comprise the overwhelming bulk of the capital's population. Of course, a small fraction of Muscovites can be identified in some senses as politically mature. But, Levinson observes, they have constructed for themselves an esoteric discourse that is not only inaccessible to the great majority of people, but is also laced with the sorts of issues of principle that invite ongoing argument and continual fissure.[10] Indeed, one often gets the impression that debates within this stratum today do not concern politics or programs as much as philosophy.[11]

Context, again, can help us to elucidate this phenomenon. The decades of depoliticization maintained under the old order have resulted in a situation in which the reappearance of political expression assumes initially a primitive form. Moreover, the socioeconomic structure associated with the old order, in which everyone appears as an employee of the state, is not conducive to the generation of interests that parties might represent. As Sergei Mitrokhin has remarked:

> One of the strange things about the depravity of our political situation is that there are no links between material interest and party affiliation. We have parties, of course, that are oriented toward certain economic interests--the Peasant Party, the Party of Free Labor, and so on--such that a person from the West might easily think that these parties express the interests of these producers or those entrepreneurs. But as a matter of fact what we find here are people concerned with abstract, purely political, purely--how might we say--"higher interests." . . . Social interests play a role, but an insignificant one. They are less a stimulus than are simple emotions.[12]

Since social differentiation, then, has not proceeded to the point at which identifiable interests can be picked up and articulated by individual parties, those parties currently on the scene remain divorced from social bases for whose allegiance they might compete. Instead of authentic competition among party leaders, we find, in the words of one Russian sociologist, "a feud [that] develops, not true partisanship but partiality expressed in irrelevant arguments."[13]

Even at the critical phase of party activity--namely, the electoral campaign--the issue of organizing national constituencies has been occluded by these factors. As a result of the amorphousness of public opinion and the attendant preoccupation of voters with immediate, local issues,[14] as well as their tendency to embrace candidates who appear trustworthy and capable of delivering the goods, elections in certain respects actually have retarded party formation. As one observer noted with respect to candidates in both the national elections of 1989 and the republic and local elections of 1990, all of whom put forward their own individual platforms, "each candidate for office was 'a party unto himself.' "[15] Even in those cases in which local groups have been able to field slates of successful candidates to district and city soviets, their deputies often find themselves deadlocked in the legislature with other similar groups, each arguing, say, that the planned industrial plant or refuse dump should be located in someone else's neighborhood. It seems that in not a few cases the stalemate among representatives of these local interests has been overcome by invitation from the deputies to the corresponding committees of the CPSU to intervene as arbiter and thus settle the dispute. By virtue of the very fact that the CPSU apparatus is regarded as unrepresentative of the community, its impartiality does not appear to be in question.[16]

From Political Movement to Political Parties

Our discussion thus far might serve as a caution against the reification of political activity along the lines of parties, platforms, interests and so forth that appear as discrete "things." While this caveat is valuable in any context, it seems especially so in the Russian one. Indeed, simply to take at face value Russia's new political parties would be to read more into these organizations than is, for the moment at least, there. Yet something, surely, is there, and even were it the case that extrapolating a future from the current array of political parties would be a misguided enterprise, parties--however unsteadily--are emerging. By focusing on them, we cannot hope to predict accurately their futures, but we can learn something about the dynamics that lie behind their formation and how these dynamics might express themselves in the years to come.

As we have noted, the organization of political forces on Russia's democratic left tends to oscillate between their combination into a movement and their differentiation into separate parties. The formation of the Inter-regional Deputies' Group (IRDG) within the first Congress of People's Deputies would seem to contain an element of each. On the one hand, it arose as a parliamentary opposition (with a membership that eventually peaked at about 450) to the dominant bloc of deputies in the legislature, which was tied closely to the CPSU apparatus and was led by, if anyone, Mikhail Gorbachev.[17] The initial conception underlying its formation appeared to be that of a parliamentary party, although open party activity remained illegal at the time. As its leader, Boris Yeltsin, remarked at its founding meeting: "We understand that our group must have not only its own approaches to problems, but also its own leadership, structure, system of ties to the electorate and, possibly, some sort of fund of material support."[18] Accordingly, the IRDG endeavored, but with small success, to publish its own newspaper and to organize democratic groups at the grassroots, enlisting the Interregional Association of Democratic Organizations as a base of support.[19]

On the other hand, however, these steps toward party formation were rather quickly arrested by the fact that the IRDG simply contained too many dissonant political elements to evolve very far in that direction.[20] As a discourse analysis of IRDG speeches at the second Congress of People's Deputies (December 1989) revealed, while IRDG leaders were solidly united in their opposition to the current government and its policies, their own positions on issues of mutual concern varied greatly, revealing in turn the presence of a number of differing political orientations within the group-- ideologies--each with the capacity for conflict and cooperation with others on a given question. In short, a number of identifiable tendencies had been dwelling inside the spacious tent of the parliamentary opposition and would soon emerge from it to announce themselves political parties.[21]

The Social Democratic Party of Russia

Organizational efforts that culminated in the founding of the Social Democratic Party of Russia (SDPR) began with the first meeting of the Social Democratic Association of the Soviet Union (SDASU) in Tallinn in June 1989.[22] This meeting was restaged in January 1990 on an expanded basis--drawing representatives from some 200 groups and clubs from 90 cities and regions of the USSR--as SDASU's founding congress.[23] A parallel effort at establishing a social democratic center for the USSR had been undertaken by the Social Democratic Confederation--which drew members from such "informal" political organizations as Moscow's Democratic Perestroika, Leningrad Perestroika, Leningrad's Rebirth, and the social democratic faction from the Democratic Union; but soon after holding its own inaugural meeting in Tallinn in July 1989, this group merged with SDASU.[24] Although officially registered as a public organization in February 1990, SDASU's organizational net--encompassing Marxist-Leninists, advocates of the Swedish model of socialism, anarcho-communists, and liberal democrats-- was cast too broadly to provide much coherence or lead to any action.[25] Accordingly, when the constitutional prohibition against the formation of political parties was lifted in March 1990, Russian social democrats called a founding congress for the SDPR which met the following May in Moscow. This meeting, attended by 237 delegates representing 4,216 members in 92 cities,[26] inaugurated a Russian social democratic party whose political course would be charted without appreciable connection with, or influence from, SDASU.

Beyond electing a leadership (presidium) composed of IRDG member Aleksandr Obolenskii, Oleg Rumiantsev, and Pavel Kudiukin, this congress confined its work to speechmaking on the theme of what the SDPR should stand for--opposition to class struggle or dictatorships of any type, endorsement of a market economy and a system of social security, a commitment to representing a balance of class and group interests, and a general strategy of forming coalitions with other democratic parties in order to remove the CPSU from power and establish a democratic republic.[27] While SDPR labor (Sotsprof) and voter-organizing (Golos) affiliates were creating a financial basis for the party,[28] the SDPR's political subcommission translated the general principles, expressed at the first congress, into a draft program that was adopted, amid considerable debate, at the party's second congress the following October in Sverdlovsk.[29]

Despite formal protestations to the contrary, the concept of class struggle has been central to SDPR thinking at this juncture. That is, its leaders regard the matter of how the coming market economy is to be defined as the pivotal issue for Russia's future and see in this respect two competing definitions, each the product of class forces locked in struggle. One side of this conflict is made up of the old ruling group--the *nomenklatura*, led by Gorbachev and supported by foreign capital--which is attempting to reestablish its privileges within a market framework that, together with organized criminal elements, it will dominate as *komsobstvenniki* ("communist property owners"). A "new middle class," composed of the intelligentsia, the emerging business sector, the progressive elements in state industry, and skilled workers, is said to stand in opposition to the *komsobstvenniki* and in favor of an open market and democratic polity wherein their talents and efforts would be rewarded as real contributions to the development of the country. It is this new middle class that the SDPR seeks to lead.[30]

Although the SDPR boasts among its members a few of the more prominent people's deputies of the USSR and RSFSR and may soon be attracting more people's deputies to its ranks, for the foreseeable future it remains incapable of taking on the task of dislodging the Communist Party from power. Consequently, a rather bizarre situation has resulted in which the repeated denunciations that it has leveled (along with effectively all parties on the democratic left) at the CPSU for its refusal to disband its party organizations within the military, the police, and other state and economic institutions have given way to a decision on the part of the SDPR to organize its own members within the armed services in precisely this fashion.[31] This internal reorganization of the SDPR from a "normal parliamentary party," to use its own language, to one structured on the "totalitarian" model, has found a rather odd complement externally in its coalition arrangement with other parties which, as we see below, has markedly reduced its salience as an identifiable institution.

The Republican Party of Russia

The roots of the Republican Party of Russia (RPR) lie in Moscow's informal political movement. By spring 1988, a number of Communist Party members who had become active in various groups and clubs in the capital decided to form an "inter-club party group" that would hopefully act as a medium for transmitting ideas sprouted in the hothouse of informal meeting halls and *samizdat* publications into the CPSU itself. By the end of 1989, this strategy had caught on in some 102 cities of the USSR, from which delegates were dispatched to a conference of party clubs in Moscow.[32] Although the initial intention of democratizing the CPSU from within was to prove a futile effort, the movement of party clubs resulted in the formation of the first openly organized faction to have appeared in the CPSU in some sixty-five years, the Democratic Platform.

In January 1990 the Democratic Platform was officially inaugurated in Moscow by over 400 CPSU members calling for thoroughgoing reforms in the ruling party: the abolition of democratic centralism, the disbanding of CPSU organizations in state and economic institutions, and "the creation of a multiparty democracy" in which the CPSU would function as a "normal party of the parliamentary type."[33] Prominent among the leaders of Democratic Platform at this time were IRDG luminaries Boris Yeltsin, Gavriil Popov, Iurii Afanas'ev, and Nikolai Travkin. Their participation in this group, however, would be short-lived, and when the Democratic Platform eventually cut its ties with the CPSU, it began an independent life without leaders approaching the stature of these figures.

The rationale behind the organization of the Democratic Platform was summed up in its accusation that the CPSU had not only betrayed its announced project of *perestroika*, but had itself become the principal impediment to *perestroika*'s success.[34] Hopes to democratize the CPSU and thereby break the hold of its conservative apparatus on power were dashed in the wake of the procedures employed for delegate selection to the Communist Party's twenty-eighth congress, which ensured a lopsided majority (68 percent) for officials of the party-state apparatus.[35] Similarly, talk of bolting the Communist Party altogether grew in proportion to threats to expel members of the Democratic Platform from the CPSU that were emanating from numerous Communist Party organizations around the country, capped off by the Central Committee's notorious "Open Letter to All Communists" urging expulsion of those in the Democratic Platform who refused to the see the error of their ways.[36]

At regional conferences and at its second all-union conference, the Democratic Platform gradually arrived at the position, in the advent of the twenty-eighth congress of the CPSU, that it would fight for its proposals on the congress floor; but, should a critical minimum of these fail to be adopted, the Democratic Platform would walk out and constitute itself as a new political party.[37]

With survey research showing that 35 percent of CPSU members supported the Democratic Platform[38] and with their proposals roundly defeated at the twenty-eighth CPSU congress, the Democratic Platform nonetheless balked at the decisive hour. At the press conference called on 13 July to announce its decision, Democratic Platform leader Viacheslav Shostakovskii spoke of "splitting" with (or within) the CPSU rather than simply leaving. This hedging on the matter of not cutting all ties with the Communist Party was explained, rather unconvincingly, as a way to lay claim to some of the property owned or possessed by the Communist Party.[39] A more likely, though unmentioned, reason was the fact that leaving the

Communist Party almost certainly meant that a great many of the Democratic Platform's leading figures would be expelled from their positions in the academic world, a penalty immediately visited on Shostakovskii, who was sacked from his post as rector of Moscow's Higher Party School by the Moscow City Committee of the Communist Party.

At its organizational meeting of 14-15 July with some 250 members in attendance, the issue of "splitting" versus "leaving" the CPSU was bitterly debated and finally resolved (without a formal vote) in favor of cutting all ties to the CPSU and founding a new political party. But in certain respects the discourse evident at this meeting indicated otherwise. A number of speakers urged that the Democratic Platform constitute itself as a "normal, parliamentary party" while simultaneously addressing those assembled as "comrades," a title associated with the underground, revolutionary, and then totalitarian, party that they had just left. Moreover, the formal declaration adopted referred to the Democratic Platform as oriented toward the creation of a political party that "rejected all dogmatism" and based itself instead on "scientific analysis."[40] It would seem, then, that the break with communism was less than complete, as the Democratic Platform rather second-naturedly announced its independence not with the intention of a "normal parliamentary party" to articulate the demands of the populace or those of certain constituencies, but with a Leninist reflex awarding the determination of program in the final analysis to the party's theoreticians.[41]

Having delayed the convocation of its founding congress for some two months, the Democratic Platform finally staged it in November 1990 and took for itself a new name--the Republican Party of Russia. In a number of respects, however, this event oddly resembled more a prelude to, rather than the climax of, its transformation into a party. First, no leaders were officially elected at the congress. Instead, the more prominent members of its coordinating council--Shostakovskii, Vladimir Lysenko, Igor Chubais, and Stepan Shulakshin--have simply continued to act as an informal collective leadership,[42] but one in which deep divisions and personal rivalries have long been inscribed.[43]

Second, the organizational structure adopted by the RPR is especially loose and decentralized. With the exception of three rubles per member that are deducted for the support of the central party organs, membership dues--assessed on the basis of one percent of a member's annual income (with lower rates for students, pensioners, and the unemployed)--remain entirely at the disposal of the RPR's local and regional organizations.[44]

Finally, outside of the leaders' intentions to prevent the RPR--composed as it is of former communists--from becoming an anticommunist mirror-image of the CPSU, this party has exhibited no clear identity that would distinguish it from others on the democratic left. Indeed, not only is its program essentially the same as that of the SDPR,[45] but SDPR leaders Rumiantsev and Obolenskii addressed the RPR's founding congress with calls for a merger, an idea endorsed by 51 percent of the delegates. Consequently, a joint RPR-SDPR commission has been created to work out the terms of a union, and a new congress at which it will be consummated has been projected for February 1991.[46] Given what each side could bring to such a merger (the SDPR has some leaders of prominence in both Russia and the USSR, as well as a relatively well developed party infrastructure; the RPR, on the other hand, has perhaps the greatest legislative presence among all the new parties, with ten deputies in the USSR Congress of People's Deputies, sixty in the Russian parliament, and fifty in the Moscow City Soviet),[47] their combination into a single party would represent a serious political force and a great stride in party formation on the democratic left.

The Democratic Party of Russia

As if to circumvent the minefield of party ideology and its attendant squabbling over "correct" policies, the leaders of the Democratic Party of Russia (DPR) explained at an organizational meeting held in preparation for a founding congress that theirs would be a "parliamentary party oriented to the real needs of the people."[48] Toward that end, the structure adopted for the DPR at its first congress in late May 1990 made small provision for internal party machinery and instructed its members, who had been elected to soviets at all levels, to form factions responsible primarily to their constituents.[49] Moreover, the DPR purposefully organized itself as an umbrella party that other groups could enter as "collective members" (to date the writers' association April, the Memorial society, and the servicemen's union, Shield, have done so), while it maintains considerable space for internal factions and ensures their representation on its central bodies.[50] Having corked the divisive genie of ideological contention, however, schism of another sort struck the DPR's founding congress: Marina Sal'e of Leningrad's Popular Front and Lev Ponomarev of the Moscow Voters' Association walked out with the bulk of their supporters when their proposal for a multiple presidency (to which they expected to be elected) was rejected in favor of a single president, a post all knew would be occupied by the DPR's prime mover, Nikolai Travkin.[51]

Travkin has been a key figure in the IRDG, as have other DPR leaders such as Iurii Afanas'ev and Arkadii Murashev, and has established a national reputation as a capable organizer untainted by past association with political work within the Communist Party or the long-winded ways of the intelligentsia.[52] His stature is such that the DPR is commonly referred to as "the party of Travkin." Yet Travkin's history, and that of other DPR leaders such as Iurii Afanas'ev and Georgii Khatsenkov, illustrates a deeper affinity with many of their counterparts in the RPR and tends to account for some otherwise inexplicable aspects of the party that colloquially bears his name.

Many of the leaders in each of these new parties had been prominent communists who at the same time exercised little if any real influence within the CPSU. Just as Shostakovskii had been rector of Moscow's Higher Party School, Travkin had been among the brightest pupils there and for a while had held a seat on the Bureau of the Moscow Regional Party Committee. Similarly, Afanas'ev, director of Moscow's Institute of Historical Archives, had earlier been within the inner circle of the Democratic Platform, while Khatsenkov came to the DPR directly from his position as consultant to the CPSU's Central Committee.[53] It is perhaps this personal element, this urge to settle accounts with their own prior associations with the Communist Party, that explains both the strident anticommunism of the DPR's leaders and their tendency to replicate certain patterns of communist thinking, albeit in inverted form. With respect to the former, the DPR has structured itself so as to accommodate nearly all manner of diverse political tendencies in hopes of becoming a coalition party of all democratic forces. Equally, it has repeatedly offered to enter into coalitions with other parties.[54] Yet it has announced its intention of eschewing all cooperation with members of the Communist Party regardless of situation and circumstance. Perhaps here its otherwise pragmatic leaders are rather dogmatically washing their hands of their own communist past.[55]

Regarding the second side of this question--the tendency to replicate communist forms of thinking in inverted fashion--the DPR's program serves as a case in point. Not only is the content of this program, with its emphasis on "equal opportunity in a free market system," a flat tax on profit, and the absence of provision for assistance to the unemployed, suggestive of communist shibboleths turned inside-out,[56] but this abstract project of a free market society is distinctly reminiscent of equivalent communist constructs regarding the "radiant future" toward which it claimed to be leading society. In either case, the projection of an idealized tomorrow would seem to bulk larger than a responsive attitude toward the concrete demands and aspirations of actual people today.

At the moment the DPR is considered the leading, and perhaps only "serious," new party on the Russian scene by a number of well-informed observers.[57] It claims 80,000 individual members[58] and hundreds of thousands more who are affiliated with organizations holding collective membership in it.[59] Due to the largess of one of its co-vice chairpersons (chess champion Garii Kasparov, who is said to have donated some 12 million dollars to the party),[60] the DPR has been able to publish a 16-page monthly newspaper in editions of one million whose print quality rivals or surpasses that of its Communist Party counterparts. With the appearance of its third issue in September 1990, however, the DPR's official organ, *Demokraticheskaia Rossiia*, announced that henceforth it would no longer be published by the DPR but by the "union of democratic forces."[61] This statement recorded the fact that the DPR had submerged itself in a comprehensive coalition with the Democratic Platform and the SDPR, a development that we return to below in our discussion of tendencies in the system pushing away from party formation and toward continuation of movement politics.

Minor Parties on the Democratic Left

Immediately to the right of the parties thus far considered buzzes a swarm of smaller groups, nearly all of which bear the appellation "political party." They are of little concern to us as organizations that appear to be developing in the direction of genuine parties, but they intersect our topic nonetheless. Not only do their brief histories reveal a great deal about our principal interest--the *process* of party formation--but their aim to occupy roughly the same political niche as that sought by the RPR, the SDPR, and especially the DPR involves them directly in the formation and development of those parties as well. A number of these minor parties--the People's Constitutional Party, the A.D. Sakharov Union of Democratic Forces, and others--seem to find their only significance in a "coalition" maneuver in which they have been participating with the Gorbachev government. We return to them, therefore, in the following section of this chapter. Others, while claiming a more substantial membership, have remained but diminutive versions of the DPR. This point would apply to the Free Democratic Party of Russia, which formed around the Sal'e/Ponomarev group that walked out of DPR's founding congress over the issue of Travkin's leadership,[62] as well as to the Democratic Party, inaugurated some six months prior to the founding of the DPR but rancorously sundered at its second congress in early October 1990.[63]

Two other political tendencies, however, have attempted to distinguish themselves from the DPR. One, which emerged from a union of the informal group "Civic Dignity" and "the democratic faction" of the Moscow Popular Front in October 1989, sought to anchor its identity in Russia's pre-revolutionary political heritage and took for itself the name Constitutional Democrats (or "Kadets"). Although their program in no way differentiates them from liberal democrats,[64] the Kadets have stubbornly maintained that the principles of constitutional democracy are not identical with those of liberal democracy. Indeed, this issue of identity has been so potent for the Kadets that it split the party at its founding congress. At present, two Kadet parties exist, the Party of Constitutional Democrats and the Constitutional Democratic Party, each accusing the other of a lack of understanding of the principles of constitutional democracy.[65] While the latter "splinter" group has been joined by two prominent deputies in Russia's parliament, the former, without members in legislatures at any level, has steadfastly rebuffed efforts to reunite the constitutional democrats.[66]

The last of the minor parties on the democratic left that might merit a word would be the Liberal Democratic Party of the Soviet Union (LDP), which officially formed in March 1990 out of splinters from the Kadets, the Democratic Union, and others.[67] The LDP's membership has been purported by its leaders to range from 3,000 to 500,000,[68] but even the 3,000 figure would seem highly doubtful.[69] The LDP's program has been adopted wholesale from that initially penned by its leader, Vladimir Zhirinovskii, for another "social democratic" party that foundered and eventually collapsed.[70] Its primary concerns have been to restore the country's pre-revolutionary administrative system, with Russian as the single, officially recognized language[71] (thus seeking to dilute if not erase non-Russian national identities), and to establish a capitalist economy.[72] The freedom of opportunity that it has preached has seemed to have been liberally practiced by Zhirinovskii, who has frequently spoken at rallies of the fascist organization Pamiat',[73] and who was himself expelled from the LDP in October 1990 for collaboration with the KGB.[74] Counter-expulsions followed, resulting in a situation in which two of the same parties--in this case the Liberal Democratic Party led by K. Krivonosov and V. Bogachev, and a Liberal Democratic Party of the Soviet Union led by Zhirinovskii--have taken the place of one.[75]

From Parties Back to Movement?

Together with a number of other--not always savory--political characters, Zhirinovskii seems to have been instrumental in the organization of the "Russian Democratic Forum," a coalition formed on 23 September 1990 by some twenty-six political parties and organizations distinguished by their small memberships, near-complete absence in the legislatures of the USSR, and, not coincidentally it would appear, the good rapport they have come to enjoy with Gorbachev's government.[76] Together with "Soiuz"--the right-wing legislative faction in the Congress of People's Deputies whose patron seems to be Egor Ligachev--most of the Russian Democratic Forum reconstituted itself as the "Centrist Bloc" and entered into negotiations with Supreme Soviet chairman A.I. Luk'ianov and then prime minister N.I. Ryzhkov for the purpose of forming a "coalition government of national accord."[77] At least in the minds of the leaders of those parties on the democratic left that indeed have formed an opposition movement substantial enough to pose a concern to the present Soviet authorities, this Centrist Bloc is comprised exclusively of "parties" that have been invented by or have become the tools of the KGB or the Central Committee of the CPSU.[78] Accordingly, it would appear that the relative success of the SDPR, the DPR, the RPR, and others in developing an opposition movement has accounted for this ploy on the part of the current Soviet leadership to test the waters of (bogus) coalition. And with no bargain struck by January 1990, the Centrist Bloc has all but disappeared from the political map, abandoned by all but two of its constituent organizations.[79]

The majority of those leaders and groups who would found separate parties in the spring of 1990 had participated in winter election campaigns under the broad banner of "Democratic Russia," whose candidates swept to power in Moscow, Leningrad, and Sverdlovsk while emerging in the Congress of People's Deputies of the Russian Republic as the largest parliamentary faction.[80] The experience of governing, however, has been mixed. On the one hand, an analysis of voting patterns in the first Congress of People's Deputies of the Russian Republic has disclosed a remarkable cohesion within each of the legislature's two main factions--Democratic Russia, primarily composed of those not occupying important party or state offices, and "Communists of Russia," represented in the main by the *nomenklatura*.[81] On the other hand, however, Democratic Russia's cohesive voting patterns on such matters as the organization of the legislature or demands for the resignation of the USSR's government have frequently disassembled when matters that would divide socialists, liberals, and others have been on the table.[82]   Moreover, even if Democratic Russia were able to contain the disparate tendencies within it, its development into a parliamentary party would still be impeded by the very weakness of these legislatures themselves. The maintenance of the vertical line of authority in administration--represented above all by centralized ministries' continued use of the *nomenklatura* system of appointing officials at lower levels[83]--has meant that those formally charged to implement the laws issued by a given legislature can often ignore this duty and suffer no unpleasant consequences in so doing. In Moscow and Leningrad, although a rapprochement had been attempted with the old officials whereby effectively all were retained in their posts by the newly governing "democratic forces" and working relations with communist leaders were eagerly sought, the city soviets have appeared almost helpless to command the very administrative machinery that is formally responsible to them.[84] As Moscow mayor Gavriil Popov has lamented: "That democrats are in power does not mean that they wield any power. I ought to tell my voters honestly that I essentially have no real power. I don't command anything. I cannot provide a building, I can't ensure protection for privately run shops. I can't do a lot of things."[85]

As a consequence of their frustrations with attempts to exercise genuine power, those on the democratic left seem headed at the moment for a return to a movement form of political activity. United in opposition to what they regard as the totalitarian structure of the prevailing political order--if not on the issue of what structure should be built to replace it--1,700 left democrats (representing the DPR, SDPR, RPR, the Peasant Party of Russia, the Party of Free Labor, and others) convened a congress in Moscow on 21-22 October 1990, to inaugurate officially Democratic Russia as an opposition movement whose goals have been to pressure the CPSU into surrendering power and permitting genuine and free national elections in 1991.[86]

Yet this movement is itself beset by serious internal divisions, not the least of which is the fact that, unlike the situation faced by Democratic Russia during the halcyon days of its successes in the March 1990 elections, political parties now exist. Accordingly, political action now has alternative channels to pursue, and political ambition, which once had contributed so much energy to the democratic movement, now expresses itself in ways not always conducive to unity. Political ambition is, of course, a "normal" element in party politics. Yet the adjective "normal" here would presuppose the existence of structures within which separate ambitions could be modified, harmonized, and conjoined, thus improving chances for collective action. With respect to the conditions faced by Russia's democratic left, such structures--a modicum of political institutionalization and political culture, and a stock of material resources (especially jobs, both in and out of government) that political leaders can deploy to cement bargains and bolster coalitions--are only beginning to develop. As a consequence, political ambitions appear to express themselves in especially divisive ways, perhaps accounting for much of the fragmentation that we have observed in the process of party formation hitherto.[87]

The expression of political ambition within the conditions described here also sheds some light on the current stage of political organizing, falling as it does between the stools of forming parties and (re)building a democratic movement. For instance, a number of luminaries on the democratic left--Yeltsin, Popov, Afanas'ev and others--either had failed to attend, or had kept entirely silent at, Democratic Russia's founding congress.[88] Moreover, only some 40 out of 178 of the deputies of the Moscow City Soviet who have registered as members of Democratic Russia had managed to put in an appearance at this gathering.[89] Given the importance of this event for the democratic movement and, relatedly, for the parties that comprise it, truancies of this magnitude are difficult to explain unless it is the case that many of those concerned perceive their status as inversely proportional to accessibility. Similarly, Travkin, who was reported to have aspirations for the Russian presidency, participated in the congress reluctantly (and in response to the overwhelming sentiment in favor of Democratic Russia expressed by members of his party) since Democratic Russia would almost surely back Boris Yeltsin in the presidential election.[90] At the Kharkov meeting (26-27 January 1991) inaugurated by the RPR, the United Democratic Party of Belorussia, and the Ukraine's Party of Democratic Rebirth, where representatives of some thirty parties and movements from across the USSR assembled to coordinate non-violent actions aimed at bringing down the Communist regime, Travkin withdrew the DPR from formal participation.[91] His party's role within Democratic Russia may, then, prove to differ from that of the RPR and the SDPR, whose possible merger would mean that pooled membership would place them in a stronger position to jockey for influence inside the larger movement, one that already is represented by one-third of the deputies to soviets at all levels in the RSFSR.

These and a number of similar instances of internal politicking at present[92] appear both to express and to reinforce a situation in which the forces on the democratic left appear suspended between parties and movement. The task of dislodging the CPSU from power understandably dominates their current agenda, as evinced by the purely negative content of the speeches delivered at the Kharkov meeting--summed up by one observer as: " 'No' to the policies of the central government and 'no' to the empire."[93] Should the movement prove victorious in this effort, it will have established a necessary, but by no means sufficient, condition for the development of a "normal" party system in Russia.

Notes

This study was funded in part by a grant from the International Research and Exchanges Board.

1. Maria Markus, "Overt and Covert Modes of Legitimation in Communist States," in T.H. Rigby and F. Feher, eds., *Political Legitimation in Communist States* (New York: St. Martin's Press, 1989), pp. 82-93; Rainer Paris, "Class Structure and Legitimatory Public Sphere," *New German Critique*, 6 (1975), pp. 89-105; Michael E. Urban, "From Chernenko to Gorbachev: A Repoliticization of Official Soviet Discourse?" *Soviet Union*, 13, no. 2 (1986), pp. 131-61; idem, "Conceptualizing Political Power in the USSR: Patterns of Binding and Bonding," *Studies in Comparative Communism*, 18 (Winter 1985), pp. 207-26.

2. Robert C. Tucker, *Political Culture and Leadership in Soviet Russia* (New York: Norton, 1987), pp. 3-10.

3. See my "Popular Fronts and 'Informals,' " *Detente*, no. 14 (1989), pp. 3-8; Vladimir Brodkin, "Revolution from Below: Informal Political Associations in Russia 1988-1989," *Soviet Studies*, 4, no. 2 (April 1990), pp. 233-57; A.V. Gromov and O.S. Kuzin, *Neformaly: Kto Est' Kto?* (Moscow: Mysl', 1990); V.N. Berezovskii and N.I. Krotov, eds., *Neformalnaia Rossiia* (Moscow: Molodaia gvardiia, 1990); Vera Tola, *The USSR's Emerging Multiparty System* (New York, Praeger, 1990).

4. See the series of articles by Sergei Mitrokhin: "Sensatsiia, kotoruiu zhdali," *Khronograf*, no. 4 (18 May 1988), pp. 1-3; "Den' vtoroi: Demokratiia i MVD," ibid. no. 5 (25 May 1990), pp. 2-3; "Den' tretii: Est' takaia partiia!" ibid., pp. 1-7.

5. Mikhail Maliutin, "Za kem poidut massy," *Narodnyi deputat*, no. 5 (1990), pp. 40-42.

6. P. Anatol'ev, "Raspad DS, Raspad KPSS," *Novaia zhizn'*, no. 15 (June 1990), p. 2.

7. Irena Fomicheva, "Chas udachnykh reshenii," *Soiuz*, no. 4 (22-28 January 1990), p. 17.

8. Aleksandr Verkhovskii, "Problema radikalizma vchera i zavtra," *Panorama* (Moscow), no. 10 (September 1990), p. 4.

9. Fomicheva, "Chas udachnykh reshenii."

10. Alexei Levinson, "Predictable Surprises," *Moscow News*, no. 10 (18-25 March

1990), p. 4.

11. I am indebted to Graeme Gill for this observation.

12. See his remarks in Michael E. Urban (moderator), "The Soviet Multi-Party System: A Moscow Roundtable," *Russia and the World*, no. 18 (1990), pp. 1-6.

13. Simon Kordonsky, "Too Much Ado," *Moscow News*, no. 28 (22-29 July 1990), p. 9; Aleksandr Verkhovskii's interview with Polish Senator Zbigniew Romaszewski, "Demokratiia ponimaetsia u Vas ochen' abstraktno," *Panorama*, no. 12 (October 1990), p. 4.

14. V. Kamarovskii and V. Korniak, "Kak nastroen izbiratel'," *Izvestiia* (30 January 1990); M. Mikhaleva and L. Morozova report that 70 percent of successful candidates in 1990 scored at the upper end of a survey questionnaire concerning knowledge of local issues. See their "Pobedil tot, kto luchshe gotovitsia," *Narodnyi deputat*, no. 7 (1990), p. 36. On the local factor in the 1989 elections, see Michael E. Urban, *More Power to the Soviets: The Democratic Revolution in the USSR* (Brookfield, VT: Edward Elgar, 1990), pp. 107-9.

15. Pavel Gutiontov, "Kakoi vybor my sdelali," *Izvestiia* (6 April 1990).

16. Interview with Dmitrii Levchik (19 October 1990).

17. On the formation of the IRDG, see Urban, *More Power to the Soviets*, pp. 131-34; Elizabeth Teague, "Gorbachev Criticizes Leaders of Parliamentary Group," *Radio Liberty Report on the USSR*, RL 489/89 (19 October 1989), pp. 1-5. Andrei Vasilevskii has provided a useful analysis of IRDG members and leaders in his "Demokraty v parlamente," *Panorama*, no. 8 (September 1989), p. 6; IRDG member Valentin Logunov has recorded the first year of the group's remarkable history in his "Mezhregional'naia deputatskaia gruppa: god v oppozitsii," *Narodnyi deputat*, no. 12 (1990), pp. 19-27.

18. Quoted in A. Ivanov, "Rassudit zhizn'," *Sovety narodnykh deputatov*, no. 9 (1989), p. 31.

19. Aleksandr Verkhovskii, "Na puti k edinoi oppositsii," *Panorama*, no. 10 (October 1989), p. 1.

20. This was noted by IRDG leader Gavriil Popov in his "Deputy Pluralism," *Moscow News*, no. 1 (1-7 January 1990), p. 6.

21. Michael E. Urban and John McClure, "Discourse, Ideology and Party Formation on the Democratic Left in the USSR," in Michael E. Urban, ed., *Ideology and System Change in the Soviet Union and Eastern Europe* (London: Macmillan, forthcoming).

22. V. Levichev, "Anatomiia neformal'nogo dvizheniia," *Izvestiia TsK KPSS*, no. 4 (April 1990), p. 153.

23. Valentin Davidov, "Neformal'noe dvizhenie: voprosov bol'she chem otvetov," *Soiuz*, no. 20 (May 1990), p. 9.

24. Vladimir Pribylovskii, "Esdeki," *Panorama*, no. 8 (September 1989), pp. 1-2.

25. Idem, "Samizdat i novye partii"; Vadim Lifshits, "Mysly posle s"ezda," *Esdek*, no. 6 (April-May 1990), p. 6.

26. *Al'ternativa*, no. 1 (30 May-12 June 1990), p. 2.

27. Ibid., pp. 2, 4.

28. "V neskol'ko strok," *Al'ternativa*, no. 3 (September 1990), p. 1.

29. "Social Democrats Adopt a Program," *Moscow News*, no. 44 (11-18 November 1990), p. 2.

30. "Situatsiia v strane," *Al'ternativa*, no. 3 (September 1990), pp. 1-2. A remarkably similar analysis of this struggle has been offered by Tat'iana Zaslavskaia in an interview given to the independent press agency Interfax: "Situatsiia chrezvychaino slozhnaia," *Izvestiia* (17 December 1990).

31. *Panorama*, no. 12 (October 1990), p. 1.

32. Iu. Gladysh, "Ot partiinogo kluba k 'Demokraticheskoi platforme,' " *Narodnyi deputat*, no. 6 (1990), pp. 59-60.

33. Julia Wishnevsky and Elizabeth Teague, " 'Democratic Platform' Created in CPSU," excerpted from *Report on the USSR* (2 February 1990) in *World Peace Report*, 6 (March 1990), pp. 1-2.

34. See the statements of its leaders: Viacheslav Shostakovskii, "Partapparat: imitatsiia perestroiki," *Kar'era* (March 1990), p. 3; idem, "Esli v KPSS ne proizoidet peremen, razmezhevanie neizbezhno," *Soiuz*, no. 19 (May 1990), pp. 8-9; V.N. Lysenko in "Est mnenie," *Izvestiia* (20 June 1990).

35. Vladimir Lysenko, "Reflections on the Eve," *Moscow News*, no. 24 (24 June-1 July 1990), p. 4; Stepan Troyan, "A Congress or a Party Apparat Conference?" ibid., pp. 8-9.

36. *Pravda* (11 April 1990). On the background behind the formulation of this letter, see Georgii Khatsenkov, "A Purge," *Moscow News*, no. 18 (13-20 May 1990), p. 7.

37. On the debates within the Democratic Platform that led to its decision to leave the CPSU, see: V. Orlov and I. Iakimov, "For Consolidation But Not with the Partocracy," *Moscow News*, no. 17 (6-13 May 1990), p. 6; Aleksander Mekhanik, "The Last Frontier of the Democratic Platform," ibid., no. 22 (10-17 June 1990), p. 6; Pavel Gutiontov, "Demokraty pred"iavliaiut trebovaniia," *Izvestiia* (10 June 1990). The minimum conditions for remaining in the CPSU that were not met at the twenty-eighth congress included "converting the [CPSU's] antidemocratic totalitarian structure opposed to the people into a democratic political party . . . depolitization of state institutions, the KGB, [the Ministry of Internal Affairs], the courts and procurators . . . [and ending] the CPSU's monopoly on the means of mass information." These were listed in the Democratic Platform's resolution on leaving the Communist Party, "Zaiavlenie deputatov-storonnikov Demplatformy," *Novaia Sovetskaia rech'*, no. 2 (August 1990), p. 3.

38. Dawn Mann, "Cracks in the Monolith," *Radio Liberty Research Reports*, RL 257/90 (10 June 1990), p. 4.

39. Viktor Sadikov, "Nazad k dvoemysliiu?" *Soiuz*, no. 29 (July 1990), p. 3.

40. "Zaiavlenie Demokraticheskoi platformi" (14 July 1990).

41. I queried two members of the Democratic Platform's organizing committee on this matter. In each case, my remarks--to the effect that this formulation simply repeats the Leninist mistake of assuming some higher consciousness on the part of party leaders and relegating the expressed interests of the population to secondary

status--were met with smiles, agreement, and the reply that "You must understand who we are; these are our stereotypes."

42. Sergei Mulin, "Mensheviks Turn Republican. Only for Three Months?" *Moscow News*, no. 47 (2-9 December 1990), p. 6; P. Gutiontov, "Budet novaia partiia," *Izvestiia* (18 November 1990).

43. Interviews with Viacheslav Igrunov (9 July 1990) and Mikhail Maliutin (13 July 1990). These divisions were readily apparent at Democratic Platform's organizing meeting (14-15 July 1990) which set it on the course toward becoming an independent party.

44. Viacheslav Shostakovskii, interviewed by Nikolai Kas'ianov, "Respublikantsy vykhodiat na politicheskuiu arenu," *Soiuz*, no. 47 (November 1990), p. 5.

45. Ibid.

46. Mulin, "Mensheviks Turn Republican."

47. Gutiontov, "Budet novaia partiia."

48. Valerii Zaikin, "DPR--Partiia bez apparata," *Izvestiia* (8 May 1990).

49. V.F. Levichev and A.A. Neliubin, "Novye obshchestvenno-politicheskie organizatsii, partii i dvizheniia," *Izvestiia TsK KPSS*, no. 8 (1990), pp. 153-54.

50. Dmitrii Miknev, "Democratic Party of Russia," *Moscow News*, no. 21 (3-10 June 1990), p. 6.

51. Andrei Vasil'evskii, "Metamorfozy partii Travkina," *Panorama*, no. 6 (June 1990), pp. 1-2.

52. For a sketch of Travkin's background, see Natal'ia Iraminova, "Hero of Our Time," *Moscow News*, no. 34 (2-9 September 1990), p. 16.

53. In October 1990, Khatsenkov was censured for discrediting the DPR and resigned his post as vice-chairperson. *Moscow News*, no. 42 (28 October-4 November 1990), p. 2.

54. "Prilozhenie k vypusku No. 1," *Demokraticheskaia Rossiia*, no. 1 (July 1990), pp. 2-6.

55. This was noted in an interview with Il'ia Kudriavtsev (6 July 1990).

56. See the program enunciated in "Prilozhenie k vypusku No. 1," pp. 3-4.

57. Interviews with Il'ia Kudriavtsev (6 July 1990), Anatolii Papp (6 July 1990), and Vladimir Pribylovskii (16 June 1990).

58. *Moscow News*, no. 42 (28 October-4 November 1990), p. 2.

59. Interview given to B. Popov by Aleksei Mazur in *Novaia zhizn'*, no. 16 (July 1990).

60. Ibid.; Vladimir Pribylovskii, "Zakrytoe soveshchanie 'levykh,' " *Panorama*, no. 9 (August 1990), p. 8.

61. *Demokraticheskaia Rossiia*, no. 3 (September 1990), p. 1.

62. Vladimir Reikin, "Obshchestvo chistykh pelenok," *Panorama*, no. 9 (August 1990), p. 5.

63. Levichev/Neliubin, "Novye obshchestvenno-politicheskie organizatsii . . . ," pp. 152-53; Dmitrii Khrapovitskii, "Partii nachinayut i . . .," *Soiuz*, no. 17 (April 1990), p. 19. On the Democratic Party's second congress, at which its leader, Lev Ybozhko, expelled one sizable faction (which retained the name, Democratic Party) and

renamed his followers the Conservative Party of the Soviet Union, see Andrei Romashevskii, "Po zakonam partogeneza," *Panorama*, no. 13 (December 1990), p. 8.

64. The Manifesto of the Party of Constitutional Democrats can be found in their newspaper, *Grazhdanskoe dostoinstvo*, no. 21 (June 1990), p. 2.

65. Pribylovskii, "Samizdat i novye partii," pp. 6-7; Levichev and Nelyubin, "Novye obshchestvenno-politicheski organizatsii," pp. 148-50; Ol'ga Golenkina, "Zapiski na mandatakh," *Grazhdanskoe dostoinstvo*, no. 21 (June 1990), p. 3.

66. "V mire Kadetov," *Panorama*, no. 12 (October 1990), p. 6.

67. Pribylovskii, "Samizdat i novye partii," p. 6.

68. Varying estimates of party membership, going from the low end to the high one, can be found in: "Sozdana liberal'no-demokraticheskaia partiia," *Izvestiia* (1 April 1990); Sergei Gryzunov et al., "Novye partii," *Soiuz*, no. 24 (June 1990), p. 10; Natal'ia Iziumova's interview with Vladimir Zhirinovskii, "LDP Set to Hold Congress in Kremlin," *Moscow News* (6-13 May 1990), p. 7.

69. For instance, the 250 "delegates" attending the LDP's first congress joined the party minutes before receiving their delegate credentials. "Coup or Operetta?" *Moscow News*, no. 45 (18-25 November 1990), p. 6.

70. Stepan Orlov and Vadim Prokhorov, "Pervoaprel'skia partiia," *Panorama*, no. 7 (July 1990), p. 5.

71. Ibid.

72. Valentin Davydov, "Neformal'noe dvizhenie," p. 8.

73. Orlov and Prokhorov, "Pervoaprel'skia partiia."

74. "Coup or Operetta?"

75. Vladimir Pribylovskii, "Po zakonam partogeneza," *Panorama*, no. 13 (December 1990), p. 8.

76. Ibid.; S"ezd Rossiiskogo demokraticheskogo foruma," *Panorama*, no. 12 (October 1990), p. 7; Vladimir Pribylovskii, "Kem nas pugaet TASS," ibid., no. 13 (December 1990), pp. 7-8.

77. "Coup or Operetta?"; G. Alimov, "A. Luk'ianov; 'My otkryty dlia dialoga,' " *Izvestiia* (2 November 1990).

78. "Demokraticheskie sily o perspektivakh demokraticheskogo razvitiia," *Demokraticheskaia Rossiia*, no. 3 (September 1990), p. 4

79. "A est' li tsentriskii blok?" *Izvestiia* (29 March 1991).

80. Dmitrii Ostalskii, "Is a Coalition Possible?" *Moscow News*, no. 24 (24 June-1 July 1990), p. 4; Aleksandr Davydov, "V gorsovete formiruiutsia fraktsii," *Izvestiia* (27 March 1990).

81. L. Efimova, A. Sobianin, and D. Iur'ev, "K voprosu ob antagonizme" (mimeo; Moscow: Voters' Club, Academy of Sciences USSR, July 1990).

82. A. Dikhtar', "Na osnove edineniia," *Narodnyi deputat*, no. 8 (1990), pp. 22-24; O. Belikova, "Trudnaia vesna Lensoveta," ibid., pp. 25-28.

83. Eduard Cherny, "The Minister Ignores the USSR Constitution," *Moscow News*, no. 41 (21-28 October 1990), p. 6.

84. Gavriil Popov, in the interview given to Valerii Vizhutovich, "Vkus vlasti," *Izvestiia* (28 June 1990), has claimed that the inexperience of the left democrats with

the exercise of power made alliance with the old functionaries and their patrons in the Communist Party imperative. A. Savel'ev, a deputy on the Moscow City Soviet and a member of the Social Democratic Party of Russia, regards Popov's strategy--in which the mayor works with the old officials while bypassing the legislators entirely--as the reason why the soviet's power, and the mayor's along with it, has been nil. See his "Mossovet: Vzgliad iznutri," *Al'ternativa*, no. 3 (September 1990), p. 2.

85. Gavriil Popov, interviewed by Yegor Yakovlev, "The Times are Getting Tougher," *Moscow News*, no. 42 (28 October-4 November 1990), p. 7. For a description of this same problem in Leningrad, see the interview given to Sergei Kraiukhin by Anatolii Sobchak, "Ia ishchu v Lensovete edinomishlennikov," *Soiuz*, no. 49 (December 1990), p. 5.

86. Arkadii Murashev and Evgenii Sevast'ianov interviewed by Valerii Platonov, "Kurs Demokraticheskoi Rossii," *Izvestiia* (5 October 1990); Aleksandr Davydov, " 'Demokraticheskaia Rossia' gotovitsia k s"ezdu," *Izvestiia* (13 October 1990). The organizational form taken by Democratic Russia is clearly one of a coalition movement, based on no general political program other than removing the CPSU from power, and affording guaranteed autonomy in strategy and tactics for all member organizations. See Davydov, " 'Demokraticheskaia Rossiia.' "

87. For an analysis of one case--the founding of the SDPR--in which divisive ambitions were with some success contained, see N. Solianik, "Pomen'she by ambitsii," *Narodnyi deputat*, no. 12 (1990), pp. 75-77.

88. Elena Bonner, "Trevoga moia--ot kakogo-to ranee nebyvalogo chuvstva razryva," *Soiuz*, no. 47 (November 1990), p. 15.

89. Natal'ia Davydova, "Not Everybody Takes a Break," *Moscow News*, no. 50 (23-30 December 1990), p. 4.

90. Andrei Vasil'evskii, "Demokraty: Ob"edinenie i razmezhevaniia," *Panorama*, no. 13 (December 1990), p. 3.

91. Sergei Tsikora, "Gotovitsia Demokraticheskoi Kongress, *Izvestiia* (4 December 1990); O. Medvedev, "Demokraticheskii Kongress v Kharkove," *Izvestiia* (28 January 1991).

92. Vasil'cvskii, "Demokraty," p. 3.

93. Vladimir Orlov, "Democratic Congress: Future Prospects," *Moscow News*, no. 5 (3-10 February 1991), p. 5.

THE FUNCTIONING OF THE
NEW SUPREME SOVIET

8

LEGISLATIVE-EXECUTIVE RELATIONS IN THE NEW SOVIET POLITICAL ORDER

Eugene Huskey

Legislatures are peculiar institutions even in the most democratic polities. They derive their authority from society yet their power is contingent on the forbearance of the executive. A study of a national legislature cannot limit itself, therefore, to analysis of the internal politics and procedures of the assembly or the linkages between the legislature and society. It must address the effects of legislative deliberation, rule-making, and oversight on the executive, which commands the machinery of state. Responding to Aristotle's claim that a polity should be ruled by laws, Hobbes reminds us that the words and paper of the assembly only take effect when they are executed by men.[1]

The tension between legislative and executive power has been a staple of the liberal democratic order. To assure the accountability of the state to society, legislatures in the West have struggled over the centuries to influence and restrain the power of the executive.[2] For the Bolsheviks, however, this conflict between legislature and executive was not a universal principle of modern government but a vestige from the bourgeois order, a contradiction to be overcome in a socialist revolution. Where capitalism subordinated the parliamentary "talking shop" to the class-aligned executive, socialism in Russia promised to combine legislative and executive functions in a new "working parliament," the soviets.[3] Thus, Lenin's slogan "All Power to the Soviets," advanced in April 1917, was more than a tactical assault on the Provisional Government. It was also a summons to unite permanently the diverse functions of state into a single institution.

The Leninist vision of a "working parliament" did not accord, however, with the demands of revolutionary rule or with Bolshevik intolerance of opposition and open debate. Once in power, the revolutionary leadership quickly abandoned attempts to govern through the unwieldy and unreliable soviets. Instead of channeling all power to the soviets it siphoned all power from the soviets and into a separate executive hierarchy (the Sovnarkom, later renamed the Council of Ministers) and the professional apparatus of the Communist Party.[4] By the mid-1930s, the soviets were functioning as a caricature of what Lenin considered the lifeless legislatures of capitalist societies. Selected by a ruling bureaucratic class and not by the people, the soviets assembled only long enough each session to give unanimous approval to policies and laws advanced by the party and the government. Thus, the Soviet political leadership overcame the tension between legislative and executive power not by fusing government and parliament but by completely emasculating the soviets as legislative institutions.

As the democratization campaign of Gorbachev breathed new life into the soviets at the end of the 1980s, it rekindled tensions between legislature and executive. In so doing, it raised an array of elementary questions about the realignment of power and responsibility in the Soviet political system. What is the division of labor between legislature and executive in the new Soviet political order?[5] How effective is the Soviet parliament in restraining the executive? What means does it use to achieve that end? How have the mounting crises of power and authority in the USSR shaped the development of legislative-executive relations? To assess these and related questions, this chapter examines three traditional sources of legislative power as they developed in the first two years of the new Soviet parliament (June 1989-January 1991). These legislative prerogatives are the confirmation of executive personnel, law-making, and the oversight of executive agencies.

Legislative Powers over Executive Appointments

In European parliamentary systems, the power of the legislature rests most directly on its ability to approve and remove a government. The leading members of the government come from parliament and rule at the pleasure of parliament. Subject continuously to immediate recall by the legislature, the executive must offer policies and personnel that can sustain a parliamentary majority and hence the support of society.

In its formal rules, the Soviet state system followed the parliamentary model. Yet the traditional patronage monopoly enjoyed by the Soviet Communist Party apparatus eliminated the accountability of government to parliament, which is at the core of the liberal democratic order. Governments were made and unmade not in parliament but in the party. This patronage monopoly of the Communist Party ended, however, in the spring of 1989, when competitive elections in many districts returned legislators who refused to accede to party diktat. Characterized by open debate, weakened party discipline, and a politically diverse body of deputies, the new parliament[6] exercised its long-dormant prerogative of approving a government. For the first time in Soviet history, the parliament vigorously challenged, and in some cases rejected, personnel nominated for the country's leading executive posts.

The new parliament had two sets of candidates for executive offices to consider when it assembled for its initial session in June 1989. The first group, nominated by the chair of the USSR Supreme Soviet, Mikhail S. Gorbachev, included the leading figures of state--the prime minister (Nikolai I. Ryzhkov), the head of the People's Control Committee (Gennadii V. Kolbin), the chair of the USSR Supreme Court (Evgenii I. Smolentsev), the procurator-general of the USSR (Aleksandr Sukharev), and the chief state arbiter (Iurii S. Matveev). In nominating the incumbent Ryzhkov to the post of prime minister, Gorbachev admitted that while he alone had the constitutional authority to propose the candidate for head of government, "in view of the real position that the CPSU occupies in our society as the ruling party, consultations were held with the party Central Committee regarding the nomination."[7] Thus, while the party could no longer assure confirmation of its nominees,[8] it at least retained the power to veto candidates for high executive office.

Ryzhkov won confirmation handily from the 542-seat assembly (9 deputies voted against him and 31 abstained), but only after intense questioning from the floor.[9] More than thirty deputies directed questions at the prime minister or commented on his candidacy, which some regarded as sullied by "miscalculations" in economic policy. The parliament reserved its most serious criticism of the opening session, however, for the nominee to the People's Control Committee, Kolbin. Having led the powerful, though troubled, Communist Party of Kazakhstan for the preceding three years, Kolbin seemed an unlikely candidate for the unglamorous post of chair of the People's Control Committee. When asked by the deputies whether he would be willing to assume the new post, Kolbin replied that the Communist Party had made its decision to nominate him for the position and he would therefore accept it. This explicit statement of fealty to party over parliament troubled many deputies, including the historian Roy Medvedev, who sought to scuttle Kolbin's candidacy by nominating Boris Yeltsin for the position. Even after Yeltsin turned down the nomination and threw his support behind Kolbin, almost 20 percent of the deputies refused to support Kolbin's candidacy.[10]

Once the prime minister and the heads of free-standing legal institutions had been approved, the parliament turned to the confirmation of the ministers and other executive personnel who would comprise the new government. Nominated by the prime minister,[11] this second, and larger, group of candidates also stood for confirmation individually. Thus, instead of approving the government as a team, the Soviet legislature scrutinized separately government personnel and policy in each of the areas of ministerial competence. By examining candidates for high executive office individually, in the tradition of the United States Senate, the Soviet parliament was able to exercise a finer, more discriminating, and more pervasive influence on the formation of a government.[12]

Discussions of the candidates for executive office began in legislative committees amid much confusion about appropriate procedures for examining the nominees. While most candidates were examined by a single committee, others came before several committees, with one serving as the guiding committee for the nomination (*golovoi komitet*).[13] For example, the minister of health, Evgenii I. Chazov, appeared before committees on the family and ecology in addition to the joint Committee on Public Health. Within the committees, deputies struggled to define their role in the confirmation of executive personnel. The central issue was how much information to obtain before making a decision about a nominee. Where some deputies were satisfied with the brief official biographies distributed to the examining committees, many other deputies did not wish to recommend confirmation until the candidates had given detailed testimony before the committees about their political record and plans for their ministry.[14]

Judging by the published accounts of confirmation hearings, the more insistent deputies prevailed. The consideration of nominees in committee lasted three weeks, during which many committees subjected candidates to vigorous and lengthy questioning. Although the candidate for vice-chair of the Ministry for Social Questions, Aleksandra P. Biriukova, received the recommendation of the committee, the questioning of her was so hostile that Ryzhkov personally intervened at the hearing to demand greater respect for the aging former Politburo member. "After all, we're talking about a lady. Aleksandra Pavlovna is here and every word leaves its mark. Let's be kinder to one another."[15]

Very few nominees escaped what Ryzhkov called the "purgatory" of the committees.[16] Of the senior ministerial appointments, only Eduard A. Shevardnadze (Foreign Affairs) and Valentin S. Pavlov (Finance), passed parliament with a unanimous or near unanimous recommendation of the deputies. The committee hearings were especially difficult for Lira I. Rozenova, nominated to chair the State Committee on Prices. Only one member of the examining committee voted to approve her candidacy.[17] In all, eight of the 72 nominees for ministerial posts failed to win committee recommendation.[18] Moreover, the Committee on Legislation and Legality refused to recommend the Leningrad procurator, Aleksei D. Vasil'ev, for the post of first deputy procurator of the USSR, and Aleksandr M. Filatov, Sergei I. Gusev, and Robert G. Tikhomirnov as members of the USSR Supreme Court.[19] The most controversial appointments, therefore, were those to legal institutions, which had become a favorite target of popular and parliamentary criticism.

The committee decisions were not binding, however, on the prime minister or parliament. In submitting his final list of nominees to the full Supreme Soviet at the end of June 1989, Ryzhkov included several candidates rejected in committee as well as one new candidate advanced by the antireformist labor collective movement. He also excluded from the final list two nominees who had been approved in committee. These nominees were reform-oriented candidates for places on the military collegium of the USSR Supreme Court.[20]

The confirmation debates in the full Supreme Soviet illustrated the awkward coexistence of old and new politics in the USSR. In a dramatic departure from tradition, the head of the KGB, Vladimir A. Kriuchkov, came before the parliament to defend his candidacy and to respond to the many critical comments directed against the KGB. In his remarks, Kriuchkov offered an unprecedented statement on the functions and operation of his agency.[21] Likewise, the minister of defense, Dmitrii T. Iazov, appeared before the Supreme Soviet to answer pointed questions about the armed forces. In the interpellation of Iazov, the more insistent deputies behaved as Western parliamentarians. They sought to elicit new information about the activity of the ministry, to clarify the candidate's perception of the division of responsibility in military affairs between legislature and executive, and to receive assurances of his commitment to reform.[22]

Alongside these indications of a new parliamentary assertiveness were reminders of traditions of political deference and secrecy. The selection of ministers often followed what one observer called "Young Pioneer" logic. "Fellows, I know him. He's a good man!" (*Rebiata, ia ego znaiu--khoroshii muzhik!*).[23] At times one could hear cries from the floor: "Comrades, let's give Nikolai Ivanovich [Ryzhkov] a chance to form his own team!"[24] While Gorbachev generally refrained from using his post as head of state to support individual candidates, he threw aside protocol in the confirmation of the minister of defense. Gorbachev concluded the confirmation debate on Iazov with a vigorous speech in support of the defense minister. Although most of these debates reached a large and attentive national audience by television, on occasion coverage was suspended when the questioning of candidates raised volatile political issues. The most controversial appointments in this regard appear to have been nominees to the USSR Supreme Court and the USSR Procuracy.[25]

The consideration of Ryzhkov's nominees by the full Supreme Soviet resulted in a defeat for the prime minister in several portfolios. The parliament rejected nominees to head the Ministry of Rails, the Ministry of the Timber Industry, and the Foreign Economic Commission, even though candidates for the latter two posts had received committee recommendations. If the parliament in fact contained an "aggressively obedient majority," its loyalties lay elsewhere than with the prime minister. It was evident from both the committee and parliamentary debates that the Supreme Soviet in most instances was using its confirmation prerogative to express its displeasure with government policy in the minister's area of competence and not with the nominees themselves. A case in point was price policy. Echoing popular fear of rising prices, parliament refused to approve the promotion of Lira I. Rozenova from deputy chair to chair of the State Committee on Prices. Yet the chair of the State Committee on Prices, Valentin S. Pavlov, won confirmation easily as the new minister of finance.

Conservative and reformist legislators appear to have united to defeat Ryzhkov's nominees for what might be termed thankless posts, where ministerial performance was both unpopular and unlikely to improve. With the Ministry of Rails threatened by strikes and pilloried in the press, the parliament refused to confirm a new railroad minister. One deputy admitted that the nominee "was not to blame and probably should be elected . . . [but] we should make it understood that we are able to protect the people's interest from the department. I am going to vote against him."[26] Similarly, candidates failed to receive confirmation to head departments responsible for environmental degradation, such as the Water Resources and Timber Industry ministries. The newly created Environment Ministry was the target of such popular anger that Ryzhkov offered the post to four persons before he found someone--the only noncommunist in the government--willing to be nominated for the position.

Once the government was in place,[27] the confirmation power of parliament would be used sparingly until a new parliamentary election or a political crisis led to the formation of a new government. Such is the logic of parliamentary politics. During its subsequent sessions in 1989 and 1990, the Soviet parliament confirmed only a handful of nominees for vacant or newly vacated ministerial positions before being asked at the beginning of 1991 to review candidates for a new institution, the Cabinet of Ministers, discussed below. But while the confirmation prerogative was used only episodically, it established an important precedent of executive accountability to the legislature. Gorbachev reminded deputies in closing the initial session of the new Supreme Soviet that "for the first time in the entire post-Lenin period we have created a government each member of which must pass rigorous muster with the deputies."[28]

One must be cautious, however, in using the parliamentary confirmation of the government in 1989 as evidence of a fundamental and permanent realignment of executive-legislative relations. Executive power was broader than the Ryzhkov government, and therefore in restraining Ryzhkov and the government the parliament strengthened contending forces in the Soviet executive. Gorbachev and supporting elements in the party Central Committee apparatus may have encouraged a free vote, or even a no vote, on selected nominees for government posts. Such a strategy would have enhanced Gorbachev's position by providing evidence that his campaign for democratization was taking root, by undermining the personal authority of his sometime rival Ryzhkov, and by refocusing elite and mass anger away from Gorbachev and the party and toward the government and individual ministries. But whatever the role of Gorbachev in the formation and confirmation of the Ryzhkov government, his relations with Ryzhkov were recast in early 1990 with the creation of the office of president of the USSR. This hastily conceived institutional reform realigned executive power and weakened significantly parliament's ability to restrain and influence that power.[29]

At the end of 1989, amid mounting economic and ethnic crises, Gorbachev found himself without an effective institutional base from which to govern. He could no longer rely on the party as an instrument of rule. Its authority was collapsing, and the logic of his own campaign of democratization favored a shift of power from the party to the state. Yet his position as head of state (chair of the Supreme Soviet) enabled him to wield power only indirectly, through government and parliament. There appeared to be only two avenues of escape. The first would be to unseat Ryzhkov and rule as prime minister. Besides the political firestorm that a confrontation with Ryzhkov might have unleashed, this course would have exposed Gorbachev to direct parliamentary accountability and to the rigors of managing the national economy, a task for which he was ill prepared. The second, and more attractive, path for Gorbachev was to create a strong presidency for himself on the French model. The presidential option would give Gorbachev a base of power independent of government and parliament. From this position well above the political fray, Gorbachev, like de Gaulle, could set the tone for the political debate and intervene at decisive moments to impose presidential rule.

In grafting a strong presidency onto its traditional parliamentary system, the Soviet Union pushed executive-legislative relations even further in the direction of executive dominance. A hybrid presidential/parliamentary system, born in France of the frustrations with the overbearing parliaments of the Third and Fourth Republics, was now transplanted to a country with virtually no legislative tradition much less legislative power.[30] This addition of the presidency to government and parliament altered the politics of 1989 in two important respects. First, the government gained an additional institutional master. The prime minister now looks up to the president as well as down to the parliament. The parliament, therefore, is forced to share its oversight of government with a president whose powers to dismiss and nominate ministers (the latter with the approval of parliament) make him a potent contender for the attention of the government.[31] Furthermore, the president acquired new executive powers not enjoyed previously by the prime minister or the chair of the Supreme Soviet. Some enable the president to restrict legislative action (e.g., the right to veto parliamentary legislation), while others enable him to rule without reference to parliament (e.g., the right to issue binding decrees). Outlining the responsibilities of the presidency, Anatolii Luk'ianov, Gorbachev's protégé and replacement as chair of the Supreme Soviet, explained that "the USSR government, ministers, and state committees are guided in their activity not only by USSR laws [passed by parliament] but also by the decrees of the president."[32] At the very moment when the Soviet parliament was beginning to assert its long dormant lawmaking power, the presidency appeared on the scene to challenge this traditional prerogative of the legislature.

Lawmaking in the Old and New Soviet Politics

The new politics in the USSR gave birth to a "war of laws." On one level, this war set legislation adopted by the central government and parliament against laws enacted by republican institutions. At stake was nothing less than the sovereignty of Soviet rule in the republics. But another war of laws was occurring at the center of the Soviet state. The combatants in this war were the laws of the parliament, the regulations of government and its ministries, and, after March 1990, the decrees of the president. At stake here was the distribution of power within the executive and between the executive and the legislature.

Until 1989, the Soviet parliament had shown very few signs of life as a lawmaking institution. Each year the Supreme Soviet adopted on average only three to five laws and fifteen to twenty normative edicts.[33] The parliamentary laws that did appear were often ignored by the executives of the party and government who were responsible for implementing policy.[34] But if the Soviet Union lacked a sizable and cohesive body of authoritative parliamentary laws, it was awash in a sea of normative acts issued by the Council of Ministers and its constituent ministries. Each year the government issued more than a thousand decrees and the ministries tens of thousands of departmental instructions.[35] While most of these departmental instructions were internal directives designed to regulate the operation of a single bureaucracy, many ministries and state committees issued instructions that were binding on other central government institutions and on the citizenry.[36] In 1987, approximately 10,000-15,000 all-union departmental instructions were binding beyond the issuing institution.[37] Alongside these governmental acts was a vast number of party directives and joint party-government decrees that had the force of law even if they lacked its pedigree.[38]

Not only did government and party decrees swamp parliamentary laws in number, they took precedence over them in shaping the behavior of the state and society. Although government decrees were formally subordinate to the Constitution and the laws of parliament, they outranked them in the daily administration of Soviet life. "One holds a bureaucrat accountable not for a 'violation' of the Constitution," one legal scholar remarked, "but for a violation of an instruction."[39] There was simply no enforcement mechanism in place to insure that the hierarchical principle of legislation was respected in the Soviet Union.

The rulemaking power of the executive was one of the least visible but firmest pillars of traditional Soviet politics. It denied society the stability of laws found in even the most authoritarian modern states. Facing government rules that were pervasive, obscure, and mercurial, Soviet officials sought refuge in networks of party patronage that could protect them from "state discipline," a term used to describe the respect due government regulations. All Soviet citizens sought protection from the vagaries of government rules by avoiding risks, by "overinsuring" themselves in the Soviet vernacular. "Everyone, from ministers to primary school teachers, is waiting for instructions. Any act is preceded with the question: 'Tell us first, is this all right?' For everything there is a need to secure preliminary consent and guaranteed success."[40]

Two institutional innovations at the end of the 1980s began to challenge this role of government rules in the Soviet political system. The first was the invigoration of the Soviet parliament, the second the formation of a Committee on Constitutional Supervision, one of whose tasks was the settlement of disputes in the war of laws. The new parliament formed in 1989 broke the virtual monopoly enjoyed by the government and party in the purveying of legal norms. In its first year and a half, the new parliament adopted sixty-nine laws,[41] an unprecedented level of legislative activity for a Soviet parliament. The new body of parliamentary laws was impressive in its breadth and detail. By enacting laws that contained more specific provisions than was traditional in Soviet legislative practice, the new parliament sought to hinder attempts by the government to fill the interstices of laws with regulations that violated legislative intent.

Even before parliamentary laws assumed a more prominent place in the Soviet normative order, government rules themselves had come under attack. Following the Communist Party plenum of June 1987, commissions of the Supreme Soviet as well as internal working groups in government ministries began to eliminate some substatutory legislation that had been overtaken by newer regulations or that stood in the path of reform legislation. A prominent legal official reported that by the summer of 1989 tens of thousands of government decrees and departmental instructions had been annulled.[42]

At the end of the 1980s, the secrecy as well as the scale of government rulemaking became a subject of reform. Traditionally, only the parliament's laws and a small portion of the decrees of the Council of Ministers were published. The vast body of government instructions that gave direction to Soviet life was obscured from public view, distributed in effect as internal government memoranda.[43] Unable to discover rules governing such basic questions as residence permits (*propiski*) and housing and labor rights, Soviet citizens operated in ignorance of the legal consequences of their actions. Lacking the direction of authoritative parliamentary laws and knowledge about most substatutory acts, government officials regularly issued instructions that contravened other substatutory acts. The Soviet normative order, in short, was an impenetrable labyrinth that encouraged *proizvol* (arbitrariness) and not a rule of law.

In a decision with potentially far-reaching implications for executive-legislative relations in the USSR, the Committee on Constitutional Supervision ruled in November 1990 that the Soviet government could no longer withhold publication of acts affecting the rights of citizens. Citing as authority Article 59 of the USSR Constitution as well as international treaties to which the Soviet Union was a signatory, the committee held that when citizens' rights were at issue, publication must precede implementation. The committee gave the government three months to publish these instructions. Instructions affecting citizens' rights that remain unpublished at the end of February 1991 would lose legal force.[44]

The rulemaking prerogative of the executive has come under attack, then, from two sides. The parliament has sought to assert its claim to legislative sovereignty by adopting more detailed laws more frequently and by pruning from the normative pyramid large numbers of substatutory acts that are politically or legally compromised.[45] The Committee on Constitutional Supervision, for its part, has taken a dramatic first step in asserting the primacy of constitutional principles enacted by the legislature over the detailed instructions issued by government. In this and other rulings that address disputes between legislature and executive, this proto-constitutional court has used its authority to strengthen the parliament's role in the Soviet political system.[46]

A major question outstanding is whether the executive will respect the laws of parliament and the rulings of the court. In the first years of Gorbachev's rule, the government and its ministries issued a wave of substatutory acts designed to block any reform-oriented legislation enacted by the still party-controlled parliament. No sooner had the USSR Supreme Soviet adopted the Law on the State Enterprise than "ministries and departments so overloaded it with instructions that economic officials confirmed with one voice: the Law is not taking effect!"[47] The available evidence suggests that since 1989 the resistance of some ministries to the laws of parliament may have lessened. The mere threat of a ruling by the Committee on Constitutional Supervision on the question of residence permits (*propiski*) led the Council of Ministers to annul thirty decrees where the rules on *propiski* discriminated against the rights of certain categories of citizens.[48] But even officials as conservative as Anatolii Luk'ianov have recently admitted that "new norms and principles meet with harsh resistance from old structures, which in essence are blocking laws."[49] When asked by the journal *Argumenty i fakty* in the fall of 1990 why the laws passed by parliament were not being enforced, Luk'ianov responded that we do not yet have "implementation discipline."[50]

Who is blocking the implementation of the laws? Most immediately, individual ministries that have traditionally pursued their own narrow branch or departmental interests with scant regard for written norms from above. A basic ingredient of the old "command and administer" system, "departmentalism" (*vedomstvennost'*) has remained largely unaltered in the Gorbachev era. "Our ministries and ministers continue to feel themselves independent," complained a deputy at the end of 1990.[51] Another noted that "the Supreme Soviet calmly looks on as the laws it has adopted go unfulfilled. The executors--ministries, departments, and officials--explain, in a mocking way, that your laws have no mechanism for implementing legal norms. Who should call to account those people who sabotage legislative acts adopted by the supreme body of power?"[52] Undoubtedly, resistance to parliamentary legislation is at times encouraged, or at least acquiesced in, by the prime minister and other leading government and party officials. But the continued existence of departmental fiefdoms devoted to economic and political autarky is as much a challenge to president or prime minister as it is to parliament.

It was in part to combat departmentalism that Gorbachev expanded the powers of the new presidency at the end of 1990.[53] Where the original presidential mandate was to control the executive through the prime minister, subsequent changes granted the president more direct leadership of government ministries. The Council of Ministers was transformed into a Cabinet of Ministers, signaling its direct subordination to the president and the loss of status and authority of its head, the prime minister. The creation of a vice-presidency weakened further the office of prime minister. Individual ministries with responsibilities in the areas of law enforcement, national defense, and foreign affairs were linked in a new Security Council, which answers directly to the president. In a move reminiscent of Lenin's formation of a workers' and peasants' inspectorate, Gorbachev is seeking the creation of a new state inspectorate that would serve as the president's personal corps of observers of ministerial behavior.[54] Moreover, to direct that behavior into desired channels, Gorbachev has issued numerous executive decrees in his first year as president.

These reforms have done little thus far to enhance implementation discipline but much to erode the power of parliament. In streamlining the executive, Gorbachev has begun to uncouple the government from parliament, thereby shifting its formal as well as de facto accountability from the legislature to the supreme political leader. "If my perspectives begin to differ from those of the president," Prime Minister Valentin S. Pavlov noted in February 1991, "it would be better for me to resign immediately. Under presidential rule, disagreements between the prime minister and president are not acceptable."[55] According to revisions in the constitution adopted in 1990, the Supreme Soviet no longer confirms (*utverzhdaet*) the members of the government but merely gives its agreement (*daet svoe soglasie*) to nominees appointed by the president.[56] Whereas previously the prime minister proposed ministerial candidates to parliament, the president now formally appoints (*naznachaet*) them through a decree (*ukaz*). Parliament then has the option to overturn the appointment. There is thus a presumption of confirmation not present in 1989. In parliamentary debates in February

1991 on nominees to the Cabinet of Ministers, the new prime minister, Pavlov, asserted that deputies could no longer use the occasion of reviewing a candidate to raise issues of policy within the nominee's area of competence.[57] Parliament was increasingly being forced into "take it or leave it" decisions on executive proposals, a traditional mark of executive dominance of the legislature.

Openly frustrated with what he perceived to be the lack of discipline and efficiency of the parliament, Gorbachev began to circumvent the legislative process altogether by issuing presidential decrees on pressing issues of public policy.[58] In September 1990, he succeeded in convincing the parliament to grant him extraordinary power for approximately 500 days to issue directives on economic policy that had the standing of law.[59] Although parliament retained the right to annul these decrees, it appears unlikely to restrain presidential power in the midst of a deepening economic crisis. By acquiescing to the expansion of presidential power in 1990, an obedient and intimidated majority in parliament reduced significantly the ability of the legislature to hold the executive politically accountable. The parliament's action also diminished its own accountability to the nation.

Legislative Oversight of the Executive

A universal feature of modern government is the executive's superior access to information and expertise. A monumental challenge for the new Soviet parliament has been to develop from scratch access to information and expertise, both from the executive and from its own and independent sources. The policy of *glasnost'* and the rise of a vigorous press have given the new parliament knowledge about executive behavior and social and economic conditions unrivaled since the early years of Soviet power. Parliamentary committees and commissions, for their part, have been able to draw heavily on the expertise of specialists from universities and research institutes to educate deputies and to assist in legislative drafting. In addition, there are small but growing committee staffs,[60] though as yet most parliamentary support personnel work in the presidium, whose close political ties to the executive leadership make it as much an appendage of executive as of legislative power.[61]

To oversee effectively the execution of the laws, a parliament must also have the means to extract information directly from government agencies. While the interpellation of ministers making reports to parliament generates some information, it is the deputy's *zapros* that is designed to allow parliament to probe with depth and regularity into the bureaucracy.[62] An oral or written question posed by one or more deputies to an executive agency, a *zapros* must be answered within a month by the official to whom it is directed. When a violation of the law is at issue, a response must be made within three days.[63] From the middle of 1989 to the middle of 1990, deputies addressed 8,200 *zaprosy* to the USSR Procuracy alone.[64] This avalanche of *zaprosy* directed to executive agencies is more than a request for information. It also serves to remind government officials of the intensity of parliamentary concern about problems within their jurisdiction.[65]

The heavy usage of *zaprosy* notwithstanding, it is as yet difficult to reach firm conclusions about the effectiveness of the *zapros* as an instrument of parliamentary oversight. Perceptions vary according to the observer as well as the subject of the *zapros*. Aleksandr M. Iakovlev, a reformist legal scholar, insists that deputies are granted ready access to information possessed by the executive.[66] Some deputies, however, are dissatisfied with responses to *zaprosy*, particularly on matters of foreign affairs, national security, and finance.[67] The Western analyst Mikhail Tsypkin reports that "to counteract Ministry of Defense stonewalling, the more radical committee members [in the Committee for Defense and State Security] are coming to rely on individuals they euphemistically refer to as 'consultants.' These are in reality whistleblowers--defense industry specialists and military and KGB officers who, despite threats of retribution, are said to provide information that their agencies are trying to conceal."[68] What is needed, one Soviet journalist argued, is a law on information for deputies that would hold accountable those in the executive who provide disinformation to parliament.[69]

The vigor of parliamentary oversight of the executive is limited on a very practical level by the deputies' continuing dependence on the state for the provision of scarce goods and services. As Peter Solomon illustrated in a study of the roots of localism in Soviet political culture, legal and political officials often abandon professional and institutional loyalties to bind themselves to individuals or networks of officials who can supply the essentials of life--apartments, telephones, transportation, and education.[70] Soviet legislators continue to be subject to many of the same pressures that this "goods dependency" creates.[71] Indeed, the radical deputy Galina Starovoitova claimed that, at the end of 1990, deputies succumbed to Gorbachev's pressure to shift power from parliament to presidency because they had been bought off by apartments and other goods provided by the executive.[72] In a country without a market, where one still tends to make a life from politics and not for politics, the executive's virtual monopoly of economic resources encourages deference in the attitudes and behavior of deputies.[73]

The Soviet executive has also learned to court deputies by pursuing policies that benefit certain electoral districts, a practice widespread in the United States and many other Western countries. In deliberations on the budget, for example, deputies have sought to obtain from the ministries special projects for their constituencies. Ministerial officials, in turn, attempt to mobilize the support of potentially sympathetic deputies who will assist them to acquire resources above plan or budget.[74] This cooperation between "localist" and "departmentalist" interests, long a feature of behind-the-scenes bargaining in Soviet budgetary politics, is a revealing example of the adaptation of longstanding traditions to the new structures of Soviet politics. It is an adaptation that is viewed with alarm by both Gorbachev and radical reformists, who share a distaste for Madisonian principles that legitimate the open pursuit of partial interests.

Conclusion

At the end of the 1980s, the democratization campaign in the USSR set off a chain reaction in Soviet politics that has yet to run its course. Competitive elections brought the rise of a vigorous, if poorly organized, opposition in the USSR Supreme Soviet. The parliamentary opposition then transformed executive-legislative relations by challenging, for the first time in modern Soviet history, the personnel and policies advanced by the party and government leadership. To be sure, these challenges usually failed. The Soviet government, like governments in all parliamentary systems, could rely on a majority in parliament to sustain most of its proposals. It could also rely on a fifth column within the parliament, the presidium of the Supreme Soviet, headed by Anatolii Luk'ianov, to serve as a kind of institutional whip for the executive leadership. But some policies and personnel did not receive the support of parliament. Moreover, the mere use of parliamentary prerogatives so long ignored heightened the expectations in government, in society, and in parliament itself that the executive would be, and should be, accountable to the legislature.[75]

The appearance in 1990 of a new executive institution, the presidency, dashed these expectations by reclaiming for the president much of the power that had flowed to the parliament from party and government in 1989, most notably in the areas of lawmaking and government oversight. In assuming the presidency, Gorbachev appeared to be less troubled by the realignment of executive-legislative relations than by the inability and/or unwillingness of the legislature to bring under control independent-minded ministries and republics.[76] Originally frustrated with the Communist Party as a vehicle of reform, Gorbachev has now abandoned the parliament as well in favor of the presidency, an instrument of rule at once more responsive and powerful. The question for the future is whether parliament can reassert its authority without Gorbachev's support and indeed against Gorbachev's own executive institution.

Notes

1. Thomas Hobbes, *Leviathan*, H. Schneider edition (Indianapolis: Bobbs-Merrill, 1958), p. 17.

2. The rise of modern, disciplined parties has, of course, moderated this tension in political systems that have strong parliamentary majorities.

3. V. Lenin, *The State and Revolution* (New York: International Publishers, 1932), pp. 35-44.

4. The most compelling account of this process remains Leonard Schapiro, *The Origins of the Communist Autocracy: Political Opposition in the Soviet State, First Phase, 1917-1922*, 2nd ed. (Cambridge: Harvard University Press, 1977).

5. Soviet scholars began in the mid-1980s to discuss the problem of the separation of powers in the Soviet government. See B. Lazarev, " 'Razdelenie vlastei' i opyt sovetskogo gosudarstva," *Kommunist*, no. 16 (1988), and Iu. Tikhomirov, "Vlast' v obshchestve: edinstvo i razdelenie," *Sovetskoe gosudarstvo i pravo* [hereafter SGP], no. 2 (1990), pp. 35-43.

6. Unless otherwise specified, the term parliament will be used to refer to the USSR Supreme Soviet. The term legislature will be used more broadly, to embrace both the USSR Supreme Soviet and the USSR Congress of People's Deputies. The latter is an assembly of 2,250 people's deputies that selects from among its members 542 persons to sit in the USSR Supreme Soviet, which is in effect the country's standing parliament.

7. "The First Session of the USSR Supreme Soviet," *Izvestiia*, 9 June 1989, in *Current Digest of the Soviet Press* [hereafter CDSP], no. 31 (1989), p. 25.

8. Dawn Mann reports that nominees for government posts in the summer of 1989 were still approved first in the Central Committee of the party. "Gorbachev's Personnel Policy: The USSR Council of Ministers," *Report on the USSR*, 17 November 1989, pp. 11-12.

9. "The First Session of the USSR Supreme Soviet," *Izvestiia*, 9 June 1989, in CDSP, no. 31 (1989), p. 25.

10. Ibid. The candidate for procurator-general, A. Sukharev, proved to be almost as unpopular among the deputies as Kolbin. He was attacked from the right for losing the war against crime and from the left for failing to take more decisive measures to humanize Soviet justice. Sukharev's position was weakened further by a reputation for indecision within the Procuracy.

11. Formally, the prime minister presents only the leading members of government to the parliament for confirmation. These include the deputy prime ministers, the Council of Ministers administrator of affairs (*upravliaiushchii delami*), the ministers of foreign affairs, defense, internal affairs, and finance, and the head of the KGB. The deputy prime ministers in turn propose the remaining ministers and present their resumes to the parliament. "N.I. Ryzhkov: Learning to Work Together," *Izvestiia*, 24 June 1989, p. 1, in *Foreign Broadcast Information Service* [hereafter *FBIS*], 26 June 1989, p. 45.

12. If the performance of the government as a whole is regarded as unsatisfactory, the parliament may by a two-thirds majority express no confidence in the government and "raise the question" about changing the composition of the government. "Reglament S"ezda narodnykh deputatov SSSR i Verkhovnogo Soveta SSSR," *Vedomosti S"ezda narodnykh deputatov SSSR i Verkhovnogo Soveta SSSR* [hereafter *Vedomosti SSSR*], no. 29 (1989), st. 565.

13. The distribution of committee responsibilities in the confirmation process was

made by the presidium of the Supreme Soviet.

14. "A Good Beginning Is Half the Job," *Izvestiia*, 20 June 1989, in CDSP, no. 34 (1989), pp. 17-18; A. Grobov et al., "Examination for Minister," *Izvestiia*, 23 June 1989, in CDSP, no. 34 (1989), p. 19.

15. A. Luity et al., "The Soviet Government Is Being Formed," *Pravda*, 23 June 1989, in CDSP, no. 34 (1989), pp. 20-21.

16. "N.I. Ryzhkov's Report at the First Session of the USSR Supreme Soviet," *Pravda*, 28 June 1989, in CDSP, no. 35 (1989), pp. 13-14.

17. V. Dolganov et al., "A Most Demanding Test," *Izvestiia*, 24 June 1989, in CDSP, no. 34 (1989), pp. 19-20.

18. Two of the nominees were withdrawn before being voted on by the committees.

19. Luity et al., "The Soviet Government Is Being Formed."

20. V. Dolganov et al., "They Will Stand Guard over the Law," *Izvestiia*, 7 July 1989, in CDSP, no. 36 (1989), pp. 11-12.

21. E. Gonzalez et al., "The Formation of the Government Nears Completion," *Izvestiia*, 14 July 1989, in CDSP, no. 36 (1989), p. 16; V. Dolganov and I. Korolkov, "The USSR State Security Committee in the Light of Glasnost," *Izvestiia*, 15 July 1989, in CDSP, no. 36 (1989), p. 17.

22. I. Korolkov et al., "Ministers Get the OKAY," *Izvestiia*, 3 July 1989, in CDSP, no. 35 (1989), p. 17.

23. P. Voshchanov, "Portfel' dlia ministra," *Komsomol'skaia pravda*, 22 July 1989, p. 3.

24. Ibid.

25. G. Alimov et al., "Two Weeks of Debates are Behind Us," *Izvestiia*, 8 July 1989, in CDSP, no. 36 (1989), pp. 12-13.

26. V. Dolganov et al., "The Situation in the Branch and the Minister's Program," *Izvestiia*, 6 July 1989, in CDSP, no. 36 (1989), p. 11. The same nominee would be confirmed by parliament several weeks later. V. Dolganov and R. Lynev, "The Session Is Over, the Work Continues," *Izvestiia*, in CDSP, no. 38 (1989), p. 18.

27. On the composition of the new government, see Alexander Rahr, "Ryzhkov's New Cabinet," *Report on the USSR*, 30 June 1989, pp. 13-16.

28. "Speech by M.S. Gorbachev on the Conclusion of the Work of the First Session of the USSR Supreme Soviet," *Pravda*, 5 August 1989, in CDSP, no. 38 (1989), p. 19.

29. On the formation of the presidency, see Elizabeth Teague, "Executive Presidency Approved," *Report on the USSR*, 9 March 1990, pp. 14-16; and idem, "The Powers of the Soviet Presidency," *Report on the USSR*, 23 March 1990, pp. 4-7.

30. On the functions and powers of the presidency, see "Ob uchrezhdenii posta Prezidenta SSSR i vnesenii izmenenii i dopolnenii v Konstitutsiiu (Osnovoi Zakon) SSSR," *Vedomosti SSSR*, no. 12 (1990), st. 189.

31. The president was denied the power to dismiss members of the Supreme Court or the Committee on Constitutional Supervision, reportedly a compromise forced on him by the legislature. Teague, "The Powers of the Soviet Presidency," pp. 6-7.

32. "On Making Changes in and Additions to the USSR Constitution (Basic Law) and Establishing the Post of President of the USSR," *Izvestiia*, 13 March 1990, in CDSP, no. 11 (1990), pp. 7-8. On the formation of the presidency, see B. Lazarev, "Prezident SSSR," SGP, no. 7 (1990), pp. 3-14.

33. The following account of lawmaking in the Soviet Union draws heavily on Eugene Huskey, "Government Rulemaking as a Brake on Perestroika," *Law and Social Inquiry*, no. 3 (1990), pp. 419-32.

34. On the distinction between "declarative-propagandist" and "working" legislation, see A. Obolenskii, "Kakuiu politicheskuiu sistemu my unasledovali (anatomiia 'doaprel'skogo' politicheskogo rezhima)," SGP, no. 10 (1990), pp. 69-71.

35. "O verkhovenstve zakona i stikhii podzakonnykh aktov," *Izvestiia*, 20 February 1989, p. 2.

36. These norms, variously labeled as generally obligatory (*obshcheobiazatel'nye*) or extradepartmental (*nadvedomstvennye*), emerge primarily from the most powerful governmental institutions, such as the Ministry of Finance, the Ministry of Internal Affairs, and the State Committee on Prices.

37. S. Polenina and N. Sil'chenko, *Nauchnye osnovy tipologii normativno-pravovykh aktov v SSSR* (Moscow: 1987), p. 93; "Opiat' ob instruktsiiakh," *Izvestiia*, 23 September 1987, p. 3.

38. On the role of party directives and joint party-government decrees in the Soviet normative order, see S. Alekseev, *Pravo i perestroika: voprosy, razdum'ia, prognozy* (Moscow: Iuridicheskaia literatura, 1987), p. 51; and Donald D. Barry, "The *Spravochnik Partiinogo Rabotnika* as a Source of Party Law," in Dietrich Loeber, ed., *Ruling Communist Parties and Their Status under Law* (Dordrecht, Netherlands: Martinus Nijhoff Publishers, 1986), pp. 37-52.

Since the nineteenth party conference, the party and government were to have halted the publication of joint decrees. But as V. Sazonov points out, because high-ranking officials of the government still comprise a large share of the Central Committee, central party ties with the ministries are still very close, if at times troubled. "TsK KPSS i perestroika," *Argumenty i fakty*, no. 5 (1990), p. 6. In fact, there have been instances of continued use of such party-government decrees. See, for example, "O merakh po finansovomu ozdorovleniiu ekonomiki i ukrepleniiu denezhnogo obrashcheniia v strane 1989-1990 gg. i v trinadtsatoi piatiletke," of 15 March 1989. *Sobranie postanovlenii Pravitel'stva SSSR*, no. 22 (1989), st. 69. E. Primakov reports that the Central Committee often complains that the Council of Ministers fails to implement party directives, while the Council of Ministers believes that the party issues unfulfillable orders. "O vlasti i privilegiiakh," *Argumenty i fakty*, no. 10 (1990), p. 2.

39. E. Luk'ianova, *Zakon kak istochnik sovetskogo gosudarstvennogo prava* (Moscow: Izdatel'stvo moskovskogo universiteta, 1988), p. 33.

40. N. Belyayeva, "Rule Out Loopholes in the Law," *Moscow News*, no. 21 (1989), p. 12.

41. This figure is based on a count of substantive laws (*zakony*) enacted by the USSR Supreme Soviet and published in *Vedomosti SSSR* from June 1989 through

December 1990.

42. ". . . s S. Emel'ianovym," *Sovetskaia iustitsiia*, no. 1 (1989), p. 6.

43. If only the entire ministerial "kitchen" was opened up, one reformist argued, there would be an end to the politics of stagnation. V. Krichagin, "Vedomstvennaia glasnost'," *Argumenty i fakty*, no. 23 (1990), p. 3.

44. "O pravilakh, dopuskaiushchikh primenenie neopublikovannykh normativnykh aktov o pravakh, svobodakh i obiazannostiiakh grazhdan," *Vedomosti SSSR*, no. 50 (1990), st. 1080.

45. In order to insure the implementation of laws, some reformists advocate that parliament review in committee all ministerial instructions issued on the basis of laws. M. Buzhkevich, "V dvukh ipostasiakh," *Pravda*, 29 June 1990, p. 3.

46. The head of the Committee on Constitutional Supervision, S. Alekseev, recognizes, however, that "a purely parliamentary solution historically has led to blind alleys." In arguing for a strong and effective government alongside a strong parliament, he referred to the lessons of France before the Fifth Republic. "The Extraordinary Third Congress of USSR People's Deputies," *Izvestiia*, 13 March 1990, in CDSP, no. 11 (1990), pp. 2-3.

47. "Pravovoe gosudarstvo: kakim emu byt'?" *Pravda*, 2 August 1988, p. 2.

48. S. Alekseev, "Tret'ia vlast'," *Izvestiia*, 23 February 1991, p. 3. This is an article of major significance for understanding the Committee on Constitutional Supervision, written by its head. See also D. Kerimov and A. Ekimov, "Konstitutsionnyi nadzor v SSSR," SGP, no. 9 (1990), pp. 3-13. On the question of *propiski* generally, see T. Merzliakova, "Izgoi po . . . zakonu: sovmestima li sistema propiski s pravama cheloveka?" *Izvestiia*, 6 February 1991, p. 3.

49. "Vysokaia otvetstvennost' zakonodatel'noi vlasti (doklad Luk'ianova)," *Izvestiia*, 10 September 1990, p. 3. See also A. Stepovoi, "Posle parlamentskikh kanikul," *Izvestiia*, 4 September 1990, p. 1.

50. "Nel'zia idti vpered, gliadia nazad," *Argumenty i fakty*, no. 39 (1990), p. 2.

51. Interview with V.A. Shapovalenko, USSR People's Deputy, Moscow Television Evening News (*Vremia*), 30 November 1990.

52. V. Dolganov and A. Stepovoi, "Time Is Running Out," *Izvestiia*, 1 June 1990, in CDSP, no. 23 (1990), p. 10.

53. For an outline and justification of these changes, see "The President Proposes His Program," *Izvestiia*, 17 November 1990, in CDSP, no. 46 (1990), pp. 10-11; S. Chugaev, "The USSR President's Proposals Are Supported," *Izvestiia*, 5 December 1990, in CDSP, no. 49 (1990), p. 13; and "Bring Life into the Constitution, and Bring the Constitution into Life," *Pravda*, 22 December 1990, in CDSP, no. 2 (1991), pp. 13-15. On parliament's response to the proposed changes, see A. Stepovoi and S. Chugaev, "Once Again about the Situation in the Country," *Izvestiia*, 23 November 1990, in CDSP, no. 47 (1990), p. 13.

54. In theory, "the functions of the Supreme State Inspectorate cannot and must not overlap either the functions of parliamentary control or the functions of prosecutor's supervision." "Bring Life into the Constitution," p. 14. It is inconceivable, however, that there would not be considerable overlap in practice.

55. M. Krushinskii, "Plan, rynok i . . . kartoshka (Press-konferentsiia V.S. Pavlova)," *Izvestiia*, 23 February 1991, p. 1.

56. "Ob uchrezhdenii posta Prezidenta SSSR i vnesenii izmenenii i dopolnenii v Konstitutsiiu (Osnovnoi zakon) SSSR," *Vedomosti SSSR*, no. 12 (1990), st. 189. The powers of the presidency are set out in Article 127 of the revised Constitution.

57. A. Stepovoi and S. Chugaev, "Obsuzhdaetsia zakon o Kabinete ministrov," *Izvestiia*, 28 February 1991, p. 1.

58. Some deputies have sought, unsuccessfully thus far, to challenge the legal standing of presidential decrees. L. Aksenov et al., "Otkrylas' sessiia Verkhovnogo Soveta SSSR," *Izvestiia*, 10 September 1990, p. 1.

59. Dawn Mann, *"Ukaz* and Effect: Gorbachev is Granted Additional Powers," *Report on the USSR*, 5 October 1990, pp. 1-4. Even before this formal shift of lawmaking authority in economic affairs, the government appeared to be preparing drafts for presidential decrees on economic matters rather than submitting the legislation to parliament. "Vysokaia otvetstvennost' zakonodatel'noi vlasti (doklad Luk'ianova)," *Izvestiia*, 10 September 1990, p. 3.

60. Unlike American congressmen, members of European-style parliaments have modest personnel support, often only a single secretary. In the new Soviet parliament, individual deputies have no permanent staff but they do have the right to request that enterprises in their districts assist them with secretarial support. The response of enterprises to such requests varies widely, and therefore some deputies are much better supported than others. Dawn Mann, "Supreme Soviet Adopts Laws on the Status of People's Deputies," *Report on the USSR*, 28 September 1990, pp. 1-4. The use of enterprises as support bases began in the parliamentary elections of 1989, when candidates for the USSR Congress of People's Deputies were given the right to draw on factories and institutes for campaign assistance.

61. The secretariat of the presidium of the Supreme Soviet reportedly spent 6.5 million rubles on its staff in 1989, compared with 16.3 million rubles for the administrative staff of the USSR Council of Ministers. The central apparatus of the individual ministers and state committees reportedly costs the country 465 million rubles a year. The latter figure does not include the central staffs of the KGB or the Ministry of Internal Affairs, and presumably also the Ministry of Defense, all of whose budgets are secret. G. Alimov et al., "The Difficult Path of Parliamentary Decisions," *Izvestiia*, 3 August 1989, in CDSP, no. 38 (1989), p. 17.

For criticisms of the presidium's lack of accountability to parliament, see the speeches of Sobchak and Lubechenko in "The Extraordinary Third Congress of USSR People's Deputies," *Izvestiia*, 17 March 1990, p. 21.

62. Oversight is also exercised by standing committees and by the select commissions created to investigate topical issues, such as the massacre in Tbilisi and the Gdlian-Ivanov affair. Most committees, however, appear to be chaired by establishment politicians who do not encourage vigorous oversight of executive institutions.

Furthermore, the membership of the committees is stacked in favor of the government sector being overseen. As two research associates of the Institute of the

USA and Canada pointed out, "The military and the top figures in the defense industry form the overwhelming majority in the Defense and National Security committees of the USSR Supreme Soviet. Among its members there is no civil lawyer or economist. This would be an unthinkable situation for any Western parliament, where the nomination of the head of a defense-industry complex as chairman of the parliament's committee for matters of national defense would be taken only as a bad joke." A. Iziumov and A. Kortunov, "The Monster: A Profile of the Soviet Military-Industrial Complex," *Moscow News*, no. 8 (1991), p. 9.

63. "Reglament S"ezda narodnykh deputatov SSSR i Verkhovnogo Soveta SSSR," *Vedomosti SSSR*, no. 29 (1989), st. 565; "O statuse narodnykh deputatov v SSSR," *Vedomosti SSSR*, no. 29 (1989), st. 567. The latter law also grants deputies the right to conduct inspections of government departments and to request immediate action by law enforcement organs if a violation of law is discovered.

64. "Gde nuzhno, vlast' upotrebit'," *Literaturnaia gazeta*, no. 25 (1990), p. 12.

65. In September 1990, for example, the head of the Social Democratic bloc in the Supreme Soviet, S. Belozertsev, directed a *zapros* to the Minister of Defense and the head of the KGB concerning the movement into the Moscow region of elite divisions of the armed forces. "Pervoi zakon chetvertoi sessii," *Izvestiia*, 25 September 1990, p. 2.

66. Interview with A.M. Iakovlev, 11 July 1990, Moscow.

67. Deputies have also found it difficult to receive information about the perquisites of leaders. "E.A. Pamfilova, secretary of the USSR Congress of People's Deputies Commission on Reviewing Privileges Enjoyed by Certain Categories of Citizens, complained to the members of parliament that all the commission's inquiries to the Council of Ministers, particularly to first vice-chairmen L.A. Voronin and A.P. Biriukova, have been met with complete silence and a refusal to provide necessary information and documents." V. Dolganov and A. Stepovoi, "A Week for Reflection," *Izvestiia*, 12 September 1990, in CDSP, no. 37 (1990), p. 6.

68. M. Tsypkin, "The Committee for Defense and State Security of the USSR Supreme Soviet," *Report on the USSR*, 11 May 1990, pp. 10-11.

69. B. Sergeev, "Chelovek prokhodit kak khoziain," *Argumenty i fakty*, no. 37 (1990), p. 2. There is also concern among radical deputies that the parliament's right of oral *zapros* is being limited illegally by the chair, A. Luk'ianov. In a heated debate in February 1991, a deputy directed a *zapros* to the Minister of Justice, asking him to comment on the legality of registering the Communist Party under the new law on public associations. Luk'ianov intervened to seek a vote on whether to accept the *zapros*, even though this right of deputies is not subject to a vote. In the event, the vote succeeded, by the slimmest of majorities, in preventing the request from being posed to the minister. A. Stepovoi and S. Chugaev, "Sessiia obsuzhdaet plan raboty," *Izvestiia*, 19 February 1991, p. 1. As if the defeat of the vote were not enough, V. Ivashko, the deputy general secretary of the Communist Party, attacked the "political" character of the deputy's *zapros* and warned that unless the deputy could prove all of his insults directed against the party, "we" reserve the right to take "appropriate measures." Ibid.

70. Peter Solomon, "Local Political Power and Soviet Criminal Justice, 1922-1941," *Soviet Studies*, no. 3 (1985), pp. 305-329.

71. The parliament is unable to oversee the government, one deputy lamented, "because we're drowning in apartment problems and other such matters. Some bodies of power find it very advantageous to have USSR People's Deputies like that." Dolganov and Stepovoi, "Time is Running Out."

72. "Power Structure Reform: Supreme Soviet Upstaged?" *Moscow News*, no. 50 (1990), p. 8.

73. Ministries may also seek to coopt deputies by offering them personal "benefits." The Ministry of Foreign Affairs, for example, has been operating seminars for deputies to expose them to international law and diplomatic practice. Response to Reader's Question, *Argumenty i fakty*, no. 45 (1990), p. 8.

74. V. Dolganov and V. Romanyuk, "Everyone Needs Money--Where Is It to Come From?" *Izvestiia*, 22 September 1989, in CDSP, no. 38 (1989), p. 22.

75. The expectations of fundamentally new legislative-executive relations were evident in Ryzhkov's comments in June 1989 following the first days of confirmation debates. "We must work together, constantly remembering the enormous tasks facing the country. . . . Those who come through this parliamentary procedure successfully cannot, of course, fail to have a sense of satisfaction in winning a vote of confidence from people's deputies. An important new quality will thereby appear in the position of the future government members--reliance on the support of the people's representatives. And the formal act of appointment to a post thereby acquires fundamentally new importance as a democratic act that is part of the restructuring of our political system." "N.I. Ryzhkov: Learning to Work Together," *Izvestiia*, 24 June 1989, in *FBIS*, 26 June 1989, pp. 46-47. How different the politics of 1989 from the politics of 1990!

76. In a revealing speech to the cultural establishment at the end of November 1990, Gorbachev justified the subordination of the Council of Ministers to a strong presidency as essential to hold together the Union. "Speech by M.S. Gorbachev," *Pravda*, 1 December 1990, in CDSP, no. 48 (1990), pp. 1-5.

9

PARLIAMENTARY GOVERNMENT IN THE USSR

Thomas F. Remington

One of the most remarkable developments in Soviet politics since 1988 is the beginning of a transition from a system that concentrated immense nominal power in executive institutions toward one more closely resembling Western-style parliamentary democracy. The concept of separation of powers--*razdelenie vlastei*--has gained widespread acceptance in discussions of constitutional reform. Gorbachev's own proposals at the 1988 party conference offered a slightly less radical vision of the future, calling for a substantial increase in the decision-making powers of soviets at all levels, the creation of a two-tiered union legislative structure, and a new Committee on Constitutional Supervision to rule on the constitutionality of legislative and executive enactments. The new framework of state power was described by Gorbachev as a "socialist system of checks and balances." As we know, his proposals were adopted virtually *in toto* by the outgoing Supreme Soviet at the end of 1988 after scarcely a month of public discussion.[1]

In this chapter we shall examine the record of the newly elected Supreme Soviet in its first convocation, that is, from the spring of 1989 until the end of 1990.[2] The question addressed is the degree to which legislative power in the Soviet Union has become a counterweight to the executive branch. Theoretically the problem is conceptualized as one of legislative institutionalization, which, following Samuel Huntington's theoretical definition of institutionalization, is understood in terms of four attributes: *autonomy*, or freedom of agenda-setting and decision-making vis-à-vis the state bureaucracy, the Communist Party, the new presidency, and the presidium of the legislature itself; *cohesiveness*, the capacity to act in defense of institutional prerogatives in the face of internal and external pressures;

175

adaptiveness, the capacity to address the full range of policy issues faced by the Soviet state; and *complexity*, or the ability of specialized units of the legislature to perform separate functions.[3] Although no final judgment about the effectiveness of legislative power in the USSR can be drawn at present, this chapter is concerned to identify trends of development that might help predict whether the Supreme Soviet of the USSR might eventually succeed in performing functions analogous to legislative institutions in liberal democracies in three critical areas: representation of the electorate, enactment of laws, and checking the power of the executive. My premise is that an effective legislative branch is one of the essential components of a working democracy in the modern era, though by no means a sufficient condition for one; only a legitimate legislature can reconcile the competing requirements of popular representation and responsible decision-making that democracies confront.

As we know from the literature on transitions from authoritarian rule, there is no particular set of requisites that guarantee that democratic institutions will prevail against concerted efforts by powerful political actors to suppress them.[4] There are only conditions that make the emergence of democratic institutions more or less likely. Certainly we may agree that the Soviet Union lacks many of the characteristics that facilitate the emergence of a competitive and open political system: a property-owning middle class interested in protecting its rights and freedoms through law; a low degree of social polarization; a pluralistic infrastructure of social and civic institutions that draw support across the entire national political community; and diffusion of economic resources. On the other hand, the period of liberalization inaugurated under Gorbachev in 1987-90 encouraged a rapid, even explosive, spread of independent associations.[5] In turn, partly under the stimulus of national and subnational elections in 1989 and 1990, political organizations, including parties and party-like formations, have begun aggregating social interests across territorial boundaries.[6] Moreover, the record indicates that new norms of legislative independence and assertiveness have become widely diffused and internalized among the Soviet deputies, some of whom have begun to play a new role of professional parliamentarian.[7]

By the same token, some deeply disturbing trends were evident in early 1991. One hundred ninety-seven members of the Supreme Soviet--36 percent of the membership, as compared with the 20 percent that had been anticipated in the law--resigned at the time of the December 1990 rotation of membership. Many were disenchanted by the inability of the Supreme Soviet to solve the country's urgent problems; some were frustrated by the impossibility of combining their duties as Supreme Soviet member with their regular occupational responsibilities. Amid a worsening political and economic crisis (in which the resignation of Foreign Minister Shevardnadze, the replacement of Interior Minister Bakatin by Boris Pugo, a series of decrees expanding the civil authority of the KGB and the military, violence by the military and MVD special forces against unarmed citizens in Lithuania and Latvia, the departure of the most independent and democratically oriented advisors from Gorbachev's circle, and a number of other alarming developments stand out), the question of the degree to which the USSR Supreme Soviet constitutes a meaningful check on the apparent slide to authoritarianism becomes critical.

What are realistic criteria for measuring the degree of legislative institutionalization in so fluid a setting as Gorbachev's USSR? I am not arguing that legislative *supremacy* over the executive is in any sense a necessary condition of democracy, since legislatures everywhere are the object of criticism for their insufficient influence.[8] Yet even a parliamentary arrangement, in which the legislature is normally subordinated to the executive's will, imposes a "daily dependence of the government upon its legislative majority for continuation in office."[9] Gauging the influence of the new parliament in the USSR is as difficult as trying to measure the speed of one body in motion while standing on another body in motion; influence is relative. At the moment central political authority in the Soviet Union is in decline generally. By what standard, then, should the power of the new parliament be measured? Shall we compare it to the old Communist Party machinery, which has relinquished its sovereign hold over political life, or to the old Supreme Soviet? Neither comparison is especially edifying. The criterion we shall apply is institutionalization of the legislative power in the three major domains of political activity in which a legislature specializes: representation, law-making, and oversight of the executive branch.

The chapter is divided into three parts. The first reviews some of the influences on the emergence of the new Soviet parliamentary institutions that stem from its peculiar genealogy and the political environment in which it works. The second turns to a particularly rich case of its activity, the history of the law on the press, in order to trace the interaction of the new parliamentary institutions with their environment in the course of the legislative process. The third part reviews the record of the legislature's activity over the past two years from the standpoint of our criteria of institutional development.

Before beginning, it may be useful to say a word about how to locate the emerging Soviet system among political systems. The Soviet system currently combines elements of both the parliamentary and presidential types of government and retains a strong residual influence of the communist regime's traditional separation of effective power, vested in the Communist Party and state bureaucracy, from dignified power, in Bagehot's term, which was assigned to the facade of elective soviets. The new system introduced by the 1988 constitutional amendments preserved the old system's parliamentary framework whereby the national executive, the Council of Ministers, answers to the Supreme Soviet, although since 1990 the president has had the right to propose the composition of the government and to direct its work.[10] The new system also departs from usual parliamentary models to the extent that the parliament itself is bifurcated into a large and broadly representative congress and a smaller, quasi-professional Supreme Soviet formed from and accountable to the Congress of People's Deputies.

Under the Constitution, these two tiers of legislative power have separate and complementary, but also overlapping, spheres of competence.[11] To the Congress is assigned exclusive jurisdiction over certain issues, particularly constitutional changes. To the Supreme Soviet are given most specific powers of legislative regulation. Their powers are complementary in certain details. The Supreme Soviet is given the right to appoint the chairman of the council of ministers and several other state officials, while the Congress is empowered to confirm the appointments. Both are, however, given broad mandates. The Congress has the right to consider and decide any question falling under the competence of the union; the Supreme Soviet has the same right except in the case of those issues assigned to the exclusive jurisdiction of the Congress. Likewise the Congress is given the right to set the basic lines of domestic and foreign policy. Constitutionally, therefore, there is no guarantee that disputes will not arise if the two tiers adopt contradictory decisions over the same policy issue, but final power is vested in the Congress since it is given the power to annul legislative acts of the Supreme Soviet, as well as to elect it and its leadership.

Of course the system continues to evolve. After their first year, the new arrangements were upset by Gorbachev's sudden decision to create a powerful executive presidency. The president acquired powers comparable to those of the French president: the freedom to appoint and dismiss the prime minister and other ministers; certain broad powers to ensure the stable and effective functioning of the national government generally; the right under emergency conditions to exercise presidential power directly; and the right to dissolve parliament. The French and American presidencies were taken as models in the drafting of the Soviet presidency law, and the French Fifth Republic's combination of presidential and parliamentary structures seems to have been a source of particular inspiration. Nevertheless the Soviet system deviates substantially from the French or any other mixed presidential-parliamentary system (the Finnish and Swiss systems offer potentially useful features). Above all it lacks the extraparliamentary play of national political parties that organize government and opposition programs, mobilize voter support for competing teams of professional politicians in elections, and link legislators with more or less effective bonds of loyalty and discipline to produce majorities for government bills.

In September 1990, at Gorbachev's behest, the Supreme Soviet granted the president exceptional powers to implement measures through presidential decree "on economic problems and questions of the preservation of law and order." This action followed a prolonged impasse in the elaboration of a general program for the economy that would decisively move it to a market footing; in the face of the deadlock of the government economic bureaucracy, the parliament, and the Russian republic, which were unable to reach a consensus, the Supreme Soviet on September 24 took two decisions that relinquished control over economic policy to the president. By overwhelming majorities (323 for, 11 against, and 56 abstentions for the first vote; 305 for, 36 against, and 41 abstentions on the second), the Supreme Soviet agreed, first, to allow Gorbachev to force into a single program the utterly incompatible schemes advanced by the Council of Ministers and by Stanislav Shatalin's 500-days team, and, second, to grant Gorbachev additional powers lasting until March 31, 1992, to implement such measures as he deemed necessary to overcome the worsening economic crisis. These decisions followed the failure of the Supreme Soviet to reach any consensus on a strategy for economic policy and effectively represented a surrender of its policy-making power in this area.

At the end of 1990 Gorbachev again unexpectedly proposed and readily obtained both Supreme Soviet and CPD consent for yet another reorganization of executive power.[12] Eliminating the Presidential Council, he sought an expanded role for the Federation Council--which was now charged with coordination of the activities of the union and the republics as well as with carrying out nationality policy. He also replaced the old Council of Ministers with a smaller Cabinet of Ministers which the president directly oversees through a new prime minister (*Prem'er-Ministr*). Third, he created a national Security Council (*sovet bezopasnosti SSSR*) with broad but vague responsibilities in the areas of defense policy, "economic and ecological security," and responses to states of emergency. Finally, a vice-presidency was established, an office apparently much in the American mold; the vice-president is to succeed the president in case of death or disability but is not otherwise assigned much to do. These amendments to the system of executive power did not in the first instance alter the rights and duties of the legislative branch, but they reflected a broader trend toward the accumulation of nominal power in the executive.

There is general agreement among Soviet officials and academics that the system itself is continuing to evolve. The Congress of People's Deputies, for example, is commonly agreed to be obsolete, whatever its utility in the first period, when the legitimacy of a representative legislature needed to be secured by ensuring the participation of all major social groups and bodies. That it is generally considered to be unnecessary in the next round of constitutional reform is indicated by the fact that none of the drafts of a union treaty currently circulating nor the draft constitution of the Russian Republic published for public discussion leaves room for a Congress of People's Deputies. Rather, they all establish a bicameral legislature in which one chamber represents national territories and the other equal popular districts.[13] Given the highly unsettled state of political arrangements at present, further significant changes are more than likely.

To summarize my conclusions here, I argue that the process of legislative institutionalization is slow and uneven. In some respects, especially in regulative policy domains, the USSR Supreme Soviet has certain accomplishments to its credit, but that these have been overshadowed by its failures to grapple with fiscal and economic policy, its weakness vis-à-vis the presidency, and its inability to enforce adherence to the laws it passes. Even looking beyond the accumulation of political and economic crises that cast the process of Soviet democratization in grave doubt, I would also argue that the future effectiveness of parliamentary power will require the development of modern partisan institutions for articulating and aggregating interests-- party electoral machines, information resources, and legislative caucuses.

Rise of the Two-Tiered Parliament

In a a recent essay, Jeffrey W. Hahn has reviewed the constitutional changes that resulted in the elections of 1989 and establishment of the Congress of People's Deputies and Supreme Soviet.[14] Hahn concludes that the new system has already demonstrated "a significant departure from past practice" and that it has "restored the idea, if not yet the reality, that real power should belong to the soviets and to those who elect them."[15]

As many Soviet and Western commentators have pointed out, a persistent pattern in the record of the new parliamentary system is Gorbachev's exercise of extralegal powers to shape it. The first instance is the rushed pace at which the new institutions were enacted into law.

The idea of a new, effective, and two-tiered parliament was first mooted by Gorbachev in June 1988 in his address to the nineteenth party conference. Perhaps responding to the calls for some sort of "popular front" to complement the party's leading role or even serve as a loyal opposition, Gorbachev proposed an expansion of the seat of state power by adding another 750 deputies to the 1,500 currently elected to the Supreme Soviet. These new deputies were to be named directly by public organizations such as the party, the trade unions, the Komsomol, and so on. The existing division of the Supreme Soviet into two sets of deputies, half elected on a basis giving equal representation to ethnoterritories of like status on the four-runged hierarchical ladder (union republic, autonomous republic, autonomous province, and autonomous district), and the other half elected by more or less equal popular territorial districts, would be retained. The new and expanded body would be renamed, however, suggesting its role as a representative and deliberative congress, while from it another and smaller working parliament would be elected. To the latter would go the name "Supreme Soviet." Gorbachev's proposals were quickly embodied in two draft documents, a set of constitutional amendments and a corresponding electoral bill, and these were submitted to the country for national discussion.

But in contrast to the usual previous practice of allowing several months for deliberation, this campaign lasted only five weeks. Opinion in a number of republics was opposed to the proposed system, on the grounds that the corporate representation for all-union public organizations would over-represent the interests of the union at the expense of republican interests. Nevertheless, Gorbachev railroaded the proposals, slightly amended, through the Supreme Soviet session in late November 1988, and the country immediately prepared itself for an electoral campaign.

In the haste of the sponsors of the new parliamentary legislation to win the adoption of the reform and proceed with elections as quickly as possible, several crucial aspects of the process of nominating, registering, and electing deputies were given scarcely any attention at the time. Later these proved to be sources of serious difficulties. One was the mechanism for supervising the electoral process, the electoral commissions. Although the commissions had enormous power, they were formed very casually, often by the executive committees of soviets. Often they simply extended the power of the local ruling establishment over the electoral process, allowing powerful officials to manipulate the election meetings and other components of the nomination, registration, and election stages. At the top, the Central Electoral Commission was the body that ruled on how many seats various public organizations would receive among the 750 reserved for them. They ruled, for example, that the new independent cooperative associations would not be permitted any seats, whereas the book-lover's society, the stamp-collectors' society, the society for the struggle for sobriety, and other amateur associations would be given one seat apiece, and the sports associations would have three seats. Another flaw was the absence of clear guidelines governing the raising and spending of campaign funds and the use of other campaign resources. Still another was the curiously unbalanced attention given to the procedures for nominating, selecting, and registering candidates. Although the elections provided for residential district nominations, it was in fact very hard for organizers of neighborhood-based candidacies to meet the 500-voter quorum set for nominating meetings. The great majority of candidates were therefore nominated through their workplaces or other organizations.

A still more troublesome requirement was the provision that when a particular electoral district ended up with more than two nominees, an election meeting was to be held to determine which of the candidates should be registered. (Legally there could be any number of candidates on the ballot; but when there were more than two, each had to pass a kind of certification process intended to ensure they had sufficient popular support to justify inclusion on the ballot.) To qualify for registration, a candidate had to receive at least 50 percent of the votes at such election meetings. Norms of representation of delegates to the election meetings were set by the Central Electoral Commission in excruciating detail in an attempt to ensure that no single nominating collective would have undue influence over the meeting. On the other hand, the conduct of the meetings often permitted the chairman of an electoral commission to exercise power in arbitrary and undemocratic ways to defeat insurgent candidates. Of all the institutional flaws of the first round of parliamentary elections, the election meetings occasioned the most criticism. Because they were widely considered to be obstacles to the free democratic expression of the voters' will, Estonia simply dispensed with them in 1989, and in 1990 the RSFSR and most other republics did so as well.[16] This in turn created still another problem--the very high number of candidates listed on ballots in the 1990 races, making it difficult if not impossible for many voters to choose among them. Once again, the lack of a party system created serious problems, in this case imposing an undue burden on the electoral process of determining which candidates should run for election.

In fact, the absence of competitive national party organizations has proven to be the origin of many difficulties because of the strain placed on parliamentary structures to compensate for them. Certainly the Communist Party performed almost none of the roles of a parliamentary party. The CPSU's role in the 1989 election was not uniform or consistent. Its leadership mobilized the party's organizational machinery to produce a slate of 100 candidates for its 100 reserved seats. This had the effect, presumably intended, of guaranteeing deputies' mandates for all Moscow-based senior party leaders without the need to face the test of popular vote. Otherwise the party was little more than a congeries of regional political machines which enjoyed varying degrees of success in influencing the outcomes of the electoral process. There seems to have been little effort to impose a consistent ideological line or organizational campaign across the party's territorial branches. (The Central Committee did produce an anodyne platform, but it simply was not a reference point for candidates. Local party organizations also issued their own platforms, usually responding to local concerns about crime, the environment, and greater autonomy.)[17] Regional leaders accordingly sought to exercise as much control over the elections as they could get away with, some misjudging their ability to manipulate the process, and others successfully using it to preserve most of their former power. In the Russian Republic, 23 of the obkom and kraikom first secretaries who ran for seats were defeated (two failing even to win nomination); 32, however, won. In the autonomous regions of the Russian republic, however, nineteen were elected and only two were defeated. As Jerry Hough reminds us, 80 percent of the republic and obkom secretaries who ran did win their races, with apparat dominance most evident in Central Asia.[18] Setting aside the Communist Party, then, as a special case, there were no national party organizations active across the Soviet Union. Independent political groups operated only on a local and regional basis. The most broadly aggregative independent political organizations active in the 1989 election were the Baltic popular fronts, although other municipal and republican popular fronts contested some local seats in other areas. The Lithuanian Sajudis, for example, won 36 out of the 39 districts where it ran candidates.

The weakening of the CPSU as a national force together with the absence of other national parties shifted the weight of political organization to localities and regions for legislative delegations as well. This pattern was reinforced by the tradition of leaving legislative leadership to delegations organized along regional lines and represented by "elders." To some extent this practice of relying on the ranking members of territorial delegations for leadership in agenda-setting has been formalized in the standing orders of the Supreme Soviet. Each chamber of the legislature uses a "council of elders" (*sovet stareishin*) to meet before sessions to discuss the agenda.[19] Regional caucuses were not only used to decide the make-up of slates for election of members of the Congress of Deputies to the Supreme Soviet in June 1989, but this practice was embedded in the standing orders of the parliament as well (Article 51). As might be expected, many regional caucuses are dominated by the old guard. For example, during the first session of the Congress of Deputies in May-June 1989, some heads of regional delegations briefed their deputies on how to vote. The obkom first secretary from the Chuvash autonomous republic, A. Petrov, met with his delegation each morning of the congress in the Rossiia Hotel and instructed them to follow the lead of the chairman and presidium in voting. During the second session of the congress, in December, he warned them against the influence of the Interregional Group of Deputies, which, he darkly intimated, was fighting for "soviets without communists."[20] The absence of developed party organizations and the compensatory strength of territorial ties tended to reinforce the power of traditional party-state apparatus leaders.

Another illustration of the point that there is a competitive relationship between the old territorial principle for grouping deputies and political parties as bases of legislative organization was the radical change in certain local soviets after the 1990 elections. The deputies affiliated with the "Democratic Russia" coalition won a decisive majority of seats in the Moscow city soviet and in several other city soviets. After the election they agreed to retain a relatively cohesive bloc structure in the republican and local soviets. At the first meeting of the Moscow soviet, the DR bloc demanded that the organizational committee, which corresponds to the presidium of the Supreme Soviet in that it determines the legislative agenda, be composed of representatives of political tendencies instead of by the old territorial principle (i.e., by district). The motion carried by a vote of 249 to 106. Each bloc was to name its own representatives, one for every ten members of the bloc. In this way, DR got 28 out of the 46 members of the committee.

The same principle--organization of the directive committee of the legislature along party rather than territorial lines--is not presently observed at the union level. The presidium of the Supreme Soviet comprises the chief executives of the union republics and a symbolic number of lesser autonomous units, together with the chairs of the legislative committees and commissions and of the two chambers. Movement in the direction of granting greater recognition to parties is evident, nonetheless, in the draft RSFSR constitution, one version of which would officially register in its proposed "parliament" parties and groups with at least ten members and would give party fractions certain acknowledged rights to proportional membership on committees.[21]

Because parties remain far stronger at the republican and local levels than at the national level, the Congress of People's Deputies and Supreme Soviet of the USSR have experienced much greater difficulty in asserting autonomous leadership over legislative acts and setting the agenda generally. It seems fair to say that the initiative has fallen to three sets of actors: the Presidium of the Supreme Soviet, the committees, and nuclei of activists among the deputies. Over the Supreme Soviet's first two years, the liberally oriented Interregional Group of Deputies has been the most successful source of legislative initiative among deputies' groups, but in the fall 1990 term, a conservative group, "Soiuz," or union, became considerable more visible and numerous than the Interregional Group. At the Congress of People's Deputies session in December 1990, the presidium agreed to register deputies' groups. The reported figures indicated something of the distribution of interests and affiliations in the congress (but note that there is no formal requirement of membership in these groups and many deputies are affiliated with more than one group):[22]

Soiuz	561 deputies
Interregional Group	229
Group of autonomous formations	239
Communists	730
Constructive interaction	153
Ecology	220
Young deputies	125
International servicemen (the "Afghantsy" or Afghan war vets)	52
Justice	40
Workers	~400
Agrarians	431
Life (a group formed by women deputies)	261
For a civil society ("za grazhdanskoe obshchestvo")	38
Cultural issues ("gruppa po voprosam kul'tury")	112
Science and Industry	87
Academic deputies ("akademicheskaia deputatskaia gruppa")	87
Social Democrats	19

Until the beginning of the fall term of 1990, the Interregional Group was the most effective group in exerting influence in the legislature, although its victories were often minor or symbolic; much of its attention, moreover, was devoted to the development of democratic institutions in republican and local government.[23] It has, however, successfully won concessions both from the presidium and from Gorbachev in confrontations with them. For example, it organized sufficient support from the Supreme Soviet in the fall session that began on September 10, 1990, to reject the agenda proposed by the presidium. Speaking for the group, Anatolii Sobchak criticized the agenda proposed by Anatolii Luk'ianov for containing several issues that are only of secondary importance, and in turn he proposed others, including a call for a vote of no confidence in the Ryzhkov government, a review of Gorbachev's presidential decrees with respect to their effectiveness and constitutionality, an investigation of the unpublished directives and orders issued by the KGB, and a transfer of the country's gold reserves to the disposition of the Supreme Soviet. At the suggestion of Iurii Shcherbak, a member of the Interregional Group from the Ukraine, a conciliation commission was formed to work out a new, compromise agenda.[24]

The Interregional Group also won minor concessions from Gorbachev on the constitutional changes establishing the presidency, including the provisions strengthening the Supreme Soviet's ability to override a presidential veto and restricting the president's ability to declare a state of emergency.[25] Trying to sum up its record, the group's responsible secretary cited a record of failures on many major issues, together with small victories in some battles; but its most important albeit intangible effect was its role in pushing the national leadership in the direction of ever more radical change. Its positions have often been rejected at one point only to be accepted later. Moreover, it succeeded in building electoral organizations in several localities through voters' clubs and regional organizations, and a number of its members have become visible and independent political figures in their own right, such as Anatolii Sobchak, Gavriil Popov, Sergei Stankevich, Fil'shin, Nikolai Travkin, Poltoranin, and Nikolai Fedorov.[26]

It is generally accepted that the legislature has been an abject failure in its efforts to enforce bureaucratic compliance with law. A deputy wrote early in 1990 that government ministers and other officials do appear before the parliament, but often not when they are supposed to appear; and when they do submit to questioning, they often fail to provide full information. Deputies are often refused access to government offices except by obtaining special permission. [27] Clearly, traditional norms are extremely hard to reform. In the case of the RSFSR parliament, the deputy chairman of the republican council of ministers (and a chief author of the 500-days program), Grigorii Iavlinskii, stated recently that it took a special decree from Gorbachev to force the Defense Ministry and the KGB to release budget information to the republican parliament.[28] Put quite simply, the Supreme Soviet has scarcely begun to wield the most powerful tool of Western legislatures vis-à-vis executives, the power of the purse. Given the general breakdown in administrative and fiscal integration of the Soviet economy, however, it is unreasonable to expect the Supreme Soviet to have gained mastery over government appropriations or planning. As one ranking official associated with the Supreme Soviet commented in an interview, "without a market there cannot be a parliament."[29]

The Law on the Press

To understand how deputies can exercise influence successfully in the face of these obstacles to legislative power, it will be useful to review one particular case of legislation, the law on the press. Analysis of the case should help shed light on the shift in the balance of political forces between executive and legislative branches brought about by the establishment of the new parliament.

The Law on the Press and Other Media of Mass Information was adopted in June 1990 by the Supreme Soviet of the USSR. The history of this bill is illuminating because it reveals the changing relations between politically interested actors and the policy-making system. To a certain degree, it illustrates continuity between the pre- and post-reform regimes, inasmuch as under the new system as under the old, coalition-building was necessary to generate a consensus for a specific decision. On the other hand, it shows still more dramatically the opportunities democratic legislative institutions create for democratic policy initiatives: the institutional changes in the policy-making environment changed the balance of power in favor of liberal democratic forces.

The first mention of a plan for a law governing the rights and obligations of the mass media came in the unusual package of planned legislation issued by the Supreme Soviet in 1986. The plan included the law on the press among the legislative drafts to be completed by the end of 1986 and published for general discussion.[30] Very soon, however, it became apparent that the process of drafting a press law had run into snags. In January 1987 a member of the Secretariat of the Supreme Soviet Presidium announced that the widening of *glasnost'* and other changes in the media had delayed work on the bill.[31] Pressure for a law on the press came from a variety of sources, journalists as well as legal scholars, but the most persistent early advocate of a law that would limit the ability of official organizations to restrict access by the media to information and establish specific rights for journalists to obtain information from state organizations was a legal scholar, Mikhail Aleksandrovich Fedotov. Relatively young--born in 1949--he had worked for the newspapers *Vecherniaia Moskva* (Evening Moscow) and *Sotsialisticheskaia industriia* (Socialist Industry) before becoming an instructor at the all-union juridical correspondence institute. He was coauthor of an article that appeared in November 1986 in *Zhurnalist* that denounced the ability of bureaucratic organs to strangle media coverage, and called for a law laying down guidelines for the authority of investigative journalism.[32] He also published a substantial article in *Sovetskoe gosudarstvo i pravo* (Soviet State and Law) in March 1987, where he described his own proposal for a press law.[33]

Throughout 1987 and 1988, Soviet sources described the press law as being "in preparation." In fact rival conceptions of a law on the press were being elaborated and circulated. Neither group was able to build a coalition strong enough to effect a decisive victory; the result was a protracted stalemate. For three years--mid-1986 to mid-1989--the process of reaching a consensus on a law on the press was deadlocked.

The law on the press obviously touches on core ideological and organizational matters, such as how far-reaching *glasnost'* would be permitted to be, whether there is a categorical right to free expression, and how to balance journalists' rights against their obligations. At some point in 1987 the party Central Committee staff commissioned a draft law, which, according to Iurii Baturin (a coauthor of the draft that was ultimately adopted, and a researcher at the Institute of State and Law) was "inspired less by legal standards than by Party documents."[34] This was circulated for comment to various institutes, including the Institute of State and Law, where Baturin and his colleague Vladimir Entin drafted alternative language. Their text was, in turn, gutted by the authorities.[35]

Traditionally, the policy process in the Soviet Union toiled extremely slowly because of the distinctive way in which centralized policy-making structures accommodated the norm of consensus. Instead of preceding a policy decision, consensus-building has *followed* a high-level decision that a particular policy decision was needed: once a decision on the intention was reached at the top, a text of the proposal would be drafted and circulated for comment among numerous interested and affected organizations. Each of these offered comments and revisions, which in turn were taken into account by the working group responsible for the document. Points of consensus were likely to be reflected in the final version enacted by the leadership. This up-and-down process of decision-discussion-decision gives meaning to the concept of democratic centralism. Paul Lawrence's brilliant analysis of the Soviet enterprise management system, for example, notes that "the centralization of one-man leadership and the decentralization of collectivism are not conflicting forms of management, impossible to reconcile. This is because the Soviets resolve the apparent paradox by clearly alternating these forms in distinct phases of a coherent system of decision making." Lawrence identifies six phases in the process as it affects management:

1. The leader sets a goal to be attained.
2. The work collective discusses the issue.

3. The amended proposal is returned to the leader.
4. The leader considers the suggestions of the collective.
5. The leader issues a decision and transmits it to his subordinates.
6. The decision is carried out.

Lawrence observes that these phases are not only separated in time, but are identified by clear social signals and rituals, so that no phase is overlooked or forgotten. For example, during the deliberation phase the atmosphere of discussion between the leader and the subordinates is loose, even jocular, whereas the atmosphere at a meeting where the decision is announced is stiff and formal, signaling the social distance between the leader and the rest of the collective.[36]

An analogous process characterizes traditional Soviet policy-making procedures. Interested bureaucracies, institutes, and organizations were consulted by being sent drafts of documents under consideration for adoption. Lawrence's Phase 1--the basic decision to adopt a particular policy --would already of course have been completed at this point. Consultation, circulation, discussion, revision-proposing, and sign-off are all elements of the second phase. Ultimately a working group consisting of representatives of several interested parties hammered out a revised draft reflecting agreement on points in dispute, and returned it to the central authorities for adoption. They, in turn, circulated it to other senior officials for comment, before it was finally given formal ratification by any of several available decision-making authorities: the CPSU Politburo or Secretariat; the presidium of the Supreme Soviet; the presidium of the Council of Ministers; or even, for budget and plan documents and a few other legislative acts, the Supreme Soviet.

The same decision-deliberation-decision model applied to the press law in 1986-89 before it was overtaken by a very different decision framework after the new Supreme Soviet convened in June 1989. Under the direct supervision of the Propaganda Department (and after the reorganization of September 30, 1988, the Ideology Department) of the Central Committee, staff workers of the presidium of the Supreme Soviet drafted a law on the press sometime in 1987. Their draft must have made some nominal concessions to the new and expanding definition of information rights under *glasnost'*, but it was, by all accounts, a very conservative document. For example, Mikhail Nenashev-- at the time, the chairman of the State Publishing Committee (Goskomizdat), and a moderately liberal centrist--expressed his own objections to it in a November 1987 article. The draft circulated to editorial offices was, he remarked, superficial and needed major revisions. It was much clearer about the obligations of the media than about the rights of journalists to obtain information; about the latter, it simply indicated that journalists were authorized to receive information from state and public organizations "according to the established procedures" (*v ustanovlennom poriadke*)-- despite the fact that no such law or regulation was on the books.[37]

In this case the bureaucracy failed to achieve a consensus through the deliberation process. Evidently, powerful opponents expressed serious doubts. At the same time, there was probably deep division among senior policy-making officials, with some seeking to regulate journalists in the increasingly uncertain environment created by *glasnost'*, and others hoping to use the bill as a statement for a general public right to information. One can readily imagine a stand-off as each tendency sought powerful patrons, for instance the first from Egor Ligachev, the latter from Aleksandr Iakovlev. Viewed as a political struggle between reformers and conservatives, it appears that the delays were being introduced by reformers unhappy with the official draft; the conservatives were therefore eager to move the process along as quickly as possible. Meeting with local media officials in Gorkii in the summer of 1988 after the nineteenth party conference, Ligachev, for example, expressed his expectation that "very shortly, we shall examine the draft, which is already sufficiently near readiness, in the Central Committee; then publish it for discussion. From every point of view, it is necessary to hasten the appearance of this law." The tenor of Ligachev's remarks suggested that he saw the law as a way both to regularize the powers of the media under *glasnost'* and to provide a legal standard against which to evaluate critical materials.[38]

The impasse is understandable. The official draft set out the rights and obligations of the media in a traditional, ideologically dominant, and statist context. Publishers of samizdat newspapers would now be subject to punishment for publishing unauthorized matter. Opinions expressed in the official press could not advocate "changes in the existing Socialist system of the USSR." The draft was a codification of the existing position of the press, modified by the conservative conception of *glasnost'* as a means of holding officials more effectively to account for their behavior. This view clashed with the liberals' vision of *glasnost'* as a progressive expansion of the sphere of protected expression for journalists and the public which would eventually establish a constitutional right to a free press.[39]

Accordingly, frustration with the official draft drove the liberal jurists to produce an alternative draft. Its initiators were Mikhail Fedotov and the two scholars at the Institute of State and Law who had earlier tried to insinuate radically new language into the official draft. Baturin, Entin, and Fedotov then spent some months drafting their own version of a press law. In their bill, censorship would be abolished, the principle of a free press established, and any independent groups or individuals would have the right to found their own print or broadcast organizations.[40] Their draft was completed by the summer of 1988. Evidently unable to publish it in Moscow, they published it in Estonia in October, first in an Estonian-language sports newspaper, then shortly afterward in *Molodezh' Estonii*. In January 1989 they submitted it for publication as a pamphlet to the Moscow publishing house for legal materials, Iuridicheskaia literatura, which allowed them to pay for its publication in April in an edition of 5,000 copies.[41] Simply achieving the publication of an alternative draft was a significant step forward for the liberal group, making it possible for them to circulate it to scholars, journalists, and deputies through the spring in order to build support.

With the convening of the Congress of People's Deputies (May 1989), followed by the election of the Supreme Soviet and the establishment of specialized legislative committees, the new parliament became the venue for deliberation on the law on the press. Early on, three committees--the Committee on Legislation, Legality, and Law and Order; the Committee on *Glasnost'* and Citizens' Rights and Appeals; and the Committee on International Affairs[42]--acquired responsibility for the bill. These committees in turn formed a working group consisting of representatives from each committee, suggesting that the initiative in framing the consensus had now passed from the bureaucracy to the legislature. The first action taken by the group, which was headed by a deputy affiliated with the Interregional Group, Nikolai Fedorov, was to reject the inherited draft that the presidium of the Supreme Soviet's staff had developed at the behest of the party ideological apparatus.[43] Instead they preferred the Baturin-Fedotov-Entin draft and took it as the basis for the future law.

Through the summer and fall, the working group sought to build a consensus around the liberal draft. Early on they tried to publish it in the monthly organ of the journalists' union, *Zhurnalist*. But the editor refused to run it without obtaining permission from the Central Committee, and Aleksandr Kapto, head of the Ideology Department, refused to grant it. Nonetheless, work on the bill proceeded. By fall, the committees on legislation and on *glasnost'* had reported out a draft bill. Following standard procedures, they then ordered that copies be printed for distribution to all deputies. Again however, they were stymied by the bureaucracy. Although he had no constitutional power to interfere in the legislative process, Vadim Medvedev, Kapto's superior and the Central Committee secretary charged with responsibility for the ideological sphere, turned out to be the chief spokesman for the forces opposing a liberal press law. In the course of a three-hour meeting between four of the deputies and Medvedev, the cautious Medvedev hedged. He expressed his unease with the article that allowed any citizen to establish a newspaper and the provision abolishing censorship. Since these were centerpieces of the liberals' conception of a press law, it was evident that he wanted an entirely different bill. Confronted with the deputies' insistence that since the bill had now been approved by two committees, he must authorize its printing, he vaguely agreed, although it still required several days more before the bill was in fact printed and distributed. At that point the working group was shocked to discover that without the knowledge or permission of the committee chairmen, "alternative language" had been substituted for the agreed-upon language on two key points in the printed bill: the article establishing the right for any citizen to found a media organ had simply been dropped, while the article specifying the rights of those who establish media organs now gave to the publishers, not only to the founders, the right to interfere in editorial operations.

This was the draft that was then distributed to the Supreme Soviet for the first reading on November 24. The Supreme Soviet rejected the bureaucracy's "alternative language" and on November 27 approved the committees' bill by an overwhelming margin (376-8-13).[44] But the version then published in *Izvestiia* on December 5, also providing the more liberal language, was the bureaucracy's "alternative draft." A still more significant assertion of the conservative forces' power was another maneuver. Although the Supreme Soviet had reaffirmed the responsibility of the same three committees that had previously worked on the bill to continue with the mark-up process, the presidium removed this power from them and instead assigned it to a special commission, dissolving the Fedorov working group which had held the principal responsibility for the bill to that point. The presidium of the Supreme Soviet--overseen on behalf of Gorbachev by Anatolii Luk'ianov--clearly was responding to the balance of the contending forces at the top of the political system in managing this bill. In this case, it is clear that Luk'ianov, testing the wind, found the combined forces of the party apparatus, censorship agency (Glavlit), and state publishing authorities stronger than the still-untried power of the elected legislature. It seems also that an important intermediary between the liberal legislators and the apparat was Georgii Shakhnazarov, a long-time house liberal who was also deputy chairman of the Committee on Legislation. It was he, for instance, who was named to report on the bill to the Supreme Soviet on the day it was voted on for its first reading; and, according to the chairman of the working group, Fedorov, who was originally supposed to give the report, Shakhnazarov glossed over the distortions slipped into the committee print.

The reconciliation commission comprised representatives of state agencies and legislative committees. No one from the party apparatus, the KGB, or Glavlit was named to the commission. But several members were presumably representing their interests. Certain state media organizations were represented. Mikhail Nenashev (recently appointed head of Gosteleradio, the State TV/Radio Committee) was on it, as were the deputy minister of justice and the chairmen of TASS, Novosti, and the State Committee on the Press (Goskompechat'). Shakhnazarov was on it, as was Fedorov. It was chaired by Konstantin Lubenchenko, from the Committee on Legislation.[45] According to Fedorov, the commission appeared to be responsive to the will of the presidium, which in turn was influenced by the conservatives' desires. The chairman of the state press committee, for example, seconded by the deputy minister of justice, declared at the first meeting that it was necessary to find a proper legislative mechanism to keep socially harmful materials from infiltrating into the press. In short, there was a strong effort to preserve a legal basis for political control over the media. In turn, although the *glasnost'* committee was charged with the task of summing up the results of the national discussion of the published draft bill, the presidium of the Supreme Soviet was able to play the legislature off against the new commission.[46]

The commission met for three months, hearing from a variety of experts. In the course of its deliberations, the draft was further amended. Some provisions desired by the liberals were dropped, such as the article establishing penalties for refusal by state organizations to provide journalists with information, or for dilatory compliance. It did not establish a general civic right to information. It did provide a right to reply in case of slander or libel, even if it were to be shown that the information contained in the libelous utterance were true. It failed to specify how, given the state's monopoly on paper and printing facilities, nonstate groups might in fact found their own newspapers, let alone broadcast services. Finally, there were fears that the courts might levy excessive damages awards in cases when information published in the media was held to be false or defamatory.[47] However, the liberals were generally able to accept these revisions, hoping that subsequent changes in the law and civil codes might provide sufficient protections. (Amendments to the civil code were adopted concurrently which provided relief to individuals and organizations if they could prove that they had been slandered or defamed or that their rights or legal interests had been damaged. In the former case, the published information had to be shown to be false; in the latter case, no such test was specified.)[48]

Meantime, by March, the party's ability to emasculate the bill's guarantees of press freedom had weakened significantly, perhaps as a result of Gorbachev's dramatic reversal on the issue of the party's leading role. In any case, a bill reflecting the most important demands of the liberal deputies --recognizing a general principle of an uncensored press and a legal right for any group or citizen to establish a media organ--was finally ready for a vote. On April 6, the legislation and *glasnost'* committees met jointly and approved a draft bill for a second reading. Finally, on June 12, 1990, four years after the first announcement that such a law was forthcoming, the Supreme Soviet passed the law on the press.[49]

Without question, the passage of the law represented a political victory for the democratic forces, and it is equally clear that the achievement was the result of a shift in the policy-making system that allowed the liberals to prevail in their long fight with the party and state bureaucracy. But a policy enactment alone is a hollow step if the law remains a purely paper guarantee of press freedom. Has it been implemented?

Here the record is ambiguous. The most immediate impact of the law is to require all media organizations to register with the state. Newspapers and other periodicals are supposed to register with the agencies designated by the Council of Ministers.[50] They can be denied the right to register if the name of the publication has already been assigned to another organization, or if the publication calls for the forcible overthrow of the state, or puts out pornography, reveals state secrets, or incites war, cruelty, violence, or racial or national intolerance.[51] The process is grinding slowly. Only a small minority of publications has been registered in fact.[52] There is ambiguity in the legal standard for registration of independent press publications: while any association of citizens has the right under Article 7 to found a mass information medium, the law also specifies that such associations must be "formed in accordance with the law." Since there is not yet a law on registering public associations, existing independent publications are in legal limbo.

The history of the new press law began with discussion of the need to codify the rights and responsibilities governing the relations among journalists, the organizational sources, and the public. With time the issue expanded to that of the legal status of the media in a democratic society. As a result, the most important consequence of the law at present appears to be in finding a legal mechanism for media organizations to declare their independence of their state and party owners. The new press law distinguishes the role of "founder" (*uchreditel'*) from that of "publisher." Some formerly state publishing organizations have gone over to the media equivalent of "leasing" by the expedient of registering their workforces (the *trudovoi kollektiv*, or labor collective) as founders. This has been initiated, for example, by *Ogonek* and *Literaturnaia gazeta*. *Ogonek*'s request has been approved.[53] In effect, we have a kind of joint management-labor buy-out of the magazine from the state owner (which was the Pravda publishing house). The editorial freedom they win in turn will force them to seek financial independence through commercial success. In the future, therefore, we will probably see a mixed media environment: official organizations will own and finance major press and broadcast outlets, such as State TV/Radio's broadcast programs, the Communist Party's daily *Pravda*, and the army's newspaper *Krasnaia zvezda*. Other major publications will "go private" through management takeovers and will be pressed by commercial considerations to raise circulation and run extensive advertising. Still others will be the organs of independent parties and public organizations, and will be financed and editorially controlled by them. The press law will indeed have an effect, principally by having created a legally operative category of "founder" of a media organization. There would be no need for a juridical concept of "founder" if all founders were, in effect, agents of a single legal person, the state. Therefore this concept alone means that a principle of rights outside the state has been recognized in the area of media expression. The separation of a "founder" from the state gives legal support to the demonopolization of state control over the flow of information and is therefore a critical normative support to the establishment of liberal democratic institutions. Needless to say, it leaves a host of other pertinent problems unaddressed: Can the state apply the standards for judging acceptable media content in an arbitrary fashion? Will the cultural climate in which officials, journalists, and the public operate accept the commercialization of the media? How will independent groups manage to put together the productive infrastructure to reach mass audiences? Legislative acts do not in themselves resolve economic, social, and cultural problems, but to the extent that affected organizations observe the requirements of the law, the law changes the distribution of power and obligations among interacting institutions.

The Legislative Agenda

In this section I will assess the record of legislative activity of the Supreme Soviet over its first four sessions, spring 1989, fall 1989, spring 1990, and fall 1990, according to the degree to which the legislature is able in fact to decide policy and, still more important, to set its own agenda.[54]

The legislative calendar is set in various ways. Early on, several bills were inherited from the previous legislative agenda, such as the press law and the proposed laws on civic associations and on youth. In certain cases, the Congress of People's Deputies instructs the Supreme Soviet to elaborate and enact legislation on a particular issue (such as the law on the status of deputies). Gorbachev as president has initiated several highly visible legislative packages, including the constitutional reforms restructuring the executive and the extraordinary powers he sought to issue edicts on the economy in September 1990. Some actions are initiated by deputies themselves, and all deputies, both in the congress and in the Supreme Soviet, have this right. Still others reflect urgent topical problems arising from changes in the political and social environment. All are scheduled for consideration by and through the presidium, meaning in practice its staff, the secretariat. The presidium has a great deal of power to determine the agenda, to assign bills to committees, and to schedule the order of consideration of acts, and as we have seen with the law on the press, the presidium is not a politically disinterested executive organ of the legislature. For most purposes it appears to be an extension rather of the power of Gorbachev as party leader and state president. Some bills alter their title, conception, and scope with time, or are simply forgotten as more pressing business overtakes them. All in all, however, there is a high level of procedural regularity and continuity to the Supreme Soviet's activity, perhaps thanks to the institutional continuity with its rubber-stamp predecessor.

At the outset, in June 1989, the two chambers of the Supreme Soviet agreed on a set of thirteen legislative actions that it intended to begin considering beyond the basic questions of setting up housekeeping: forming its own committees, determining the composition of the Council of Ministers and other posts, and establishing its own procedures. Most of these were inherited rather than being newly introduced. These bills concerned[55]:

1. product quality and consumer rights
2. protecting inventions and innovations
3. judicial reform
4. income tax
5. reimbursement of deputies' expenses
6. public organizations
7. the criminal code
8. the press and other media
9. delineation of powers of economic management between the union and the republics
10. local self-government and economic management
11. rights of trade unions
12. youth
13. freedom of conscience and rights of religious organizations

None of these laws was enacted in 1989. The law on religion was ultimately adopted only in September 1990. The press law, the law on economic relations within the federation, the tax law, the law on the status of deputies, and the law on local self-government were all passed in the first half of 1990. The laws on public organizations and the rights of trade unions were adopted in the fall session of 1990. But the bills on judicial reform, the criminal code, inventions, consumer rights, and youth, have been sidetracked. The slow pace of legislation in the first session (June 6 to August 4) is partly explained by the sizable workload of the Supreme Soviet. Besides its hearings and votes on some sixty-three ministers and deputy ministers, the Supreme Soviet also voted on the composition of the People's Control Committee, the Supreme Court, the Procuracy, and the State Arbitration Board, and of course it determined the composition and leadership of its own committees and commissions and the leadership of each of its chambers.[56]

When its second session opened (it lasted from September 25 to November 24), there were thirty-four issues on the legislative calendar, of which nineteen were deemed to be of top priority.[57] Another twenty bills were introduced by deputies themselves. Nearly all were given some consideration. Very few bills in fact were enacted, but several major regulatory acts passed a first reading and were submitted to public discussion, including the laws on the press, local self-government, property, and land. The Supreme Soviet also considered and approved some money bills, including the government's economic plan for 1990, its report on the 1989 plan's fulfillment, and the 1990 budget. Other important bills were introduced including laws on citizenship, on state language, on the rights and duties of the Ministry of Internal Affairs, on the Committee on Constitutional Supervision, on strikes and labor disputes, on amendments to the existing law on cooperatives, and on enterprises. A bill on pensions was introduced in response to a widely shared desire among legislators to improve the lot of retired and other groups dependent on state transfer payments. (Soon this became a cause as unassailable as Social Security bills in the U.S. Congress.) Some bills were introduced in response to the deterioration of national relations and federal integration, such as a bill on the rights of citizens living outside their national borders, a bill (passed into law) trying to regularize the economic rights of the Baltic republics, together with the new proposals for laws on citizenship and state language.

But overshadowing the deliberations of the Supreme Soviet, and of the Congress of Deputies when it convened at the end of the year, was the acute economic crisis. The government's economic reform commission, headed by Leonid Abalkin, sought to forge a broad compromise for a radical and concrete plan for market-oriented reform in November, but failed, and the government plan submitted to the Congress of People's Deputies in mid-December 1989 emphasized "stabilization" (through a sharp and immediate shift of government resources to the consumer sector and a stretching out of politically painful measures such as freeing prices, denationalizing state property, and putting the ruble on a convertible basis) while deferring "transition" with its politically threatening implications of freely-rising prices and a sell-off of state assets. Ryzhkov's program passed by an overwhelming margin in the Congress (1,532-419-44) and the Interregional Group's efforts to move no confidence in the government failed by a still greater margin (199-1,685-99). The absence of an alternative program--Ryzhkov threatened to resign if the program failed--meant that the choice, for many deputies, was either acceptance of the government plan or anarchy. The Congress instructed the government to develop an integrated package of laws and decrees that would provide a legal basis for the transition to a market economy.

The agenda for the third session of the Supreme Soviet (February 14-June 14, 1990) consisted of four kinds of bills: those directly tied to the government's program for economic transition; others pending from previous sessions; those responding to specific crises or challenges to union authority; and new laws.

Among the crisis-inspired legislation were resolutions about the government's handling of Chernobyl; responses to the Lithuanian and Estonian condemnations of Soviet annexation of the Baltic republics; a resolution on the continuing violence in Azerbaijan and Armenia; a bill on the legal regime under martial law; and a decision to create a legislative committee to oversee the fight against crime. Perhaps one might also include here the law providing for the first time a procedure for republican secession from the union. Inherited from previous sessions were the law on income tax; on property; on land; on amending the cooperatives law; on the enterprise; on delineation of the respective rights of the union and republican governments; the bill on the MVD's rights and duties; and the bill on local self-government. Very little room was left for new initiatives. Among these were three tax bills: elimination of the unpopular bachelor's tax; a bill regulating the state tax inspectorates; and a bill levying uniform tax rates on enterprises and organizations. Together with the adoption of the law on pension reform, which prompted a terrific row because of the conflict between the widely understood need for reduction of the budget deficit and the immense popularity of measures providing material relief of the indigent,[58] this agenda suggests that the legislature was slowly asserting its power over fiscal policy, not merely regulatory policy. It was also beginning to discover a link between taxing and spending measures and electoral response.

Although this was the session interrupted by Gorbachev's decision to seek the elimination of Article 6 from the Constitution and from party statutes and, as part of the same package, to institute the new presidency, both requiring the convening of the Congress since both required constitutional amendments, the third session was unusually productive. In four months, the Supreme Soviet considered fifty pieces of legislation and adopted nearly thirty.[59] Many of these were fundamental regulatory acts that had been under discussion for months, such as the laws on the press, on land, on property, on local self-government, on pension reform, on enterprises, on the status of deputies, on citizenship, on cooperatives, and on the delineation of powers between union and republics.

In late May Ryzhkov reported to the Supreme Soviet on the government's current "Conception" of a transition program, requesting specifically legislative authority to raise bread prices as of July 1. The mere presentation of the proposal sparked a wave of panic food buying in major cities. The parliament responded by tabling both the general program and the price increase, instructing the government to revise the program in accordance with the comments of the Supreme Soviet and republic legislatures and governments, and to come back in the fall term with a fully developed package of legislative measures together with alternative proposals. These would then be considered during September by the committees of the Supreme Soviet. Simultaneously it instructed the presidium of the Supreme Soviet to prepare, by June 25, a provisional list of laws that would need to be adopted by the legislature in connection with the transition program.[60] With respect to the bread price proposal, it pointed out in a separate resolution that the state budget and resolution on stabilizing the consumer market had expressly ruled out any price increases on staple goods. It charged the government with reworking the proposal, consulting with the republics, and resubmitting it in the fall term. The Supreme Soviet's concerns here seem to have been, first, to avoid committing political suicide by adopting intensely unpopular measures; second, to provide a sound legislative foundation for the coming marketization of the economy; and third, to ensure that the opinion of the republics was sufficiently represented in the final program. By mid-June, when the Supreme Soviet adopted these resolutions upon its adjournment for the summer, the Belorussian and Ukrainian parliaments had rejected the government's plan, and the Russian republic was on the verge of doing so as well. Yeltsin had registered his strong opposition. The Supreme Soviet refused to adopt a program that had no chance of being implemented.

There seems now to be a consensus that the Supreme Soviet can only consider 20-25 bills in a given three-to-four month session.[61] But the Supreme Soviet has only partial control over its agenda, as we have seen. Much of its workload is a function of events in the environment or is driven by the connectedness of major policy measures. This is nowhere more evident than in increasingly tense discussions surrounding the economic reform package, which over the summer became joined with the deliberations over a new union treaty. Several indications suggest that both Gorbachev and Ryzhkov recognized the expediency of transferring responsibility for the extremely risky transition package to the legislature in order to spread the political onus widely.

By the beginning of the fall 1990 session, however, the three great crises loosed by *perestroika* had grown so interconnected that the legislature was no better equipped to resolve them than were the president and government. These were the staggeringly difficult problems of managing the economy, the breakdown of central political authority as the CPSU collapsed but the new legislative and executive institutions were unable to fill the void, and the confrontation between the union center and the republics. These crises reached a head in the summer of 1990 and became a generalized crisis of state authority. For reasons that remain a matter of speculation, Gorbachev renounced his apparent agreement with Yeltsin on the adoption of a radical reform program for the union (Shatalin's 500-day program) and instead demanded that Ryzhkov's more conservative "stabilization" program be combined with the 500 days. In all likelihood, elements of the state bureaucracy refused to tolerate the substantial delegations of economic power to the republics that the 500-day program entailed. In any case, as the confrontation between right and left and between Gorbachev and Yeltsin unfolded in late summer and early fall 1990, the Supreme Soviet proved incapable of taking the initiative and unsnarling the tangle of political and economic crises.

On September 1, the presidium of the Supreme Soviet approved a decision to place before the Supreme Soviet for its consideration an agenda that included the economic transition program, the union treaty, the problem of the "war of laws" sparked by regional declarations of sovereignty, the state plan and budget for 1991, and a series of bills that were ready for a first or second reading. At the same time it assigned various committees jurisdiction over the package of bills associated with the economic transition program. When the Supreme Soviet convened on September 10, therefore, it was confronted with the challenge of legislating solutions to problems of overwhelming magnitude for which it was grossly unequipped. Lacking either internal partisan leadership to shape a response to the competing versions of the economic transition program offered by the Shatalin team and the government, or sufficient expertise to develop an alternative plan of its own, the Supreme Soviet ultimately failed to reach a consensus on a policy and granted Gorbachev the power he sought both to decide and to implement a policy.[62]

The fall 1990 session was overshadowed by the failure of the Supreme Soviet to assert its power to make national economic policy. Its legislative achievements were considerably fewer than those of the spring session. By the time it adjourned, on December 12, it had adopted laws on trade unions, associations, religion and freedom of conscience, the State Bank, and a law to increase penalties for black marketeering and speculation, and it had ratified the treaties with the United States on underground nuclear testing and explosions. It also approved guidelines for a law on the procedures for holding national referenda and for a union treaty for consideration by the Congress of People's Deputies, and the principle of the reorganized executive structure requested by Gorbachev. All these were subsequently approved, with amendments, by the Congress of People's Deputies. The Supreme Soviet became slightly more active in foreign affairs than in the past, adopting resolutions sought by the government which supported its foreign policy. For example, in addition to ratifying the nuclear test treaties, it also ratified a UN treaty on Soviet participation in international efforts to fight the narcotics trade, and passed resolutions supporting Shevardnadze's Persian Gulf policy, on measures for the evacuation of Soviet citizens from Iraq, on the Helsinki summit meeting between presidents Bush and Gorbachev on September 9, and on friendship with the GDR in view of the impending unification of Germany. Perhaps still more significant in this regard is the adoption of a statement in the laws on religion and on public associations to the effect that where international treaties to which the USSR is party contradict provisions of the laws, international treaty law takes precedence. This principle, routinely cited as well in the decisions of the Committee on Constitutional Supervision, represents a symbolically important acknowledgment of the principle of membership in a wider international normative community.

On the other hand, the Supreme Soviet still failed to adopt bills regularizing the right of emigration, regulating the powers of the militia and the KGB, on military reform, on principles of civil law, and bills on several other issues that have been working their way through the legislative mills.[63]

The laws passed by the Supreme Soviet in its first four sessions are predominantly regulatory in nature rather than distributive or redistributive, and their implementation has been gravely hampered by the inability of the legislature to penalize noncompliance by bureaucratic or local authority, which is reinforced by the weakness of judicial instruments. As the evidence cited here indicates, the legislature lacks the capacity to guide itself because of the undeveloped nature of political organizations uniting deputies around partisan or other interests; most groups of deputies are considered at present to be largely labels rather than organizations, with the exception of the Interregional Group. It set an example of skillful use of legislative tactics in the first three sessions but has been weakened and demoralized by the worsening of the political and economic crisis generally, as well as by the preoccupation of its ablest members with their duties at subcentral levels. The weakness of internal political organization is the major reason that territorial groups remain an important source of organization and initiative, and still more for the continuing domination of the presidium and secretariat over the deputies. The presidium's position in this respect is ambiguous. While nominally answering to the Supreme Soviet as a whole, it seems to have acted as an instrument of the will of the party center and the president.

Looking at the relationship between the legislative and executive branches, it remains a serious dilemma that there is no party discipline linking the president, the government, and the leadership of the parliament, because there are no political constraints on their relations with one another except for the highly embryonic norms derived directly from the constitution. The consequences of the decisions each party in this triangle adopts will thus feed back onto the legitimacy and authority of their offices rather than onto one or another political line. The general crisis of political authority in the Soviet state brought about by the collapse of the old party-state system will not be resolved until a pluralistic infrastructure of voluntary political associations develops that will unite legislators and executives around common positions and link those in power with the citizenry.

Notes

1. A concise summary of the history of the discussion and enactment of these reforms will be found in Stephen White, *Gorbachev in Power* (Cambridge: Cambridge University Press, 1990), ch. 2. A valuable overview of the new legislative structures is Stuart D. Goldman, "The New Soviet Legislature," *CRS Report for Congress* (Washington, DC: Congressional Research Service, 20 September 1990).

2. In addition to the documentary and secondary sources cited, some of the discussion in this paper is based upon interviews with Soviet officials and scholars in the United States and Moscow in January 1991.

3. Samuel P. Huntington, *Political Order in Changing Societies* (New Haven: Yale University Press, 1968), p. 12.

4. Outstanding studies include Robert A. Dahl, *Polyarchy* (New Haven: Yale University Press, 1971); Dankwart A. Rustow, "Transitions to Democracy: Toward a Dynamic Model," *Comparative Politics* 2, no. 3 (1970), pp. 350-51; Guillermo O'Donnell and Philippe C. Schmitter, *Transitions from Authoritarian Rule: Tentative Conclusions about Uncertain Democracies* (Baltimore and London: Johns Hopkins University Press, 1986).

5. Cf. Thomas Remington, "A Socialist Pluralism of Options: Glasnost' and Policy-Making under Gorbachev," *Russian Review,* 48, no. 3 (1989), pp. 271-304.

6. For more extended analyses of the 1989 and 1990 elections, see Thomas F. Remington, "Perestroika and Pluralism: The Soviet Elections of 1989," Japan-US Joint Study on the Soviet Union, Conference VI (16-17 June 1989); and idem, "The March 1990 RSFSR Elections," Darrell Slider, ed., *The 1990 Soviet Elections* (Durham: Duke University Press, forthcoming). Also see Thomas F. Remington, "Regime Transition in Communist Systems: The Soviet Case," *Soviet Economy* 6, no. 2 (1990), pp. 160-90, for a discussion of the effects of the limited liberalization under Gorbachev on the rapid spread of democratizing pressures from society.

7. Establishment of distinctive role definitions of legislative behavior is the criterion of Loewenberg and Patterson's conception of the institutionalization of legislatures. Gerhard Loewenberg and Samuel C. Patterson, *Comparing Legislatures* (Boston: Little-Brown, 1979), p. 21.

8. Cf. Jean Blondel, *Comparative Legislatures* (Englewood Cliffs, NJ: Prentice-Hall, 1973), p. 133, who warns against either an exaggerated notion of legislative "sovereignty" or an unduly pessimistic attitude about the general decline of legislatures in the modern period.

9. G. Bingham Powell, Jr., *Contemporary Democracies: Participation, Stability and Violence* (Cambridge: Harvard University Press, 1982), p. 56.

10. Under the revisions of the Constitution enacted in December 1990, which created a Cabinet of Ministers answering to the president, the parliament is still given the right to approve the structure of the cabinet, to hear the reports of the cabinet, and to vote no confidence in it and force its resignation. See *Izvestiia*, 27 December 1990.

11. The constitutional amendments establishing the new parliamentary system are given in *Vedomosti Verkhovnogo Soveta SSSR*, no. 49 (7 December 1988), item 727.

12. The constitutional amendments that were adopted were published in the central press on 27 December 1990.

13. See the conception of a union treaty published in *Narodnyi deputat*, no. 11 (1990), pp. 61-64; the draft union treaty published by *Pravda* on 24 November 1990 (in *FBIS*, 90-227 [26 November 1990], pp. 39-42); and the draft RSFSR constitution published in *Argumenty i fakty*, no. 47 (1990).

14. Jeffrey W. Hahn, "The Soviet State System," in Stephen White, Alex Pravda and Zvi Gitelman, eds., *Developments in Soviet Politics* (Durham: Duke University Press, 1990), ch. 5.

15. Ibid, p. 103.

16. Among the numerous articles in the Soviet press detailing the process by which candidates were nominated, registered, and elected, three may be noted in particular: "From Real Struggle to Real Elections," *Moscow News*, no. 11 (1989), p. 9; Iu. Ryzhov and N.S. Starovoitov, "Shkola demokratii," *Kommunist*, no. 2 (1989), pp. 46-54; and *Izvestiia*, 24 January 1989.

17. See *Izvestiia TsK KPSS*, no. 1 (1990), pp. 84-86, for several examples.

18. Jerry F. Hough, "The Politics of Successful Economic Reform," *Soviet Economy* 5, no. 1 (1989), p. 17. *Argumenty i fakty*, no. 21 (1989), reports that 191 regional and republican party secretaries ran but 126 succeeded in running without opposition. For most, noncompetitive races produced victories: of the 38 party

secretaries who lost, 32 had faced opponents. On the other hand, in localities where the political environment permitted independent popular mobilization, uncontested races were widely condemned as antidemocratic. In Leningrad, Kiev, and certain other places, uncontested races backfired for the candidates and yielded spectacular defeats for prominent officials.

19. Article 62 of the Reglament S"ezda narodnykh deputatov SSSR i Verkhovnogo Soveta SSSR, in *Vedomosti S"ezda narodnykh deputatov SSSR i Verkhovnogo Soveta SSSR*, 29 (27 December 1989). Hereafter this source will be cited as *Vedomosti*.

20. Nikolai Fedorov, "Still Trying to Influence," *Moscow News*, no. 11 (1990), p. 14.

21. Version "B" of Section V of the draft constitution, *Argumenty i fakty*, no. 47 (1990).

22. From a report on Soviet television, in BBC Summary of World Broadcasts (SWB), AU/0957 C2/2 (29 December 1990).

23. Cf. Valentin Davydov, "Neformal'noe dvizhenie: voprosov bol'she, chem otvetov," *Soiuz,* no. 20 (1990), pp. 8-9.

24. RL Daily Reports, 10 and 11 September 1990.

25. An excellent account of the autocratic methods employed by Gorbachev to push through the presidency is David Shipler, "Between Dictatorship and Anarchy," *The New Yorker*, 25 June 1990. The concessions forced by Stankevich and the liberal forces are discussed on pp. 55-56.

26. A. Murashov, "Mezhregional'naia deputatskaia gruppa," *Ogonek*, no. 32 (1990), pp. 6-8.

27. V. Danilenko, "Utverzhdaia novuiu formu pravleniia," *Narodnii deputat*, no. 2 (1990), p. 17.

28. RL Daily Report, 17 September 1990.

29. An illustrative example of the difficulty deputies have in making sense of the government's spending and planning decisions, let alone setting policy, was a report on the hearings held by the Planning, Budget and Finance Commission of the Council of the Union on the government's proposed plan and budget for 1991. See the account in *Izvestiia*, 1 December 1990 (translated in *FBIS*, 90-235 [6 December 1990], pp. 27-28).

30. Victor Yasmann, "Drafting a Press Law: Glasnost' as an Alternative to the Free Flow of Information," RL Research, 14 (8 January 1987).

31. Victor Yasmann, "Soviet Jurists Discuss Draft Press Law," RL Research, 208 (1 June 1987).

32. Yuri Borin and Mikhail Fedotov, "Pravo na informatsiiu," *Zhurnalist*, no. 11 (1986), pp. 24-25.

33. M.A. Fedotov, "K razrabotke kontseptsii o pechati i informatiki," *Sovetskoe gosudarstvo i pravo*, no. 3 (1987), cited in ibid.

34. "Glasnost' Struggles: An Insider's Account," Meeting Report, Kennan Institute for Advanced Russian Studies, 7, no. 17.

35. Ibid.

36. Paul R. Lawrence and Charalambos A. Vlachoutsicos, et al., *Behind the*

Factory Walls: Decision Making in Soviet and US Enterprises (Boston: Harvard Business School Press, 1990), pp. 76-77.

37. M.F. Nenashev, "Koordinaty glasnosti," *Zhurnalist*, no. 11 (1987), p. 11.

38. "Povyshat' sozidatel'nuiu rol' pressy," *Zhurnalist*, no. 9 (1988), p. 2.

39. On the competing conceptions of *glasnost'*, see Thomas F. Remington, "Gorbachev and the Strategy of Glasnost'," in idem, *Politics and the Soviet System* (New York: St. Martin's Press, 1989).

40. "Glasnost' Struggles."

41. Iu. M. Baturin, M.A. Fedotov, V.L. Entin, *Zakon SSSR "O pechati i drugikh sredstv massovoi informatsii": Initsiativni avtorskii proekt* (Moscow: Iuridicheskaia literatura, 1989).

42. Evidently the international affairs committee was involved because of the leadership's desire to bring Soviet legislation into conformity with international norms as provided under the Vienna agreements of January 1989.

43. Fedorov, "Still Trying," p. 11.

44. Nearly every bill in the Supreme Soviet goes through three readings. In a sense these recapitulate the decision-deliberation-decision process. The first reading is a general approval of the principle and concept of a legislative act. It sets in motion an extensive round of committee hearings, public discussion, and committee mark-up. Most of the revisions on a bill are to be completed during this phase and a broad consensus reached. The second reading is then a vote taken on the revised bill. Having passed the second reading, the bill is then returned to committee for final--and usually minor--revisions before being reported out for the third and final readings. The third reading is the actual enactment of the legislation. The time between first and second readings can be very long, while the time between second and third readings is usually much shorter. The only time a bill is enacted on the first reading is when there are no amendments or revisions and it is unanimously approved.

N.B. The three figures in the report of the vote gives affirmative votes first, followed by negative votes, then abstentions.

45. For a full list of the members, see *Vedomosti s"ezda narodnykh deputatov SSSR i Verkhovnogo soveta SSSR,* no. 1 (3 January 1990), p. 31.

46. Fedorov, "Still Trying."

47. *Izvestiia*, 8 April 1990.

48. *Vedomosti*, no. 26 (27 June 1990).

49. The English-language text may be found in the British Broadcast Agency Summary of World Broadcasts: Soviet Union, series 3 (3 July 1990). It was published in the Soviet press on 21 June.

50. Precisely *which* agency is a matter on which sources disagree. Some sources insist that all periodicals aimed at a union-wide public must register with the State Committee on Publishing; others give the State Committee on the Press. Under the law, republican and local-level media need only register with republican or local authorities. In the RSFSR a number of periodicals are registering with the Russian Republican Supreme Soviet instead of with the union government. Does this mean that a Russian republic-level periodical cannot be circulated outside the republic? The

freedom of the press partially recognized by the law makes the old hierarchical administrative subordination of media organizations obsolete.

51. TASS in *FBIS*, 90-153 (8 August 1990), pp. 47-48. Article 5 of the law specifies the limits of permissible expression.

52. RL Daily Report, 24 September 1990.

53. RL Daily Report, 17 September 1990.

54. I am grateful to Kathleen Montgomery for her invaluable assistance in compiling much of the material reported here.

55. TASS in *FBIS*, 89-122 (27 June 1989), pp. 33-4.

56. *FBIS*, 89-121 (26 June 1989), pp. 36-7.

57. Danilenko, "Utverzhdaia novuiu formu pravleniia," p. 17.

58. See *Sovetskaia Rossiia*, 13 and 16 May 1990.

59. *FBIS*, 90-100 (23 May 1990), p. 42.

60. See the Resolution (*postanovlenie*) of the Supreme Soviet, in *Vedomosti*, no. 25 (20 June 1990), pp. 658-60.

61. *Izvestiia*, 13 August 1990, in *FBIS*, 90-159 (16 August 1990), p. 34.

62. Although the Supreme Soviet rebuked the Presidium on September 11 for presenting it with an inadequately developed set of proposals, and responded by charging its committees with the task of hammering out legislative enactments that were to be returned to the floor by October 1, on September 21, the Supreme Soviet was unable to muster a quorum to debate the issue, and on September 24, by the overwhelming margins noted above, granted Gorbachev the powers he asked to assume responsibility for an economic strategy.

63. A listing of the status of agenda items readied for the Supreme Soviet's fourth session may be found in *Vedomosti*, no. 38 (19 September 1990), pp. 928-29.

10

SOVIET DEFENSE AND FOREIGN POLICY AND THE SUPREME SOVIET

Robert T. Huber

Introduction and Framework for Evaluation

The initiation in 1989 of competitive parliamentary elections in the Soviet Union, and the resulting formation of a reconstructed Soviet parliament, is attracting serious attention from both scholars and policymakers. Changes in the Soviet political structure, like so many other remarkable developments of the Gorbachev period, have not surprisingly led to speculation about the new national legislature and its future institutional direction.

Analytical questions abound. In what areas would the legislature be likely to demonstrate influence? What would be the key indices of influence? How would legitimacy be conferred or not conferred or gathered or not gathered? Is the legislature's influence inextricably linked to the formation of political parties or could it develop without sharply identifiable partisanship? Would the legislature confine its activities primarily to matters of domestic affairs, or would it also become involved heavily in matters of defense and foreign policy?

Credibly addressing these serious questions, including the subject of this chapter, is advanced significantly by placing the activities of the new Soviet legislature in a comparative perspective. Indeed, such an approach to the study of the revitalized Supreme Soviet, where the essence of defense and foreign policy activities to date is occurring, does help analysts both to evaluate and to calibrate judgments about its present course and future direction.

Central to an assessment of that course and direction is whether in fact political institutionalization is occurring in the new Soviet parliament. Such institutionalization, defined as "the creation and persistence of valued rules, procedures, and patterns of behavior that enable the successful accommodation of new configurations of political claimants and/or demands within a given organization,"[1] can be assessed with indicators that, though far from problematic, are useful in analyzing the activities of the parliament to date.

Legislative comparativists have identified a number of such indicators. They include age of the institution, complexity of goals, structural complexity both in types and in numbers of subunits, the existence of institutional independence from other institutions identified by defined norms and methods of behavior, the extent to which resources between units are regulated, and coherence of the institution defined as "substantial consensus on the functional boundaries of the group and on the procedures, including sanctions, for resolving disputes which come up within those boundaries."[2]

In addition to these indices, scholars have pointed to the openness of elite positions within institutions, the interchangeability of elite tasks, receptiveness of existing elites to newly mobilized subgroups, widely shared performance expectations, regularized recruitment to roles and movement across roles, and "universalistic criteria applied in the conduct of internal business and impersonal codes that supplant personal preferences as prescriptions for behavior."[3]

These general indicators about institutional formation must also be complemented by a number of more specific indicators confined to the study of legislatures themselves. Such indicators include:

--the nature and intrusiveness of legislative oversight into executive agencies (e.g., how does the legislature view its role concerning day-to-day operations of bureaucracies, and does it demonstrate the ability through public hearings, private persuasion, and formal action to bring about changes in the operation of policy);

--the amount of time devoted to legislative work (full-time versus part-time legislators);

--the influence of legislative committees versus the influence of the legislative leadership (e.g. agenda-setting, consideration of legislation on the floor of the parliament, degree of preservation of committee positions on legislation after floor consideration);

--intensity of legislative involvement in budgetary matters, the creation, amendment, and enforcement of legislation and laws, and the presence or absence of informal influences on policy making (i.e., do legislative units and subunits influence policy outcomes without recourse to formal powers of budgetary approval and law-making);

--the role of partisanship in shaping decisions (e.g., significance of party identification in explaining and predicting legislative outcomes);

--the degree of perceived accountability of legislators to their constituencies;

--the self-image of legislators as policy makers.

Scholarly literature and the practical experiences of policy makers in legislatures yield a rather rich comparative analytical foundation from which to assess the legislative activities of the Supreme Soviet in the 1989-91 period. Accordingly, it is to a description of these activities in the defense and foreign policy field that we now turn.

Defense and Foreign Policy Activities of the Supreme Soviet

While the Soviet Constitution gives to the Soviet parliament's presidial body, the Congress of People's Deputies, authority over the basic direction of defense and foreign policy, the Supreme Soviet, particularly the Soviet of the Union, has operational responsibility for the ratification of and withdrawal from treaties, the appointment of responsible defense and foreign policy officials, and the making of laws in those fields, including budgetary issues affecting military activity, the proclamation of a state of war in the event of armed attack on the USSR, and the decision to send forces abroad to meet international obligations.

The office of the president is responsible for the appointment and recall of diplomatic officials, the conduct of foreign relations, the official reception of credentials from foreign countries and international organizations, the initiation of a state of war in the event of armed attack, and declarations of a state of emergency or martial law in the interests of state defense and the safety of citizens (subject to approval by two-thirds vote of the Supreme Soviet).

The day-to-day implementation of Soviet defense and foreign policy is conducted by the president's Cabinet of Ministers, specifically the ministries of Foreign Affairs and Defense, the Committee for State Security (KGB), and other bodies. The presidium of the Supreme Soviet, either through its chairman or in its own name, can issue decrees, adopt resolutions, coordinate parliamentary consideration of legislation, conduct nationwide referenda and discussions of major draft legislation, and promulgate laws passed by the Congress of People's Deputies and the Supreme Soviet. The president and relevant ministries also report to the Congress of People's Deputies and the Supreme Soviet on issues affecting defense and foreign policy and can be questioned about particular issues by parliamentarians.

If it appears, at first glance, that the initiation of policy appears to rest with the president and the chairman of the presidium of the Supreme Soviet, those appearances are clearly not deceiving. Prior to early 1990, when the office of the president was created and Mikhail Gorbachev elected to the post by the legislature, the chairman of the Supreme Soviet was Gorbachev himself. His successor in that post, Anatolii Luk'ianov, is generally recognized as a strong supporter and political ally of Gorbachev.

Since 1989, the defense and foreign policy activities of the Supreme Soviet, through its joint committees on International Affairs and on Defense and State Security, and through floor debate, have been largely responsive to issues raised and framed by the presidium and the president. Former foreign minister Eduard Shevardnadze, in his formal confirmation hearing before the International Affairs Committee, regarded the powers of the committee as confined largely to the holding of public hearings on foreign policy issues. The major exceptions to this pattern were to be hearings and enabling documents on treaties to be ratified and the discussion of relevant bills submitted for consideration.[4] Other public statements by Shevardnadze tended to minimize the committee's rights and responsibilities in receiving access to information, and the bounds of appropriate legislative activism, which were to be confined largely to open debate of issues.

Activities conducted by the International Affairs Committee and the Supreme Soviet generally bear out this confined role. The committee and the parliament as a whole have received numerous reports and testimony from President Gorbachev, former foreign minister Shevardnadze, and numerous other foreign ministry officials on foreign visits and treaties concluded. Committee members have also been engaged in seeking formal contacts with a number of foreign parliaments and have undertaken extensive foreign travel. Additionally, the committee has adopted resolutions dealing with foreign policy matters such as Soviet efforts to conclude a comprehensive nuclear test ban treaty, negotiate a global prohibition on the manufacture and stockpile of chemical weapons, and broaden the activities of the Conference on Security and Cooperation in Europe. The committee has also received many prominent foreign visitors, including U.S. Secretary of State James Baker and former president Ronald Reagan.

Nonetheless, it is certainly the case that the Soviet president and the Ministry of Foreign Affairs have taken seriously the constitutional requirement to report to the parliament about foreign policy issues and answer questions about aspects of particular policy directions. These reports have been lengthy and repeated. For example, President Gorbachev's June 12, 1990, speech to the Supreme Soviet on the Soviet leader's trip to the United States and Canada provided a full review of activities during the visit. Gorbachev relayed to parliament his assessment of the conduct of U.S. relations toward the Soviet Union, official American perceptions of *glasnost'*, *perestroika*, and new thinking in Soviet foreign policy, the development of new avenues of cooperation in U.S.-Soviet relations, the status of nuclear and conventional arms negotiations including precise descriptions of elements of the draft treaties and points of disagreement, as well as the details of agreements reached on nuclear testing and chemical weapons.

Gorbachev also described briefly to Soviet parliamentarians discussions with President Bush and American officials about the continuing civil war in Afghanistan and the political situation in southern Africa, the Korean peninsula, Kampuchea, and Ethiopia. He then described the series of economic agreements reached with the United States concerning liberalization of trade, including the extension of Most Favored Nation (MFN) status to the Soviet Union provided a law providing for unimpeded emigration was enacted by the Supreme Soviet, and the extension of American trade credits to the Soviet Union. Gorbachev cited the work of a number of Supreme Soviet members including International Affairs Committee members Georgii Arbatov, Valentin Falin, and the committee chairman Aleksandr Dzasokhov, who, he acknowledged, "conducted work directly within the framework of the visit."[5] In his concluding remarks, Gorbachev urged the parliament and its committees to conduct extensive work on the emerging outlines of the strategic nuclear weapons agreement, arguing that, with respect to treaty deliberations, "we may work on the premise the U.S. Congress will set about this treaty in earnest fashion . . . and the present composition of the Supreme Soviet [should not be] any less assiduous in discussing and examining this."[6]

In a November 26, 1990, address to the parliament, Gorbachev demonstrated a similar willingness to delve into details of foreign policy with Supreme Soviet delegates. Reporting on his participation in a Conference on Security and Cooperation in Europe meeting in Paris that helped produce general agreement on reducing conventional forces in Europe, Gorbachev defended strongly the provisions of the conventional arms treaty. He cited the reliability of verification provisions unprecedented in their intrusion, and the fact that, by Gorbachev's reckoning, the Soviet Union would be able to retain approximately one-third of the remaining military forces in Europe in major weapons categories, while the unified Germany would have to reduce about one-half of the level of equipment in the territories of the former two German states.[7] He also noted agreement by conference participants to the setting up of an all-European mechanism for the participation of parliamentarians, including members of the Supreme Soviet, on European security and cooperation issues. Finally, Gorbachev described results of his visits to France, Germany, Italy, Spain, and Finland and agreements obtained for trade credits and humanitarian food assistance.

The question and answer session that followed Gorbachev's address to the parliament indicated that legislators were not inclined to accept Gorbachev's assessment of foreign policy issues without question. Specific questions were raised about why Soviet reductions under the treaty were greater than those borne by any other signatory, and why, after political revolutions in Eastern Europe, the Soviet Union would agree to a treaty in which the numerical balance of forces in Europe would favor NATO forces. Gorbachev argued, without fully persuading deputies, that such balances were sufficiently equivalent given decisions to reduce unilaterally Soviet military forces in accordance with changed military doctrine.[8]

Deputies also pressed Gorbachev on what provisions would be made for Soviet troops affected by personnel and equipment reductions. Gorbachev, while trying to assure delegates that "our main concern today [is] to do this in a way that will allow us to take care of officer cadres, the families of officers and servicemen who are connected with this reduction,"[9] Gorbachev did not provide concrete answers about how demobilization of personnel and conversion of defense facilities would proceed.

While connected directly with his remarks, delegates also afforded themselves the opportunity to question Gorbachev on the situation in the Persian Gulf, specifically whether the United States would enter into armed conflict. Gorbachev referred to ongoing Soviet diplomatic efforts with the government of Iraq and at the United Nations. He stressed that Soviet foreign policy activities on the issue were undertaken within the framework of the UN Security Council and called for the withdrawal of Iraqi forces from Kuwait. In an interesting aside, Gorbachev cited the right of the Soviet president to conduct such activities under the amendments to the constitution approved by the Congress of People's Deputies. He also acknowledged that the Supreme Soviet should also participate in the discussion of such issues, but his remarks seemed to suggest such participation was conditional on existence of legislation or treaties proposed by the president and could not be initiated by legislators themselves.[10]

In his official capacity, then Foreign Minister Shevardnadze also frequently appeared before the parliament and the International Affairs Committee concerning matters of Soviet foreign policy. For example, Shevardnadze's addresses to the parliament on September 11, 1990, and October 15, 1990, dealt in detail with the situation in the Persian Gulf and the conclusion of a peace treaty with the newly unified Germany.

The September 11 address described the Iraqi invasion of Kuwait as an act of aggression. Shevardnadze emphasized that norms of international law, including respect for the inviolability of established borders, as well as the principles of new thinking in foreign policy compelled the Soviet Union to support UN-imposed economic sanctions. Shevardnadze stated that Soviet policy regarding the Gulf crisis stressed the need for emphasis on collective efforts to resolve the crisis, preferably through nonmilitary, political-diplomatic efforts. He described direct meetings with Iraqi officials in an effort to resolve the crisis, the efforts to obtain the release of Soviet citizens from Iraq and Kuwait, and difficulties that arose in arranging evacuation.

Shevardnadze's October 15 address to the Supreme Soviet dealt primarily with the treaty with the newly unified Germany. He argued that the division of Germany was artificial and, like the developments of 1989 in Eastern Europe, was "taking place in a controversial and very often painfully difficult way."[11] Shevardnadze argued that the conclusion of the treaty had resulted in a wave of support in Germany for the refusal of Soviet foreign policy makers to use military confrontation to prevent reunification. He also described the various treaties concluded with Germany soon to be submitted to the Supreme Soviet for ratification (the settlement of borders, economic and science cooperation, withdrawal of Soviet troops, transitional economic arrangements) and spoke in strong support of them.

Shevardnadze argued that the treaty had several real benefits for Soviet security, including the reduction of the size of the German army, the denuclearization and demilitarization (at least in terms of the presence of foreign troops) of the territory of the former German Democratic Republic, and the denunciation by the new, united Germany of possession of nuclear weapons or other weapons of mass destruction. Anticipating deputies' concerns, Shevardnadze described precisely the financial arrangements reached with respect to the withdrawal of Soviet troops from Germany, including 15 billion marks for the temporary presence of Soviet troops and transport costs associated with withdrawal. The figure, mostly provided on a grant basis, includes funds for housing construction in the Soviet Union, and training and retraining of Soviet troops discharged into reserve.

Shevardnadze's October 15 address also reiterated Soviet positions on the Persian Gulf crisis. Shevardnadze reaffirmed that Soviet military participation in a UN multinational force required approval by the Supreme Soviet, although he reiterated his support for the reinvigoration of the Military Staff Committee of the UN Security Council, which could recommend that the general staffs of the five permanent members of the Council designate military units to take actions in support of Security Council resolutions. He reiterated that should the Military Staff Committee be activated for this purpose "this is not 1979, . . . and any use of troops outside the country will require the decision of the Supreme Soviet."[12] He denied that there was any intention by the Soviet leadership to take part in military operations in the Persian Gulf. Finally, he reemphasized continuing Soviet efforts to evacuate its citizens from Iraq and Kuwait.

Questions directed to Shevardnadze by deputies were by no means wholly positive. A number of delegates regarded the current direction of Soviet foreign policy as based on "unfounded, one-sided concessions,"[13] including the withdrawal of Soviet troops from Eastern Europe, the agreement to destroy the Krasnoiarsk anti-ballistic missile radar, and the decision to support United Nations action against Iraq, which was seen as undermining Soviet influence with Arab states in the Middle East. Shevardnadze did not respond to the criticisms directly, although he did respond positively to the suggestion from Deputy En Un Kim, a member of the International Affairs Committee, for joint actions between parliament and the Ministry of Foreign Affairs[14] on major foreign policy issues.

Since Shevardnadze's resignation as foreign minister, the regularized parliamentary question hour has become even more intense. His successor, Aleksandr Bessmertnykh, has been questioned in detail about criticism by U.S. policy makers of Soviet efforts to deal with political unrest in the Baltic states. Bessmertnykh has also been questioned about the precise details of U.S.-Soviet cooperation concerning the Persian Gulf crisis, particularly after the initiation of allied military intervention in January 1991.

Unlike his predecessor, who tended to be more combative in responding to questions from deputies, Bessmertnykh has sought to reassure legislators that U.S. criticism of the government's handling of the situation in the Baltic states was inappropriate behavior for the conduct of bilateral relations. He has emphasized that the principal direction of Soviet policy has been to end military action by allied forces as soon as possible. The nature of questions concerning the Persian Gulf crisis, which have come not only from right-wing but also pro-Gorbachev deputies, as well as the nature of Bessmertnykh's answers, suggest that Soviet parliamentarians are learning the art of using forms of executive accountability like the question hour to shape at least informally the implementation of foreign policy.

While reports to the Supreme Soviet on foreign policy issues have been precise and detailed, and questions from deputies have often been contentious, there is still no clear sign that the parliament is prepared to alter substantially the foreign policy direction or implementing program of Gorbachev and the Soviet Foreign Ministry. Shortly after the above discussion in the Supreme Soviet, the parliament approved a resolution supporting the general direction of Soviet foreign policy. While debate was "far from a walk-over for Shevardnadze, who received a grilling from some deputies critical of the Soviet Union's concessions on a number of issues,"[15] the resolution passed easily, with a number of deputies, including most members of the International Affairs Committee, supporting the resolution.

In fact, most of the activity of the committee and the parliament has been highly supportive of the basic direction of Gorbachev's foreign policy. While briefings conducted for the committee by Foreign Ministry officials on the situation in the Persian Gulf have led to some concern about the loss of economic trade, and the presence of large numbers of American troops in the Persian Gulf, the committee did support, with little difficulty, the Soviet president's position.[16] The committee has also, with one notable exception described below, been quite supportive in ratifying treaties submitted to it on a variety of subjects including international drug trafficking, limited nuclear testing, and chemical weapons.

Ambassadorial appointments have also been generally approved without controversy, although Chairman Dzasokhov has noted with some satisfaction that "plenipotentiary representatives of our state in the past were a kind of secret that was kept behind closed doors somewhere deep inside the Ministry of Foreign Affairs," and that now appointments to such positions would "pass a kind of 'test' of *glasnost'* within the walls of the Supreme Soviet."[17] The committee's high level of acquiescence with foreign policy formulation and implementation by the Soviet executive branch has been generally verified by Soviet scholars studying the subject, who have decried "the passiveness of the Supreme Soviet and its committees" on foreign policy issues and warned "there is a real danger that certain committees will become simple appendages of the corresponding departments and will serve their narrow interests."[18] From what can be observed, draft legislation on foreign policy issues seems to be closely coordinated between committee members and Ministry of Foreign Affairs officials, with final legislation not likely to leave the committee without the concurrence of the ministry.

Still, there have been at least two major foreign policy issues whose handling by the Soviet executive branch appears to have raised major objections on the part of the parliament. The first concerns the German treaties. In a September 20 meeting before the International Affairs Committee, former foreign minister Shevardnadze presented the treaties for what was hoped would be rapid ratification. Shevardnadze reiterated many of the same arguments he had outlined in his earlier September 11 address to the parliament described above. Shortly after Shevardnadze's testimony, the committee recommended Supreme Soviet ratification of the treaty.

Nonetheless, the recommendation was not without subsequent controversy. Deputy Kim complained that the committee had not been adequately consulted about the terms of the treaties, most notably the renunciation of the 1975 friendship and cooperation treaty with the former German Democratic Republic. A number of questions about the implications of abrogation, including transitional financial arrangements for Soviet troops remaining in the newly unified Germany, could not be answered by Foreign Ministry officials when the Supreme Soviet was presented with the resolution on October 2. According to Kim, delegates were given the resolution only ninety minutes before floor consideration, and he asked angrily, "why is the conclusion of important agreements affecting the vital interests of the Soviet Union conducted without prior consultations with the Supreme Soviet and our committee?"[19]

Key members of the Defense and State Security Committee also complained about the haste of legislative consideration. Reflecting an opinion that was widely held within the Ministry of Defense, committee members complained that the treaties did not take adequate account of the practical and logistical problems of removing hundreds of thousands of troops from the former German Democratic Republic. They further argued that the timetable in the treaties for withdrawal was far too rapid.

Efforts by members of the Foreign Ministry to answer deputies' questions were judged to be unsatisfactory and the resolution approving the abrogation of the 1975 treaty was not adopted. A subsequent resolution deferred consideration of all the German treaties until legislative committees had an opportunity to deal with concerns expressed by deputies.

Eventually, in March 1991 the German treaties were ratified by the Supreme Soviet. Nonetheless, ratification came only after a much more deliberative legislative consideration in which both the International Affairs and Defense and State Security Committees participated. Unlike the single, desultory hearing held by the International Affairs Committee in early September, the two committees heard not only from Foreign Ministry officials but those of the Defense Ministry as well as academic specialists. Deputies opposed to the treaties were allowed to participate in committee hearings. The lengthy deliberations on the treaties helped build a more stable consensus for their approval, which eventually occurred by overwhelming majority. The consensus-building process provided the most credible evidence to date of institutionalized legislative involvement on defense and foreign policy issues.

Interestingly enough, the decision by the Supreme Soviet to defer consideration of the German treaty package, including the abrogation of the 1975 GDR treaty, was cited in Shevardnadze's resignation speech as an example of how a growing political dictatorship was forming that threatened the essence of Gorbachev's political reforms. Shevardnadze strongly condemned the introduction of the resolution by Presidium Chairman Luk'ianov:

> At Comrade Luk'ianov's initiative, literally just before the start of the sitting, a serious matter was included on the agenda about the treaties with the German Democratic Republic. As it happened, I was on my travels, and they called in deputies, and people found themselves in an utterly stupid position, and the issue was a flop. I myself had to speak the following week. How did it turn out? Those same people who are now speaking as the authors came out with serious accusations against the foreign minister of unilateral concessions, of incompetence, lack of skills, and so on and so forth. Not one person could be found, including the person in the chair [Luk'ianov], to reply and say simply that this was dishonorable, that this is not the way, not how things are done in civilized states. I find this deeply worrying.[20]

Shevardnadze's strong criticism of Luk'ianov was intriguing but puzzling. Arbitrary control of the parliamentary agenda, as will be discussed later, had hardly been without precedent since Luk'ianov's accession as chairman of the presidium, and such arbitrariness had in fact worked to the leadership's advantage in expediting consideration of foreign policy issues in the past. Furthermore, the German treaties are one of the centerpieces of Gorbachev's foreign policy, which Luk'ianov would not likely subject to some sort of parliamentary ambush. Nevertheless, the fact that the challenge to the treaties was mounted by conservative Supreme Soviet deputies, particularly the Soiuz group, which includes members of the Supreme Soviet serving in the Soviet military, is an indication of parliamentary activism on an important foreign policy issue.

Moreover, Soiuz's success in delaying ratification of the German treaties represented an effort to use legislative power to force changes not only in policy but also perhaps in the personnel carrying out that policy. While ultimately not successful in this case, Shevardnadze's eventual resignation appears in part to have been designed to forestall a major effort by Soiuz to deny his reconfirmation as Foreign Minister in the new cabinet government installed by Gorbachev in early 1991. While such a nomination would probably have been secured despite Soiuz's opposition, the use of the nomination process to constrain the policy making initiative of the Ministry of Foreign Affairs is becoming an identifiable strategy.

This strategy is also evident in Soiuz's active opposition to Soviet policy with respect to the Persian Gulf crisis. Despite Shevardnadze's public statements to the Supreme Soviet that the dispatching of Soviet troops would occur only with the approval of the parliament, Shevardnadze had implied in press statements that should Soviet citizens in Iraq be in danger, the Soviet president could authorize military action without parliamentary approval.[21] This statement brought a storm of protest from Soiuz deputies. On December 3, Soiuz issued a statement demanding an explanation of the government's intentions regarding the sending of Soviet troops to the Persian Gulf, and calling for a special parliamentary session in January 1991.

The government's response came in the form of a written but not delivered speech by Shevardnadze to the parliament. In the speech Shevardnadze argued that "even in one's wildest imagination, not one of our diplomatic acts has implied or can imply any Soviet combat participation whatsoever, as well as auxiliary or any other troops or formations, in any combat actions in the Persian Gulf region."[22] Shevardnadze did acknowledge, however, that should Soviet citizens in Iraq be in jeopardy, "the executive authority will be forced to apply extreme measures without the consent of parliament, inasmuch as it will not have time for this."[23]

Ultimately, despite Soiuz's opposition, and its success in forcing an extended parliamentary debate on Persian Gulf policy, the Supreme Soviet passed a resolution in January 1991 approving the broad outlines of Soviet policy in dealing with the crisis. Nonetheless, conservatives did persuade parliamentary leaders to support a provision in the resolution which reiterated that the dispatching of Soviet armed forces into conflict in the Persian Gulf would require parliamentary approval. The provision did not appreciably change what had been the intention of the Soviet leadership on this issue. Nevertheless, the fact that Gorbachev's parliamentary supporters felt the need to defuse the issue by including a provision regarding prior legislative approval of the commitment of troops into conflict indicated that a parliamentary majority supported the reassertion of the parliament's constitutional authority in this area of defense and foreign policy.[24]

In addition to these two areas of contention, a third issue of possibly growing contention that will likely emerge in upcoming sessions of the legislature concerns levels of assistance to foreign countries--never popular with any parliament. Indications are strong that deputies in the International Affairs Committee and the parliament generally would like to hasten the pace of reductions already taken in the foreign assistance budget. This sentiment is particularly strong concerning allies in the developing world, such as Cuba. Various forms of subsidized assistance to Eastern Europe can also be expected to come under increasing criticism, and Deputy Kim in public statements has stated that the committee "should not simply confirm the figure for credit or free aid to a particular country."[25] Kim anticipated that in 1991 grant economic aid would be reduced from 2.1 billion rubles to 300-400 million, and argued that aid should no longer be given for reasons of "prestige rather than anything else."[26]

Somewhat more active than the International Affairs Committee, the Committee on Defense and State Security has been involved in a variety of issues within its purview. Discussions within the committee have included issues such as the size of the overall defense budget, problems of conversion of defense to civilian industry in light of reductions in Soviet armed forces, military reform and problems of Soviet military personnel, housing and transitional assistance for demobilized Soviet servicemen, and the operations of the KGB. The committee also approves the confirmation of key officials of the Ministry of Defense and the KGB.

Some Soviet scholars have regarded the creation of the committee as signaling an important change in the perceptions of the Soviet political leadership concerning oversight of defense and state security functions, previously treated "as an enigmatic 'terra incognita' for the whole of society," with activities "assigned a kind of sacral character, one that did not tolerate interference by the unordained."[27] Soviet scholars have also been tolerant to some degree in acknowledging the largely acquiescent posture of the committee on defense issues, noting that "a parliamentary committee that has just obtained access to the 'holy of holies' of executive power for the first time"[28] is likely to lack aggressiveness in pursuing its authority.

Nonetheless, on many issues, the performance of the committee does not inspire great confidence. The consideration of the state defense budget has been relatively brief. In 1989, for example, the two principal changes initiated by the committee were (1) to increase, within the overall budget request of the Ministry of Defense, funds for improving living conditions for officers, and (2) the elimination of highway construction and uniformed military construction units in civilian industries from the budget of the Ministry of Defense so as to preserve scarce budgetary dollars.

However, the defense budget has not received exhaustive review. Overall consideration of the defense budget in 1989 took only three weeks, and this trend was not seriously reversed in 1990. Difficult questions of weapons priorities and numbers within defense budgets, reducing weapons design bureaus, and other more difficult budgetary tradeoffs have not been addressed in detail by the committee.

A number of other critical issues have received extensive discussion but no decisive action. With respect to conversion of defense industries to civilian production in order to improve economic conditions in the country, tangible progress is not apparent. The Ministry of Defense draft law calls for the reduction of production of 420 defense enterprises by the year 1995, and envisions that 60 percent of output at defense enterprises will consist of consumer goods."[29] However, the precise provisions of the law have been the subject of committee hearings, which have resulted in a return of the draft law to the ministry for further work. A number of controversies remain, including the nature of conversion itself and its constituent elements, into what types of machinery should products of defense industries be converted, and whether such conversion will in fact yield benefits or actually incur budgetary costs. Also creating controversy has been the question of what types of fundamental and applied research should be supported by the defense budget, to which defense enterprises it should be allocated, and appropriate bureaucratic control of the conversion process between military and civilian ministries.

Major discussions have also occurred in the committee and the parliament concerning an organic defense law for the Ministry of Defense. Unlike many other countries, in the Soviet Union there is no organizing statute for the major ministries of the government that describes and limits their authorities and powers and provides for designation and delegation of those powers. The 1988-89 political reforms envisioned the creation of such statutes to be a major activity of the new parliament. To date, the discussions on a basic defense law have been intertwined with an effort to develop a military reform statute that would deal with the myriad of force structure and equipment issues that have arisen in light of the withdrawal of Soviet troops from Eastern Europe, reductions in the defense budget, and corresponding doctrinal changes affecting the size of force structure.

Many issues remain to be sorted out in the preparation of a defense law. These include the appropriate organizational-staff structure of the armed forces, general guidelines for procurement policy, training and political indoctrination of personnel, and the nature of legal protection of military personnel in the performance of their duties. The legal responsibilities of the Minister of Defense versus the president concerning defense doctrine and equipment research, development, and procurement, and the practice of conscription versus volunteer service or variations of both approaches have also been discussed in detail.

Not surprisingly, these elements of the defense law are the subject of considerable controversy. During committee discussions of military reform and the defense law in 1990, the committee's subcommittee on the armed forces was engaged in intensive debate with the Ministry of Defense over the terms of the basic law, particularly on provisions concerning a transition to an all-volunteer army, the terms under which military doctrine would permit offensive action by the Soviet armed forces, and the appropriate balance of quality vs. quantity in weapons procurement. According to Soviet sources, the ministry pressured uniformed military members of the committee not to support drafts of the defense law introduced by Deputy Vladimir Lopatin, a major in the Soviet armed forces and an advocate of far-reaching reforms in the military.

Lopatin's activities have been among the most interesting pursued by the committee to date. Lopatin's draft defense law was developed in consultation with a number of academic and ministry institutes. Lopatin has been identified in the Soviet press as the ad hoc leader of a small group of "radical" military officers who have pressed for improved housing conditions for Soviet servicemen, prosecution of hazing incidents and deaths of Soviet servicemen, investigation of corruption among senior Soviet military officers, and other sensitive issues. Lopatin was originally successful in getting committee approval for a working group on military reform, in which he was designated chair.

The key feature of Lopatin's draft defense law, originally presented in April 1990, calls for a "phased transition to professional armed forces, smaller in number, but better in quality, manned by volunteers, exterritorial in structure, and international in composition."[30] The development of national formations, which were also used in a modified form by the Soviet military in the 1920s, would be based on service by citizens within a territory in which they reside. Each union republic would delegate defense powers to the central authorities, but could use such forces in the event of natural disasters or civil disturbances. The Lopatin draft also calls for the disbanding of political units from the military, arguing that the constitutional termination of the Communist Party as occupying the "leading role" in Soviet society and the subsequent formation of other political parties makes it essential to end political indoctrination in the armed forces.

Ministry officials have staunchly opposed the Lopatin draft law. Testimony has been inconsistent, however, providing differing figures as to the cost of such a force (though consistently saying it would cost much more). In Lopatin's view, the country would benefit economically from an end to conscription, since the size of the civilian labor force would likely increase. Ministry officials, including Defense Minister Dmitrii Iazov, have contended that severe shortages of personnel in the military would only be further aggravated by the ending of conscription, thus making it impossible to achieve defense objectives. Iazov has also been vague on how existing political units would be reorganized in the armed forces.

The achievement of defense objectives is, of course, a rather subjective judgment which has also provoked considerable debate. Lopatin has disputed the size of the official defense budget, which for 1990 was placed at 70 billion rubles, and for 1991, slightly over 96 billion rubles. He has criticized the unwillingness of the leadership to come up with a more credible figure. According to Lopatin's estimate, funds for military activities are spread across ten ministries. He has called for the merger of such activities under the control of the Ministry of Defense. With respect to procurement policy, Lopatin has criticized defense industry control of the procurement process, which, it is argued, has produced poor quality equipment.

Lopatin has a rather dismal view of the ability of the Defense and State Security Committee to deal with these fundamental problems of defense production and organization. He has argued that the committee, in part because its members have careers in the military and defense industries, "is still incapable of controlling the situation confidently."[31] Lopatin's view of committee interests was somewhat borne out by consideration of the defense budget for 1991, in which the committee proposed a budget slightly over 100 billion rubles, which was a higher figure than that proposed by either the Ministry of Defense (98 billion rubles) or the Supreme Soviet as a whole (96 billion rubles).

Deputy Committee Chairman Vladimir Ochirov has acknowledged some of the shortcomings of the committee's work although he has indicated that the committee will more seriously address the difficult questions raised by the defense law in coming sessions. On the issue of conscription, Ochirov has suggested a compromise closer to Iazov's position than Lopatin's. Under this proposal, after an initial period of conscription yet to be worked out, servicemen could contract for specific service in various parts of the armed forces, the intention being to enhance professionalism and volunteerism.[32]

Predictably, the Soiuz group has attacked the Lopatin draft. One of the group's more vocal spokesman, Nikolai Petrushenko, has argued that national formations would only increase instability in the non-Russian regions of the Soviet Union and undermine central political control and national security. Petrushenko has argued that without conscription, serious manpower shortages will develop. He has also opposed the abolition of a CPSU structure within the armed forces.

This is not say, however, that conservative deputies are necessarily opposed to any package of military reforms. The leader of the Soiuz group, Lieutenant Colonel Viktor Alksnis, has expressed his interest in seeing a major reform law passed in the Supreme Soviet, and has confined his objections to the Lopatin draft to the national unit formation issue. Other conservative deputies, supported by moderate spokesmen in the Soviet military, have pointed to the value of overhauling the procurement system to break up patronage networks between the military and defense industries that have resulted in poor quality equipment deliveries to the various armed services. Experimentation with a market system of competition has been advocated.[33] Nonetheless, conservative and liberal reformers have not been able to achieve compromises that might checkmate or overcome considerable Ministry objections to credible military reform.

The debate on the defense law and accompanying reforms dragged on throughout 1990 without resolution. Nonetheless, as of this writing it appeared the Lopatin draft was not faring well as increasing political instability led to a growing political conservatism in the parliament. While there continues to be rhetorical support for a basic law and a reform of the armed forces, evidence continues to mount that President Gorbachev has turned decisively against the Lopatin draft or any similarly ambitious package of measures designed to overhaul the Ministry of Defense.[34] Lopatin himself had his working group disbanded as a committee entity by Luk'ianov, and Lopatin has been forced to reconstitute his group in the parliament's Committee for Science, Public Education, Culture, and Upbringing.[35]

In addition to debates and deliberation on specific legislative initiatives and issue areas, the Supreme Soviet has been a forum for an ongoing debate between liberal and conservative legislators concerning military doctrine and required levels of force structure. This debate, which has been led for opposing sides by deputies Georgii Arbatov and Sergei Akhromeev respectively, has attracted considerable public attention and has also been carried out on the pages of several Soviet periodicals including *Ogonek* and *Krasnaia zvezda*.

Arbatov has argued that a reduced military threat to the Soviet Union and the formulation of the doctrine of reasonable sufficiency have made reductions in military spending justifiable, particularly in a period of economic decline. He has condemned what he has referred to as the militarization of the economy, the scientific establishment, even the process of the socialization of youth. He has characterized the Ministry of Defense as top-heavy, with leftovers from "the period of stagnation, when marshals and generals . . . were given a free hand and became subject to no control."[36] He has ridiculed the glorification of past Soviet political leaders with military ranks and awards.

Arbatov has further argued that long years of intensive military spending only worsened Soviet security by producing an impressive anti-Soviet coalition in both Europe and Asia and intensifying technological backwardness through a distorted pattern of economic investment that favored military outlays. He has also accused the military of slandering its critics and falsifying information about the Soviet force structure.[37] He has taken issue with military estimates of American defense spending and numbers of troops. Finally, he has called for placing the Ministry of Defense under the control of not only the Soviet president but also the Supreme Soviet through established procedures for budgetary appropriations. He has criticized the Defense and State Security Committee as having been "staffed to a considerable degree by representatives of the leadership of the military and the defense industry," and has argued that the committee has become the industry's lobby "rather than a parliamentary oversight organ."[38]

In response, Akhromeev has questioned Arbatov's competence in discussing matters of "military science" and has attempted to refute Arbatov's estimates of military spending as a percentage of GNP, the relative size of the U.S. and Soviet military forces, the levels of U.S. defense spending, the size of the armed forces of NATO and Warsaw Pact countries, and other issues. Akhromeev has denied that the military is not already controlled by the political leadership of the country and has labeled such charges an attempt to "set off the Army against the people and depict it as a reactionary force as well as a source of danger for the people and the country."[39] Akhromeev has also spent considerable time in debates describing the deteriorating living conditions of Soviet servicemen, and the negative attitude and alleged legal discrimination demonstrated toward them, particularly in non-Russian republics. He has indicated that critiques of the policies of the Ministry of Defense have contributed to a "crisis of state authority."[40]

Except for the marginal changes described earlier, the debates over the future of military force structure and spending have been largely declaratory in nature and have not resulted in any major legislative changes. Nonetheless, the discussions in the parliament about the most fundamental of decisions about defense and national security policy suggest that conditions may be developing for such changes in the future.

Structure of Decision Making and Perceptions of Results

To date, there remains an unclear pattern concerning the institutionalization of defense and foreign policy considerations as a legitimate activity of the Soviet parliament. The amended Soviet Constitution calls for the rotation of about one-fifth of its membership annually, with a similar rotation for the larger, part-time legislature, the Congress of People's Deputies. Mechanisms for this rotation are still not clear and the rotation is not to pertain to chairmen of standing joint committees such as International Affairs and Defense and State Security.

Additionally, joint committees are to be composed of equal numbers of the members from the Supreme Soviet and the Congress of People's Deputies. These rules of rotation and membership, at least in the view of some committee members, frustrate the development of full-time legislators and legislative business, since they make it difficult to achieve quorums (the Congress of People's Deputies is a part-time legislature and its members often are not in Moscow) and conduct committee business (rotation of members disrupts stable membership on the committee).

Conversely, there is evidence that the professionalization of legislators is in some measure proceeding. The committees on International Affairs and Defense and State Security do have a core of legislators who have been assigned to the Committees on the basis of past experience in the relevant subject areas. Deputies Evgenii Primakov, Akhromeev, Ochirov, Evgenii Velikhov, and Mikhail Simonov, serving on the Defense and State Security Committee, as well as Arbatov, Genrikh Borovik, Fedor Burlatskii, Roald Sagdeev, Anatolii Cherniaev, Valentin Falin, and, to a lesser extent, Chairman Dzasokhov of the International Affairs Committee, all have had strong careers of service with respect to defense and/or foreign policy.

Nevertheless, these deputies continue to serve in a variety of other capacities where evidence of involvement and influence in policy is greater than that exercised through service on parliamentary committees.

Indeed, Supreme Soviet deputies involved in defense and foreign policy activities have pointed to the development of full-time legislators as critical to the future institutionalization of the parliament as a policy-making body. The committees are still served by rather small staffs compared to the size of staffs that appear at committee meetings from the cabinet ministries. Neither the International Affairs nor the Defense and State Security Committee has staff for its three subcommittees, despite the fact that those subcommittees deal with critical issues such as treaty ratification, emigration law, arms control, the composition of the armed forces and defense industries, and the operation of the KGB.

The budgets of the committees are not controlled by the committees themselves and funds must be obtained largely through two sources, the budgets of the counterpart ministries and the presidium of the Supreme Soviet. With staffing limited and budgets controlled by outside sources, prospects for an activist role in policy making will be constrained severely, and committees and deputies generally will be dependent on sources of information and resources that seem likely to limit parliamentary autonomy. The shortage of staff, the rules of rotation, and other conditions deleterious to the formation of full-time legislators have led many deputies to be extremely reluctant to "relinquish their outside careers given the uncertainty of the ongoing political processes in the Soviet Union and their tenure in it."[41] These conditions have also led many Soviet legislators to conclude that unlike their peers in other national legislatures, particularly the U.S. Congress, they are "much less able to deal with the details"[42] of a variety of issues.

Nonetheless, there are some signs that the Soviet executive branch takes the committees seriously. Both the Ministry of Defense and the Ministry of Foreign Affairs have established liaison departments to deal with deputies of the Supreme Soviet and its standing committees. These liaison departments review legislation proposed by the ministries as well as amendments proposed by committees, and provide briefing papers and other information for deputies in their committee work or in their foreign travel. The liaison departments are a healthy sign of acceptance of the legislative branch as an evolving focus of decision making of some undefined nature.

Additionally, the past experiences and institutional ties of some deputies enable them to acquire information informally from the Soviet executive branch. Staff of committees are often drawn from ministries, sometimes as detailees, and academic institutes are often called on to provide information on issues in order not to have to resort to ministry expertise. Committees and deputies, however, must rely on the patrimony and volunteerism of such institutes, since the experts are on the wage bill of institutes, not the parliament, and cannot be compelled to provide information to the Supreme Soviet.

Some efforts are under way to alleviate at least partially the impediments to legislative activism. The parliamentary budget for the Supreme Soviet is estimated to be about 40 million rubles, well in excess of what was spent on the parliament prior to the political reforms of 1988-89. In addition, an agreement with the Congressional Research Service of the Library of Congress is designed to increase staff support and resource information available to deputies on both domestic and foreign policy issues, as well as assist in providing expertise drawn from Western experience on the operation of the legislative process and the writing of laws. There have also been innumerable exchange visits by Western legal experts and political scientists designed to assist in the institutionalization of the parliament as a policy making body.

While there is considerable uncertainty and doubt about the influence of committees in the parliamentary structure, there is little doubt about the power of the parliament's presidium and secretariat. The secretariat serves both the Supreme Soviet and the Congress of People's Deputies and is believed to have a personnel strength of about 700, including a number of sections providing deputies with administrative and substantive services. In addition to staff that committees may hire or contract for independently, staff is assigned to committees by the secretariat, with the approval of the presidium. One indication that service in the secretariat is clearly more important than service through committee hiring is the apparent ease with which staff is hired by the secretariat compared to the recruitment difficulties committees have faced in hiring their own staff. Furthermore, since the budgets of committees have to be approved by the secretariat, staff hired by the secretariat would clearly carry more influence.

The presidium of the Supreme Soviet serves as the parliament's rule-making body. It appoints committee members and appears to have a strong hand in selecting committee chairmen. It also plays the most critical role in directing the work of committees and determining the scheduling of legislation reaching the floor. Unlike the practice in a number of other parliaments, at the beginning of each Supreme Soviet session the presidium introduces a lengthy resolution outlining the priorities of each of the parliamentary committees, as well as an agenda of issues to be considered for the entire session.[43] Not surprisingly, the agenda has reflected the priorities not so much of the parliament as of the Soviet president. Perhaps in response to both the substance and the arbitrariness of such an agenda, the Supreme Soviet rejected the agenda proposed by the presidium for the fall 1990 session. While the parliament can reject the entire agenda, it has been unable to propose one of its own, leaving the presidium largely in control of the legislative center of gravity.

During floor debate, Chairman Luk'ianov has often shown a low threshold of tolerance for floor amendments to legislation before the parliament. As a sort of super-rules committee, Luk'ianov has been regarded by supporter and opponent alike as having a strong ability to determine--rather arbitrarily--the schedule of the Supreme Soviet on any given legislative day. Together with the ministries and agencies involved in the operational implementation of defense and foreign policy, the presidium and the cabinet ministries have often shown a minimum regard for regularized rules and orderly consideration of issues. For example, at various times during the consideration of a new emigration law, International Affairs Committee deputies have complained that draft provisions were sent to them only days or hours before committee consideration. Efforts to question ministry officials about implementing issues and provisions of the law have been largely unsatisfactory. On other issues, efforts to elicit information about various aspects of foreign policy (hard currency derived from arms sales, the details of current negotiating positions in arms control fora, information on the budgets of some parts of the Defense Ministry and KGB, the number and types of economic and security agreements with foreign countries) have not been satisfactorily answered.[44] As we have seen in the case of the German treaties, the presidium has also shown a willingness to try to rush through parliamentary approval.

The intolerance of the presidium with respect to the pace and intensity of parliamentary consideration of issues is not without some justification. Deputies themselves have not always accorded themselves well, and respect for regularized rules and procedures have often been lacking. The Soviet press contains a number of instances of both journalists and deputies complaining about the professional conduct of the Soviet parliament.[45] The parliament has frequently been bedeviled by a lack of a quorum for consideration of legislation and corresponding low roll-call voting, which has reduced political accountability. There have often been lengthy delays in the consideration of legislation scheduled, repeated efforts particularly by conservative deputies to shout down or interrupt speakers, violations of norms for recognition of speakers, and dilatory tactics of seeking explanations on provisions already considered in detail. Additionally, deputies have frequently engaged in debate nongermane to the subject under consideration, asking for votes on measures on which votes had already been taken, and preparing unprinted amendments introduced for consideration without notice to deputies. Finally, as we have seen, the enactment of a number of measures has been delayed by the formation of proliferating committees and task forces set up to study alternatives when consensus could not be reached.

Deputies also seemed quite concerned about the relevance of their activities for policy implementation. Laws passed are regarded by many deputies and executive branch officials as hasty and subject to continuing revision, thereby threatening their practical legality.[46] When enacted laws have been more capably written, oversight has been weak, despite strengthened legal provisions enabling parliamentarians to request and compel testimony from executive officials and to investigate abuses of authority and government expenditures. Compounding this problem has been the so-called "war of the laws" in which local and republican parliaments have sought to vitiate the effects of national laws that are regarded as inconsistent, inappropriate, or politically unpopular in local and republican jurisdictions. In the defense field, this problem is particularly acute, since the laws governing military conscription have been rejected in a number of republics and have led to recent efforts by Moscow to restore the authority of the Soviet central government in Lithuania and Latvia. In the foreign policy field, the Ministry of Foreign Affairs and the parliament of the Russian Republic have disagreed with the Ministry of Foreign Affairs over the scope of negotiations with Japan concerning the Northern Territories.

There are also differing perceptions among Soviet legislators about their appropriate role in the evolving political system. Some apparently feel that scarce resources and lack of full-time status make them ill-equipped to deal with "the seriousness of their country's needs, the high expectations and presumably growing impatience of the public, and the importance of the work they have undertaken."[47] A tendency to defer to the executive branch in decision making outcomes or to defer issues for further study, a tendency by no means unique to the Soviet parliament, is clearly evident. A countervailing tendency "to get on with the work of reform, perhaps even preferring to choose any issue as a starting point rather than to do nothing at all,"[48] while present among more activist legislators, seems less well-developed.

Worsening economic and political conditions in the Soviet Union have also led legislators to express great skepticism and despair about the ability of the fledgling parliament to deal with the problems presented to them by their constituencies. The plight of servicemen who were victims of violence within the armed forces or whose economic position was worsening as a result of the Soviet government's inability to absorb personnel returning from Eastern Europe are seen as two problems on which the parliament is unlikely to have a major impact. Furthermore, deputies who have served on defense and foreign policy committees have found that their constituents are more likely to be interested in issues of day-to-day survival concerning food shortages and increased crime. Public demands for results, in the view of some deputies, could threaten the existence of the parliament itself, since "the average citizen has little to show for all the turmoil that Gorbachev's reforms have created."[49]

Much like other indices of institutionalization, party formation within the parliament, particularly on defense and foreign policy issues, remains quite nascent. Lopatin's group, while it appears to have a great deal of cohesion on defense issues, taking common stands on a number of questions including the appropriate approach to defense conversion issues and the level of military threat to the Soviet Union, has admitted that it has yet to develop sufficient unity to constitute a voting bloc on defense and foreign policy issues.[50] Similarly, the Interregional Group, a large, loosely configured group of prominent individuals supportive of continuing economic and political reforms, has been a strong supporter of the basic lines of Soviet foreign policy as presented by Gorbachev and Shevardnadze and affirmed by various resolutions of the parliament. Nonetheless, the Interregional Group has been primarily focused on more contentious and nettlesome problems such as economic reform and the extent of political freedoms, executive and legislative powers, electoral reform, and autonomy of local and republican governments. Despite willingness by U.S. Secretary of State Baker to establish a dialogue with the Interregional Group should it seek to establish itself as a parliamentary opposition to the Communist Party, the group still operates in a very sporadic way, and does not appear to choose defense and foreign policy issues as a focal point for disagreements with the Soviet president, his cabinet, or right-wing parliamentarians.[51]

Perhaps the most cohesive political formation at this juncture, particularly on defense and foreign policy issues, is the Soiuz group, whose actions on such issues has already been discussed in detail. But Soiuz is difficult to characterize using an analytical framework focusing on the formation of political parties. Soiuz's leader, Colonel Alksnis, has advocated the suspension of the Supreme Soviet and political parties. Much of the bloc's political agenda, and its claimed success in effecting a rightward push to Soviet politics in the last months of 1990 and the early months of 1991, involves a political strategy of working with a variety of state institutions, particularly the Ministry of Defense, to bring about desired changes. It is not clear, in fact it is somewhat doubtful, that the Supreme Soviet is the primary focus of Soiuz's struggle to implement its political agenda.

Finally, clearly frustrating this nascent party formation has been the unwillingness of the parliament's presidium to recognize or incorporate parties or oppositional coalitions in legislative work. Anything resembling minority leaders, party whips, or caucus chairmen is absent from parliamentary proceedings. The continuing preference of both Luk'ianov and Gorbachev to work with political figures in the presidium or in the parliament with whom they are comfortable, rather than with those from various coalitions, is a serious impediment to party formation. Similarly, the leaders of coalition groups, with the possible exception of Soiuz on some foreign policy issues, do not appear to regard their coalition or the parliament as a critical channel through which influence is exercised.

Such perceptions have crippled badly the establishment of legitimacy in the Supreme Soviet as a significant and effective political institution. The procedural shortcomings described above, and the nascent and highly uncertain party and/or coalitional formation within the parliament have no doubt contributed to growing frustration both within and outside the Supreme Soviet about the effectiveness of the parliament itself. While this chapter has described significant parliamentary inability to reach consensus and compromise on defense and foreign policy issues, this pattern of irresolution has not been confined to these matters alone. It has also been manifested in ineffective consideration of legislation on price controls, emigration law, economic reform blueprints, and a whole host of other major domestic issues.

Continuing frustration with the results of Supreme Soviet deliberations in both domestic and foreign policy has led President Gorbachev to seek increasing expansions of presidential power. The fact that the parliament has largely acquiesced in this process is powerful testimony to self-doubt about the institution among its members. Many parliamentarians, by the end of 1990, were reaching the conclusion that since "the Supreme Soviet has proved itself incapable of acting decisively . . . it must now accept reduced authority."[52] The decision in September 1990, with the near unanimous approval of the Supreme Soviet, to grant to the president the power to issue decrees having the force of law without parliamentary approval, brought into sharp focus the tenuous nature of legislative power and the tentativeness of the parliament's place in the institutional setting of the Soviet political system.

Conclusion

As we approach the end of the first two years of the life of the revitalized Soviet legislature, measuring, at least in qualitative terms, the scope, intensity, and direction of institutionalization reveals a largely negative, but somewhat variegated pattern of evidence. Clearly, many of the indices of institutionalization, drawn from the comparative study of other parliaments discussed at the outset of this chapter, are not present or are barely present in the activities of the Supreme Soviet to date. This is particularly true in the field of defense and foreign policy. Largely absent are valued rules, procedures, and patterns of behavior designed to accommodate successfully new political claimants or demands. Procedures are largely undefined, and when present are initiated by the secretariat and the presidium of the parliament. Demands for reform, or for that matter reaction, are not being met through legislative action, as one measure after another is either hastily drawn or delayed in disagreement between the president and the legislature.

Coherence and regulation of functional boundaries are also not well-defined. A problem springs up, and a committee or working group with undefined powers is appointed to deal with it. Members appointed to such committees or groups do not necessarily reflect the range of political groups or individuals interested in resolving problems with which the new legislative entities are designed to deal. Committee resources for oversight activities and staff support are not regulated within the parliament but rather by the secretariat and, curiously, by the ministries on which legislative oversight and accountability are supposedly being conducted. Until this situation is changed, committee responsiveness to issue areas within its jurisdiction is badly compromised by outside political control of resources by the Soviet executive branch.

Additionally, the deterioration of parliamentary debates into *ad hominem* attacks and unstructured, ineffective consideration of amendments does not bode well for the development of substantial consensus on the agenda of issues that will be considered. Indeed, that agenda has been controlled to a remarkable extent by the executive branch appendages of the parliament, the presidium and the secretariat.

Openness of elite positions within institutions is not readily apparent although there is some room for debate on this point. The most powerful officer in the Supreme Soviet, the chairman of the presidium, cannot with any credibility be regarded as a choice of legislators but rather that of the president. Nor are elite tasks interchangeable in the sense that logical candidates for the task of chairman of the presidium, chairman of either house of the parliament, or committee chairman can be predicted with reliability by identifying leading parliamentarians who derive their prominence from recognized accomplishments within the parliament itself.

Receptivity to new elites is also not well developed. Political parties or groups represented in the Supreme Soviet do not appear to conduct their activities with the achievement of legislative goals in mind. There is no structure of party leaders, with the possible exception of Soiuz, which, ironically, has advocated the suspension of parliamentary activities. Lopatin's military reform group, which was originally sanctioned as a working group within the structure of the Defense and State Security Committee by Luk'ianov, had official sanction withdrawn, forcing Lopatin to find another institutional location for his group's work. Such arbitrariness does not suggest universalistic criteria applied in the conduct of internal business, nor impersonal codes that supplant personal preferences for appropriate legislative behavior.

The continuing impediments to a full-time professional parliament bedevil the institutionalization of the Supreme Soviet. Parliamentarians are quite reluctant to leave other official posts from which they derive their political influence, professional security, or both. Rules of rotation calling for the turnover of one-fifth of the parliament threaten further the evolution toward a body of full-time parliamentarians. Committees seem reluctant to send their own versions of legislation to the floor of the parliament unless they have been cleared by the agencies that would be affected by the legislation's provisions. Budgetary control is still beyond the parliament's reach, with budgetary review still at an early stage. Measures of partisanship are premature, since party formation, particularly on defense and foreign policy issues, is still at a very early stage. Finally, the self-image of legislators seems low, with a growing sense that the parliament is unable to deal with growing demands of constituents for resolving serious everyday concerns such as putting goods in stores and finding jobs for demobilized servicemen. This, in turn, has led to growing willingness to defer these matters to executive authority, accepting emasculation and marginalization of one's own legislative work.

Despite this highly negative portrayal, the process of institutionalization is by no means fully arrested. The more limited goals of institutionalization advocated by Gorbachev, Shevardnadze, and other political elites who played a key role in the 1988-89 political reforms have largely been achieved. Increasing transparency of the decision-making process in defense and foreign policy matters so as to prevent the kind of closed decision making that led to the Soviet invasion of Afghanistan was clearly a critical objective of the reforms which produced the current structure of the Supreme Soviet.[53] This objective has been significantly advanced. Testimony before the Supreme Soviet and its committees on defense and foreign policy issues is much more detailed and frequent than was the case before the parliamentary reforms.

Nor is the parliament simply a legitimating body for decisions already made--a change which is the source of some pride for parliamentarians,[54] who point out that they are no longer simply rubber-stamping decisions taken by a small group of political figures in the Communist Party Politburo.

In recent months, while clearly remaining a Gorbachev loyalist, Dzasokhov has helped define a substantial consensus about institutional boundaries and defined roles. The emergence of "parliament men," who in any legislature help defend legislative prerogatives and work with the executive organs of government on policy outcomes that legitimate a role for the legislature, are still only emerging in the Supreme Soviet.

Nonetheless, Dzasokhov's performance in the debates over the German treaties, the Persian Gulf crisis, and executive nominations suggests he may be evolving into one of the Supreme Soviet's "parliament men." Dzasokhov, in parliamentary debate, has reminded executive nominees always to consider domestic political considerations in the crafting of foreign policy. He has defended the right of deputies to oppose the foreign policy direction of the president and have that opposition represented in public debate. As noted earlier, Dzasokhov played an important role in developing the prior legislative approval provision in the January 1991 Supreme Soviet resolution on the Persian Gulf. With regard to formulation and implementation of Persian Gulf policy, Dzasokhov has skillfully positioned himself as an "honest broker" between those in the parliament and the Soviet foreign policy bureaucracy advocating close cooperation with the United States and the pro-Iraqi position advocated by Soiuz.

Other indices of institutionalization are also present. While in some ways proliferation of groups and committees indicates ineffective decision making, the resort to such a tactic is hardly confined to the Soviet parliament. In some ways, this response is an indication of the complexity of problems faced, and the corresponding need for structural complexity if they are to be responded to appropriately.

Furthermore, receptivity to newly mobilized subgroups in the political system has not been foreclosed totally within the parliament. Lopatin's group did, after all, find a new location in the Science Committee to continue its work. Various groupings of deputies are developing, and in the case of the Soiuz group, are beginning to feel the possible influence that derives from the threat of bloc voting. The decision of the parliamentary leadership and former foreign minister Shevardnadze to shelve the German treaties is an indication that some elements of party formation are starting to take shape. Soiuz's attempted use of legislative power, including the threat of opposing nominations to limit executive flexibility on some foreign policy issues is another indication that informal influences on policy making may be developing.

While legislative oversight has not been highly impressive, it is certainly well-advanced when considered in the perspective of the pre-1989 Supreme Soviet. Ministers of government cannot count on a ritualized presentation of policy, followed by "softball" questions from a sympathetic parliament. Indeed, Shevardnadze's outburst during his resignation speech about inappropriately intense questioning of the German treaties, and the intense questioning of Minister of Defense Iazov on military reform issues indicate that legislative oversight at the level of hearings and public criticism is becoming an accepted element of the decision-making process on defense and foreign policy matters. As a result of laws passed concerning the rights of parliamentarians to conduct oversight, request information, and question ministers of government and their associates, the potential for far-reaching involvement in the day-to-day operations of policy is in place.[55]

While progress toward a full-time legislature has been frustrated, from a historical perspective the trend toward such a process seems more evident. Compared to the two-day, twice a year meetings of the pre-1989 Supreme Soviet, the current parliament is meeting most of the year and has not been without its achievements. Scores of laws have been enacted, some of which appear to have been effective in addressing important issues of Soviet politics.[56] The decision to defer consideration of the German treaties indicates at least an implicit acknowledgment of the parliament's informal ability to influence decisions without resort to actual exercise of legislative power. Such a development has far-reaching implications for institutionalization should it continue on other defense and foreign policy matters.

Finally, the low self-image of parliamentarians regarding their own effectiveness and that of the Supreme Soviet generally is by no means universally felt. In fact, some observers have suggested that this posture of fatalism and deference to executive authority is particularly concentrated among older parliamentarians, with younger deputies still relatively eager to support the process of legislative activism on a variety of issues. Over time, therefore, support for activism may actually gain supporters in the parliament. This is particularly true if further delegations of authority to the president are not perceived as effective in dealing with problems faced by Soviet society. As of mid-1991, there is good reason to believe such delegations will not have the desired effect.[57]

What, then, of the future direction of the Supreme Soviet? The answer to this complex question goes to the heart of longstanding discussions in the social sciences about appropriate criteria for deciding what a legislature is and what it does. Without conducting a full review here of the scholarly literature and debates within it, several considerations are relevant for reviewing and defining loosely a range of expected activities. Through this review and definition, some light will also be shed on where the Supreme Soviet might be placed within that range, and what future developments are important for ongoing classification in a continuum of legislative activity.

The presence of a number of expected characteristics has been regarded as relevant to the term *legislature*. Many of these characteristics have been discussed at the outset of this chapter and are central to the institutionalization of legislatures. Such characteristics include goals, values, and structures, degree of autonomy from other political institutions, binding lawmaking ability, accountability and responsiveness to constituencies, selection rules and procedures both to enter the parliament and to operate within it, intensity of activities, policy-making initiative and influence, self-perceptions of salience of activities, and perceived legitimacy of the legislature by the executive power and elite and mass publics.

From the literature on comparative legislatures, a useful typology has been proposed for helping to analyze the Supreme Soviet. Briefly put, five categories have been described:[58]

(1) active legislatures (capacity to modify policy, fundamental legitimacy unchallenged by executive, strong support by mass and elite publics);

(2) vulnerable legislatures (tradition of extensive powers, including the modification of policy, which has been suspended or replaced by executive action; legitimacy among executive, elite and mass publics uneven and sporadic);

(3) reactive legislatures (informal influence on parameters of suitable policy making, but only rare exercises of formal power in a manner opposed by the executive, legitimacy widely accepted by executive, elite and mass publics);

(4) marginal legislatures (extensive formal limits on budgets and lawmaking; remaining powers exercised through informal negotiation with the executive; periodic suspensions of legislative power by the executive; low or degrading legitimacy among executive, elite and mass publics);

(5) minimal legislatures (no powers to modify budgets or propose laws;

symbolic ratification of decisions made by other institutions; legitimacy conferred by executive; accepted by elite and mass publics).

As the author of this typology himself concedes, the conceptualization of legislatures in this manner is not without serious difficulties.[59] Wide variations could well exist within categories and certain functions can be fulfilled by a given legislature across a number of categories. In the most extreme example, an active legislature can perform functions described of a minimalist one by acting favorably on nonbinding resolutions in support of an existing policy direction initiated by the president or through passage of legislation without amendment.

Nonetheless, the typology does serve a useful purpose in outlining possible future movement of the Supreme Soviet along a legislative continuum. There seems to be growing evidence on the basis of processes described in this chapter (and others in this book as well) that the Supreme Soviet has moved out of the minimal legislative category to which scholars have usually assigned it. Budgetary consideration of executive activities has been enhanced. No longer are oversight activities perfunctory. Legislation is no longer merely ratified symbolically. Contentious, sometimes even confrontational debate occurs on a wide variety of issues.

But if the Supreme Soviet has moved out of the minimal legislative category, how might it now be described? As we have seen, there is evidence primarily for two categories. First, some characteristics of a reactive legislature appear to be present. The debate and postponement of consideration of the German treaties, disagreement over Persian Gulf policy, the extended arguments over military reform, and the regularized "question hour" directed at Gorbachev and other executive officials suggests the development of a reactive legislature. Indeed, the concept of public accountability of policy making through a reactive legislature fits Gorbachev's own conception of the new Supreme Soviet, although Gorbachev's and Luk'ianov's actual conduct of legislative business often belies their words.

Scholarship on comparative legislatures describes an institutionalized type of reactive legislature as popularly elected, performing representative and system-maintenance roles within society. Political parties are well established, with opposition parties within the parliament exercising oversight and holding the government accountable to elite and mass publics. Party discipline is high, and the government's policy in nearly every case carries the day, though informal agreements or policy adjustments are frequently used to ensure outcomes.

This description of a reactive legislature is, on balance, not appropriate for describing the Supreme Soviet at the present juncture. Despite some evidence supporting the characterization of the Supreme Soviet as taking initial steps toward becoming a reactive legislature, the weight of evidence suggests that the Supreme Soviet is a marginal legislature. In fact, the following passage from the work of one scholar on comparative legislatures

and the characteristics of a marginal legislature bears a striking resemblance
to the current conditions describing the activities of the Supreme Soviet:

> Marginal legislatures are characterized by a lack of congruence between the
> behavior of legislators and the expectations of both mass publics and
> executive-centered elites. In addition, role consensus among the legislators
> seems to be absent. . . . These legislatures are the objects of a very heavy
> demand volume despite their limited capacities because they are the most
> accessible institution in their countries. But their members do not deal very
> effectively with this demand load because many of them do not perceive
> their role in these terms and those who do, although they devote a great deal
> of effort to the task, are stymied both by the sheer volume of requests and by
> the attitudes of uncooperative executive elites without whose assistance
> these demands cannot be met. . . . Given these "failures" there is no reason
> for executive-centered elites to support the legislature. Thus, coups or other
> extraconstitutional actions directed against marginal legislatures are quite
> common and these institutions disappear, reappear, and disappear once
> again on a more or less regular basis. [60]

The development of a marginal legislature in the Soviet Union should
hardly be categorized in some normative way as a failure. After seventy years
of Soviet history in which the national legislature dozed away in a minimalist
political position, the transformation that has occurred in the last two years is
an important systemic change. Furthermore, from a comparative historical
perspective, the transformation from one category to another in a span of
only two years is indeed a rapid transformation, particularly in the fields of
defense and foreign policy, where parliamentary activities are typically highly
restricted in all but the most active of legislatures. Parliaments emerging
from a minimalist status do not take on major new responsibilities without
great institutional uncertainties, unstable rules and procedures, unsettled
perceptions of appropriate roles, poor and unfocused resources, weak
oversight ability, and fundamental doubts about legitimacy from within and
without.

Indeed, legitimacy in particular remains a critical barometer of whether
the revitalized Supreme Soviet will remain a marginal legislature or become a
reactive or even active legislature. Critical disagreements in the fields of
defense and foreign policy concerning conscription, the composition of
military units in the republics, and elements of foreign policy affecting
neighboring states are a reflection of a whole range of disagreements that
have resulted in a myriad of national, republic, and even local laws in
contradiction to each other. While republic and local legislatures, at least in
the fields of defense and foreign policy, have in large measure supported
executive authority at each corresponding level, competing public demands,
elite allegiance, dissensus over federal and local control of resources and

jurisdictions, and nascent legislative institutionalization engender the type of centrifugal tendencies that produce countervailing support for concentration of executive power as well as mass public support for such concentration.

Ultimately, the future development of the current legitimacy crisis, along with other indices of institutionalization, will condition the political environment in which the Supreme Soviet will operate. Such indices will also perhaps determine the movement of the new Soviet parliament along the continuum of possible outcomes. Other chapters in this volume describe these processes and they need no further elaboration here. Nonetheless, the gathering of evidence on types and scope of activities in such areas as defense and foreign policy offers important signals of the trends in those larger political processes already under way in the Soviet political system.

Notes

1. Richard Sisson, "Comparative Legislative Institutionalization: A Theoretical Exploration," Allan Kornberg, ed., *Legislatures in Comparative Perspective* (New York: David McKay Co., 1973), p. 19.

2. For further discussion on this issue see Samuel P. Huntington, *Political Order in Changing Societies* (New Haven: Yale University Press, 1969), pp. 8-22.

3. For more on these points, see Nelson W. Polsby, "Institutionalization and the U.S. House of Representatives," *American Political Science Review* (March 1968), pp. 144-68; also see Sisson, pp. 2-23.

4. Shevardnadze's comments before the committee seemed to confine legislative activity to a largely passive, supervisory role. For example, while hearings were to be held on a variety of issues including foreign policy budgets, participation in international negotiations, and appointments for ambassadorial posts, Shevardnadze seemed to imply that the committee would not have powers to alter, modify, or revise proposals from the Soviet executive branch. While the legislature could reject or approve such activities, such an all-or-nothing approach severely constricts practical legislative influence. For more on these points see James P. Nichol, "Soviet Constitutional-Legislative *Perestroika* and Foreign Policy Making," paper delivered at the 1989 Annual Meeting of the American Political Science Association, pp. 3-15.

5. "Gorbachev Speaks to Supreme Soviet 12 June," Foreign Broadcast Information Service (hereinafter referred to as *FBIS*) 90-114 (13 June 1990), p. 56.

6. Ibid., p. 57.

7. "Gorbachev Addresses Supreme Soviet 26 November," *FBIS* 90-228 (27 November 1990), p. 34.

8. Ibid., pp. 7-38.

9. Ibid., p. 40.

10. Gorbachev, echoing Shevardnadze's views on the appropriate role of legislative activity on foreign policy issues, suggested that while the Supreme Soviet could choose to ratify or not ratify treaties, individual exercises of broad foreign policy powers given to the president could not be modified by the parliament. See the November 27

speech, p. 41.

11. "Shevardnadze Addresses Supreme Soviet 15 October," *FBIS* 90-200, p. 17.

12. Ibid., p. 20.

13. See comments of Deputy Nikolai Petrushenko, a leader of the Soiuz group, in ibid., pp. 20-21.

14. Ibid., p. 21.

15. "Supreme Soviet Approves Foreign Ministry Policies," *FBIS* 90-200, p. 24.

16. For more on International Affairs Committee activities regarding Soviet policy on the Persian Gulf crisis, see A. Sychev, "Committee Approves Government's Position," *Izvestiia*, 1 September 1990, p. 1; for the text of the Supreme Soviet resolution approving Gorbachev's handling of the crisis see "O positsii Sovietskogo Soiuza v sviazi s obstanovkoi v Persidskom zalive i ob itogakh vstrechi Prezidenta SSSR M.S. Gorbacheva i Prezidenta SShA Dzh. Busha v Khel'sinki," *Pravda*, 12 September 1990, p. 1.

17. L. Dekabrev, "Chrezvychainye i polnomochie--vpervye," *Pravda*, 13 April 1990, p. 1.

18. A. Kortunov and A. Iziumov, "Chto ponimat' pod gosudarstvennymi interesami vo vneshnei politike," *Literaturnaia gazeta*, no. 28 (11 July 1990), p. 14.

19. S. Karkhanin, "B sessii Verkhovnakh Sovetov SSSR i RSFSR," *Sovetskaia Rossiia*, 4 October 1990, p. 1.

20. "Shevardnadze Resigns at 20 December Congress Session," *FBIS* 90-245, p. 12.

21. Shevardnadze's offered this view during an interview with Bill Keller of the *New York Times*; for more on the controversy see Suzanne Crow, "Legislative Considerations and the Gulf Crisis," *Radio Liberty: Report on the Soviet Union*, 2, no. 50, pp. 1-3.

22. "Shevardnadze Speech Says No Gulf Force Planned," *FBIS* 90-239, p. 29.

23. Ibid.

24. For more on the controversy over Soviet policy toward the Persian Gulf among Gorbachev's foreign policy advisors, and its possible effect on parliamentary debates, see Suzanne Crow, "Moscow Struggles with Decision on UN Force," *Radio Liberty: Report on the USSR*, 2, no. 48 (30 November 1990), pp. 1-3.

25. Karkhanin, "V sessii," p. 1.

26. Ibid.

27. G. Sturua, "Komitet po voprosam oborony i gosudarstvennoi bezopasnosti: pervye mesiatsy raboty," *Mirovaia ekonomika i mezhdunarodnaia otnosheniia*, January 1990, p. 79.

28. Ibid., p. 83.

29. "Moiseyev Discusses Defense Industry Conversion," *FBIS* 90-204, p. 89; see also D.T. Iazov, "Voennaia reforma," *Krasnaia zvezda*, 5 June 1990, pp. 1-2.

30. N. Burbyga, "V komitetakh i kommissiakh Verkhovnogo Soveta SSSR: Proekt voennoi reformy," *Izvestiia*, 11 April 1990, p. 3.

31. Lopatin's remarks were included in an abridged report of a defense roundtable sponsored by and published in *Krasnaia zvezda*, 27 June 1990, p. 2, under the heading

"Armia i voennaia reforma."

32. Ochirov's views are also reported in the June 27 report, p. 4.

33. For more on the debate on military reform within the Soviet military see Stephen Foye, "Hard-Liner Calls for Military Reform," *Radio Liberty: Report on the Soviet Union*, 2, no. 43 (26 October 1990), pp. 6-8.

34. In a November 1990 meeting with Soviet servicemen holding public offices of various kinds, Gorbachev spoke out specifically against the Lopatin proposals. For more information see Stephen Foye, "Gorbachev, the Army, and the Union," *Radio Liberty: Report on the Soviet Union*, 2, no. 49 (7 December 1990), pp. 1-3.

35. For more on the transfer of the Lopatin group to the Supreme Soviet's Science Committee, see V. Kosarev, "Debate on National Security Problems," *Krasnaia zvezda*, 22 June 1990, p. 1.

36. G. Arbatov, "Armiia dlia strany ili strana dlia armii?" *Ogonek*, January 1990, p. 4.

37. Arbatov has particularly criticized Akhromeev and other senior military leaders for including reserve and national guard troops in accounting of Soviet armed forces troop strengths, thereby inflating the size of reductions required by the conventional arms control reduction agreements in Europe. See Arbatov, "Armiia. . ., p. 4.

38. Ibid.

39. S.F. Akhromeev, "Armia nuzhdaetsia v zashchite," *Krasnaia zvezda*, 28 June 1990, p. 2; for other criticisms of Arbatov by senior military officers see G. Kirilenko, "What to Consider Reasonable, What Sufficient," *Literaturnaia Rossiia*, 23 March 1990, p. 17.

40. Akhromeev, "Armiia nuzhdaetsia," p. 2.

41. United States, House Committee on Armed Services, 101st Cong., 2nd sess., *The New Soviet Legislature: Committee on Defense and State Security*, report prepared by Mark Lowenthal, Senior Specialists Division, Congressional Research Service, Library of Congress (Washington: Government Printing Office, 1990), p. 7.

42. Ibid.

43. The promulgation of such a document by the parliament's presidium is somewhat unusual for parliaments and is a clear indication of the degree of initiative exercised by the presidium, and thus the chairman, over the legislature's agenda. For an example of such an agenda, which is quite detailed and identifies priorities for nearly all of the Supreme Soviet's committees see "Ob organizatsii raboty Verkhovnogo Soveta SSSR po realizatsii reshenie vtorogo S"ezda narodnykh deputatov SSSR," *Izvestiia*, 21 February 1990, pp. 1-2.

44. For further information on these complaints from deputies see A. Kozhakhmetova, "I Do Not Want To Work in the Dark," *Rabochaia tribuna*, 9 September 1990, p. 1; also see P. Golub, "Draft Law on Free Entry and Exit Could Be Finalized in Next Few Weeks," *Izvestiia*, 3 November 1990, p. 2.

45. Some more notable examples of complaints about lack of professionalism and legislative ineffectiveness of deputies include V. Dolganov and A. Stepovoi, "Teper' slov za s"ezdom," *Izvestiia*, 7 March 1990, p. 2; V. Dolganov and A. Stepovoi, "Zakon

o presidentve: preniia zavershenia," *Izvestiia*, 14 March 1990, p. 1; and V. Dolganov and A. Stepovoy, "Povyshenie tsen otsrocheno," *Izvestiia*, 15 June 1990, pp. 1, 3.

46. This problem has been identified by the presidium, Supreme Soviet deputies, and outside observers as well. See for example, O. Losoto and A. Cherniak, "Dol'zhost': Predsedatel' Verkhovnogo Soveta SSSR," *Pravda*, 2 April 1990, p. 3; M. Buzhkevich, "Zametki parlamentskogo obozrevatelia: bez kanikul," *Pravda*, 25 January 1990, p. 2; and Lowenthal, *New Soviet Legislature*, pp. 7-13.

47. Lowenthal, p. 12.

48. Ibid.

49. Ibid., p. 15.

50. For more on disagreements within the Lopatin group see Kosarev, "Debate," p. 1.

51. For more on the activities of the Interregional Group both from within and outside the Supreme Soviet see Julia Wishnevsky, "Multiparty System, Soviet Style," *Radio Liberty: Report on the USSR*, 2, no. 47 (23 November 1990), pp. 3-6.

52. For additional information on a growing resignation among deputies to the perceived need for greater Presidential power see Dawn Mann, "*Ukaz* and Effect: Gorbachev Is Granted Additional Powers," *Radio Liberty: Report on the USSR*, 2, no. 40 (5 October 1990), pp. 1-4.

53. Nichol makes a highly persuasive case to this effect, pointing to a number of comments and statements by Gorbachev, Shevardnadze, and others to the effect that *glasnost'* should be extended to foreign policy, and that the concepts of a socialist rule of law and public control of policy making also included safeguards to ensure the consistent application of new thinking in foreign policy. Shevardnadze, in particular, pointed to the decision-making process in Afghanistan as the type of closed politics that should be avoided in the future, and saw the parliament as playing a role in that regard. For more on these points, see Nichol, "Soviet Legislative-Constitutional *Perestroika*," pp. 7-11.

54. See, for example, A. Dzasokhov, "Sovetskii parlament i diplomatiia," *Mezhdunarodnaia zhizn*, August 1990, pp. 137-55, particularly 137-43.

55. Officials of the Soviet executive branch are required by law to respond to questions from deputies, be available for questioning, and in cases of violations of or noncompliance with constitutions, laws, and decrees, respond to questions from deputies within three days. These measures, as well as others increasing deputies' access to the location and materials of all-union agencies, considerably strengthen the legal foundation for legislative oversight. For more on the law and its provisions see Dawn Mann, "Supreme Soviet Adopts Laws on the Status of People's Deputies," *Radio Liberty: Report on the USSR*, 2, no. 39 (28 September 1990), pp. 1-4.

56. In addition to the law on the status of deputies, which strengthened the legal foundation of legislative oversight, laws on local self-government, protection of individuals against ethnic violence, the electoral system, the rights of defendants in criminal proceedings, the status of judges, the operation of psychiatry, and the environment broke important new ground in the operation of domestic policy in these areas. For more information, see Julie Kim, *USSR Supreme Soviet: Major Legislation*,

Foreign Affairs and National Defense Division, Congressional Research Service, Library of Congress, 90-459F, 8 September 1990.

57. Mann makes this critical point when she argues that the expansion of Gorbachev's executive power by the Supreme Soviet "does not address the problem of how to ensure the execution of presidential decrees." She also points out persuasively that "there is little reason to expect that future decrees on property, the budget, or law and order will be executed any more efficiently than previous decrees. Gorbachev still lacks popular authority, and the present administrative structure of the Soviet Union and the legal framework that supports it are not recognized as legitimate in many parts of the country." See Mann, "*Ukaz* and Effect," p. 3.

58. For further information on this typology see Michael L. Mezey, *Comparative Legislatures* (Durham, NC: Duke University Press, 1979), pp. 6-44.

59. For more on these limitations, see ibid., p. 43.

60. Ibid., pp. 280-81.

INDEX

ABOUT THE CONTRIBUTORS

Viktor Danilenko is Professor at the Moscow State Institute of International Relations. He is a recognized Soviet scholar in the field of comparative legislative studies and American perceptions of the Soviet political system.

Stuart Goldman is a specialist in Soviet affairs in the Foreign Affairs and National Defense Division of the Congressional Research Service (CRS), Library of Congress. He specializes in political and military affairs and US-Soviet relations, and has been the principal staff in developing cooperation between CRS and the Secretariat of the USSR Supreme Soviet. He is the author of numerous reports and congressional publications dealing with Soviet affairs and US-Soviet relations.

Robert T. Huber is currently Staff Associate for the Soviet Studies Program of the Social Science Research Council. He is formerly a Staff Consultant for the Committee on Foreign Affairs of the U.S. House of Representatives. His publications include *Soviet Perceptions of the U.S. Congress: Impact on Superpower Relations*, and he has also helped prepare numerous government-sponsored studies on Soviet negotiating behavior, Soviet policy toward developing countries, and the conduct of U.S.-Soviet arms control negotiations.

Eugene Huskey is Associate Professor of Political Science at Stetson University in Florida. His publications include *Russian Lawyers and the Soviet State* and numerous articles on Soviet law and politics. He is currently editing a book on executive institutions in Soviet politics.

Donald R. Kelley is Professor of Political Science and Senior Research Fellow at the Fulbright Institute of International Relations at the University of Arkansas. He is the author of *Soviet Politics in the Brezhnev Era* and co-editor of *Khrushchev and Gorbachev as Reformers*.

Joel C. Moses is Professor of Political Science at the Iowa State University, and this year is a visiting scholar at the Hoover Institute on War, Revolution, and Peace. He is co-author of *Major European Governments* (8th ed.).

Thomas F. Remington is Professor of Political Science at Emory University. He specializes in Soviet domestic politics and the role of the media and media institutions in Soviet society. He is currently conducting research on Soviet legislative institutions. He is the author of *The Truth of Authority: Ideology and Communication in the Soviet Union*, and editor of *Politics and the Soviet System*.

Robert Sharlet is Professor of Political Science at Union College in Schenectady, NY, and has written extensively on Soviet law and politics. His forthcoming book is *The Soviet Constitutional Crisis*.

Michael E. Urban is Professor of Political Science at the University of California at Santa Cruz. He is the author of *More Power to the Soviets! Democratic Revolution in the USSR* and editor of *Ideology and System Change in the USSR and Eastern Europe* (forthcoming).